DATE			

BETTER BY
MICROWAVE

BY
LORI LONGBOTHAM
AND
MARIE SIMMONS

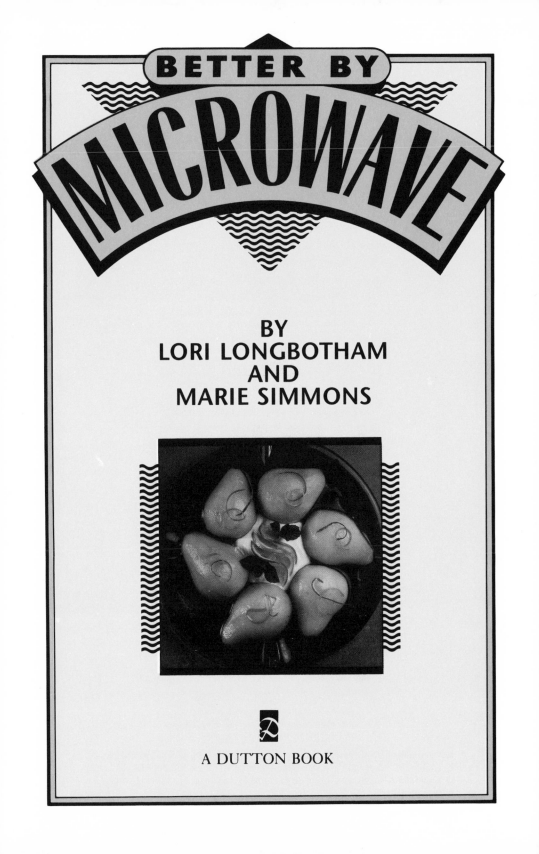

A DUTTON BOOK

DUTTON
Published by the Penguin Group
Penguin Books USA Inc., 375 Hudson Street,
New York, New York 10014, U.S.A.
Penguin Books Ltd, 27 Wrights Lane,
London W8 5TZ, England
Penguin Books Australia Ltd, Ringwood,
Victoria, Australia
Penguin Books Canada Ltd, 2801 John Street,
Markham, Ontario, Canada L3R 1B4
Penguin Books (N.Z.) Ltd, 182–190 Wairau Road,
Auckland 10, New Zealand

Penguin Books Ltd, Registered Offices:
Harmondsworth, Middlesex, England

First Printing, November, 1990

10 9 8 7 6 5 4 3 2 1

REGISTERED TRADEMARK—MARCA REGISTRADA
LIBRARY OF CONGRESS CATALOGING IN PUBLICATION DATA
Longbotham, Lori.
Better by microwave / by Lori Longbotham and Marie Simmons.
p.   cm.
Includes Index.
ISBN 0-525-24915-X : $19.95
1. Microwave cookery.   I. Simmons, Marie.   II. Title.
TX832.L66   1990   90-3548
641.5′882—dc20   CIP

Printed in the United States of America
Set in Melior Condensed and ITC Stone Sans.
Designed by Kathleen Herlihy-Paoli

CONTENTS

THE DIARY OF TWO MICROWAVE CONVERTS

We are both dedicated and enthusiastic cooks. We love the rituals of chopping and stirring while we daydream about the final results of our efforts; and the wonderful aromas of sautéing onions, roasting peppers, slow simmering soups, and baking bread make us swoon. We also love to eat good food. When the superefficient, cold, and impersonal microwave oven was introduced, we weren't interested. We were afraid that this sleek appliance without a flame would take away all the sensual pleasures of cooking.

We changed our minds. Although old habits die hard, in this instance they just sort of simmered away. True, we are passionate cooks, but we are also very busy professionals.

We found our microwaves could capture the smart, fresh, and lively flavors of the food we both like to cook. We were eating good-tasting, wholesome home-cooked meals prepared quickly and efficiently with fresh ingredients and lots of imagination. Gone was the common stereotype that the microwave was only good for reheating, for we discovered that it produced food with great flavor, color, and texture. Gradually, as we played with our microwave ovens, we realized here was a very exciting, convenient, and useful appliance.

No, it wouldn't boil water for pasta, roast red peppers, or bake a sumptuous brownie. But, it would poach a tender sweet pear, cook polenta in an astonishingly short time, and make a mean chocolate pudding. More and more, we found we were instinctively turning to the microwave for specific cooking tasks. Furthermore, we were learning how to use our microwaves to cook—and having a great time doing it. In the following recipes we share these experiences with you.

For instance, we found ourselves integrating the microwave with other cooking appliances—the broiler, an iron skillet, a saucepan filled with boiling water, or the toaster—to create wonderful recipes like Braised Fennel with Parmigiano-Reggiano Cheese, Pork Chops with Sauerkraut and Fruit, Garden Pasta Sauce, or Mozzarella and Red Pepper Melt. Or adapting some all-time favorites like puddings and applesauces—simply by learning how a microwave cooks.

Microwave cooking fits perfectly into the contemporary trend to eat healthier and lighter foods. In fact, the microwave is probably one of the best ways to cook moist, juicy skinless chicken breasts, steam fresh vegetables, or "bake" fish using much less butter or oil. This is a boon to the recent drive—on a personal and national level—to eat less fat.

Better by Microwave is a collection of sensible, flavorful, and realistic recipes that require no compromises from the dedicated cook and diner. They reflect the way we, and other busy people, like us, like to eat, cook, and entertain.

With some very hard-and-fast rules about what the microwave does best we have produced an impressive repertoire of delicious recipes with the sensual and cerebral pleasure we both enjoy still intact. We had great fun eating our way through this book, and we hope you do too.

GETTING TO KNOW YOUR MICROWAVE

The microwave is a versatile, time-saving kitchen tool. Like any tool it has its limitations, but it can also save you a lot of time and energy.

Ease into using your microwave the same way you eased into using your food processor or any other kitchen tools. Don't attempt a full-course dinner the first time around. Start out experimenting with very simple tasks and then as your confidence builds—and you develop some understanding for the way a microwave cooks—slowly expand your repertoire. A good discipline is to force yourself to use it every day for one week—experiment, have fun, and get to know your microwave.

COOKING GUIDELINES

▶ Set the timer for the **minimum** cooking time suggested in the recipe. Check for doneness and only *then* microwave for the additional suggested time—and *only* if it is necessary. Remember, even a few seconds in the microwave can make a big difference. Better to undercook first and then add more time as it is needed.

▶ Pay attention—don't miss (or ignore) the timer.

▶ Always check a dish before the suggested cooking time is up—about three quarters of the way through—to make sure all is going well. If the minimum cooking time is 60 seconds check after 45 seconds, but if the minimum cooking time is 6 minutes you might check after 5 minutes. If the dish looks like it's overcooking or cooking unevenly, stop and turn the dish or stir and rearrange the food.

▶ Like conventional cooking, cooking in a microwave is not an exact science. So continue to use the same instincts you use when cooking conventionally. Take a peek, stir, sniff, and taste as you cook—and do it often.

▶ Remember to turn the dish (if your microwave is not equipped with a turntable) and rearrange the food so that it will cook evenly.

▶ *If a dish is not done by the suggested cooking time,* continue to cook in small increments and watch carefully.

▶ Follow the suggested standing times in a recipe. The residual heat in the food will "finish" the cooking—the heat on the outside of the dish will continue to penetrate inward to the center by conduction. This is particularly true for delicate foods like fish or some vegetables. In some cases the time it takes to carry the dish to the table is enough time to finish cooking. Denser foods may continue to cook for several minutes after they are removed from the oven. Think of the standing time as just part of the cooking time. Let the food stand outside the oven. Don't worry—it will still be hot at serving time.

FACTORS THAT AFFECT
COOKING TIMES

Foods are cooked in a microwave by the heat created by the rapid vibration of molecules stimulated by microwave energy. Contrary to popular belief,

SOME VERY BASIC COOKING TIPS

STIR to redistribute heat from the hotter outer edges to the cooler inside

ROTATE encourages even cooking, or use a turntable

EVEN THICKNESS fold under the thin edges of fish fillets and other tapered foods

ARRANGING FOOD place the thick parts—broccoli stems, thick part of chicken breast—toward the outer rim of dish

ROUND DISHES food cooks and reheats more evenly in a round dish

STIR IN SALT salt attracts microwaves, so if salt lies on the surface of the food it will overcook. Stir salt in well—or add it later.

microwaves do not cook the center first. Foods cook around the outer edges first and then the heat travels to the center by conduction, cooking the center last.

▶ **VOLUME OF FOOD** The microwave cooking time increases as the volume of the food increases. For instance, four potatoes will take almost four times longer to cook than one potato.

▶ **TEMPERATURE OF THE FOOD** Just as in conventional cooking, cold food will take longer to cook or heat than room temperature food.

▶ **SIZE AND SHAPE OF FOOD** Microwaves penetrate only to a depth of about 1 inch; therefore, thin pieces of food will cook faster and more evenly than thick pieces of food, and uniformly cut smaller pieces of food will cook more evenly than large irregularly shaped pieces. The microwave is best—quicker and more efficient—when used to cook smaller cuts of food.

▶ **DENSITY** Microwaves penetrate and therefore cook porous foods more quickly than dense foods. Some foods, like broccoli, have two densities; the more dense, or slower-cooking, areas—the broccoli stems—should be placed toward the outside of the dish where the cooking begins and is therefore hotter. The less dense, or faster-cooking portions—the broccoli flowerets—should be placed toward the center.

▶ **MOISTURE, SUGAR, AND FAT CONTENT** Microwaves are more attracted to foods higher in sugar and fat than to foods high in water. Therefore, high-sugar and high-fat foods will heat more quickly than foods higher in water.

COVERING FOOD

TO COVER OR NOT TO COVER—A FREQUENTLY ASKED QUESTION

▶ A basic rule of thumb is to **cover** food in the microwave when you want it to cook faster—or when you want it to retain all its moisture (example: soup). Covered food retains more heat and therefore cooks more quickly and evenly.

▶ Leave food **uncovered** when you want some of the moisture to evaporate so that the food will "thicken" (example: sauce).

HOW TO COVER FOOD

▶ To prevent spattering, cover with microwave-safe paper towels or waxed paper. To absorb excess fat and prevent sogginess, cover with microwave-safe paper towels.

▶ For foods you want to steam or poach, use microwave-safe plastic wrap. Always vent the plastic wrap on one side by turning a section of the plastic wrap back so that some of the steam can escape. This avoids a tight seal that may cause steam buildup and the possibility of a steam burn when uncovering the food. *Do not let the plastic wrap touch the food.*

▶ For the tightest seal and fastest, most efficient cooking, cook in a microwave-safe glass casserole with a fitted lid (use a dinner plate if the dish has no lid).

WATTAGE AND POWER LEVEL

KNOW YOUR WATTAGE

All microwaves are not alike. The most significant difference is the power output, or wattage. This will affect how fast your microwave cooks. Think of it as if your conventional oven were preset to a specific temperature when it was manufactured. The larger microwave ovens are 600–700 watts; the smaller or compact ovens are 400–500 watts. The lower the wattage, the slower the rate of cooking. **Our recipes were tested and developed in a 650-watt oven.**

TESTING YOUR WATTAGE

Heat 1 cup of room-temperature (70° F.) water in a 2-cup microwave-safe glass measure on high power for 3 minutes. If the water is boiling after 3 minutes, your oven is 600 watts or more. If it takes longer than 3 minutes for the water to boil, your microwave is less than 600 watts.

EQUIPMENT

We do not encourage going out and buying a whole new battery of cookware for microwave cooking. You probably have more cookware suitable for microwave cooking right in your cabinets than you realize.

▶ We use microwave-safe glass (Pyrex) casseroles with lids, which are available in 1- through 4-quart sizes, over and over again. They are large enough to prevent boiling over, make removing the lid and stirring a simple step, and are easy to see through so you can watch the food's progress closely. The fitted lid holds the steam and heat in much more efficiently than microwave-safe plastic wrap vented on one side.

▶ Microwave-safe glass (Pyrex) measuring cups in all sizes from 1 cup right up to 2 quart are great for sauces, soups, drinks, puddings, and many more things. They are easily covered, if necessary, with a piece of microwave-safe plastic wrap vented on one side.

▸ Microwave-safe glass (Pyrex) pie or cake plates in 9- or 10-inch diameters are especially good for fish, chicken breasts, fruits, and vegetables.

▸ Porcelain ramekins or custard cups and microwave-safe glass (Pyrex) custard cups and small bowls are great for melting butter and chocolate, cooking eggs, and many other uses.

▸ Ceramics, china, pottery, and stoneware are all usually microwave-safe. If you are unsure, here is a simple test: Place the dish in the microwave; next to it place a 1-cup microwave-safe glass measure half-filled with water. Heat on high for 1 minute. If the dish is hot, it should not be used in the microwave. If it is warm, use only for reheating. If it is still at room temperature, it is microwave-safe for all cooking.

▸ *Standard metal cookware should never be used in a microwave;* nor should you use china with a metal rim. Metal causes arcing, which is an electrical current that flows from the oven wall to the metal container causing a flash and a popping sound that could damage the oven. If arcing does occur, immediately turn the oven off. Metal also reflects the microwaves and will therefore slow the cooking time.

SPECIALTY EQUIPMENT

▸ **CORN POPPERS** Corn poppers specially designed for microwave use automatically pop about 3 quarts of corn in 3 to 4 minutes without any attention from the cook. As an added bonus, you don't need any oil so you can cut down significantly on the fat and calories in this basically healthful, popular, low-calorie food. Many commercially produced popcorn products defeat the reputation of popcorn as a healthy snack food by loading it up with fats and salt.

▸ **AUTOMATIC TURNTABLES** Automatic turntables are spring-wound and slowly rotate the foods, eliminating the necessity of stopping the oven to manually turn the dish. Many microwave ovens come equipped with turntables. If your oven doesn't have one, it is a worthwhile investment.

▸ **THERMOMETERS** Specially designed microwave thermometers for meat and poultry or for candy-making can stay in the oven while it is operating. (Acu-Rite is one manufacturer.) *Never use a regular oven thermometer in the microwave.* If you don't have a special microwave thermometer, an instant-read thermometer can be used to measure the internal temperature of cooked foods when they are removed from the oven.

▶ **BROWNING TRAY** Most foods will not brown in a microwave unless the oven is equipped with a separate browning element. Microwave browning trays do the job very efficiently. First the specially formulated tray is heated in the microwave, where it absorbs microwave energy and retains heat; then the food is seared on the browning tray until it is browned and fragrant. It is great for things like ground beef and sausages, although we find ourselves browning these foods in an iron skillet on the stove and then finishing the cooking in the microwave.

MICROWAVE SAFETY

Read over the manufacturer's instruction manual before using your microwave. Some of the more important things to remember are:

▶ Don't operate your oven if the door does not close securely or is bent, warped, or damaged in any way.

▶ If your oven ever continues to operate after the door is opened, it is defective. Turn it off and have it repaired before using it again.

▶ Never operate an empty microwave.

▶ Keep your oven clean. Wipe the interior, the outer edges of the cavity, and the door frequently with a mild detergent and soft cloth.

▶ Buy plastic wraps that have been tested and approved for microwave cooking. Do not allow the plastic wrap to touch the food it is covering, since it can break down at very high temperatures.

▶ Make sure all cookware has been approved for microwave use.

▶ Always use potholders when removing food from your microwave.

▶ Microwave liquids in containers that hold two to three times the volume of the liquid to allow for expansion and prevent boil-overs.

▶ Do not microwave stuffed poultry or other meats; uneven cooking can cause salmonella.

▶ Always pierce foods with skins like potatoes, winter squash, sausage, and egg yolks to allow the steam to escape while they are cooking; steam buildup can cause these foods to explode while cooking.

* = RECIPES THAT ARE ESPECIALLY GOOD FOR YOU

The microwave oven is particularly well suited to healthful cooking, and those recipe titles followed by an asterisk are specifically low in calories, fat, cholesterol, and sodium, and high in flavor and satisfaction—especially good for you.

USING THIS BOOK WITH EASE

Better by Microwave is all about what the microwave does best. It's full of recipes that use the microwave to best advantage and just skips what we think can be done better in a conventional oven. Here are a few points you might keep in mind while using this book:

▶ We almost always cook on high power, with very few exceptions. We always specify the power in the first step, but after that simply say "microwave" unless the power changes to another level.

▶ When we call for toasted nuts and sesame seeds in the list of ingredients we assume they will be toasted in a small skillet over low heat in less than a minute or in a moderate oven for 2 to 5 minutes (depending on the quantity). Toasting nuts is not one of the things the microwave does best.

▶ Because we like the clean, fresh taste, we use fresh herbs almost exclusively. The microwave often doesn't develop the flavors of dried herbs adequately. Fresh herbs, packed conveniently in small packages, are now available in many supermarkets. If your market doesn't have them ask them to order some for you. Better yet, grow your own in pots and sow all season.

QUICK HITS

▶ **TO SOFTEN HARD BROWN SUGAR,** remove sugar from package and place sugar and an apple wedge in a microwave-safe glass pie plate; cover with microwave-safe plastic wrap and microwave on high power 20 to 30 seconds. Let stand, covered, 20 seconds. Uncover and stir to remove the lumps.

▶ **TO LIQUEFY CRYSTALLIZED HONEY,** microwave in a microwave-safe container twice the volume of the honey, uncovered, on high power for 1 to 2 minutes, or until the crystals disappear.

▶ **TO WARM LIQUEURS FOR FLAMING,** microwave up to ¼ cup on high power, uncovered, 15 seconds.

▶ **TO SOFTEN A STICK OF HARD BUTTER TO SPREADING CONSISTENCY,** microwave 1 stick on high power 20 to 40 seconds, checking every 10 seconds.

▶ **TO WARM MAPLE SYRUP,** microwave 1 cup syrup in a 2-cup microwave-safe glass pitcher or measure on high power for 30 seconds; add 15-second increments until the syrup is warm. For ½ cup syrup, cut the time in half.

▶ **WARM LEMONS, LIMES, AND ORANGES** give up more juice than cold ones. Microwave one piece of fruit on high power for 15 seconds. For icy cold or refrigerated fruit, microwave for 30 seconds.

▶ **TO CLARIFY BUTTER,** microwave 1 stick butter, cut up, in a microwave-safe 2-cup glass measure on high power for 1 to 2 minutes, or until boiling. Remove from the oven; skim the foam from the top. Let stand until separated; the clear top layer is the clarified butter.

▶ **TO PLUMP OR SOFTEN DRIED FRUITS AND RAISINS,** place them in a small bowl and sprinkle with water, juice, or other liquid. Microwave, uncovered, on high power for 15 to 30 seconds, depending on the volume.

▶ **MICROWAVED TOMATOES AND PEACHES** can easily be peeled for cooking or salads without the mess of blanching in boiling water and chilling in cold water. Microwave each piece of fruit 30 seconds on high power; let stand 2 minutes before peeling.

▶ **TO MELT CHOCOLATE,** place 1 ounce chocolate in a microwave-safe glass custard cup or small bowl; microwave on high power for 30 seconds, then stir. (Chocolate chips or chopped chocolate will melt more quickly.) Continue to heat in 10-second intervals until it stirs easily. *Don't overcook*—the chocolate will retain its shape and won't appear melted until it is stirred.

▶ **TO SOFTEN ICE CREAM THAT'S TOO HARD TO SCOOP,** just put it in the microwave on high power for about 30 seconds.

CHAPTER 1

BREAKFASTS

We begin our book just where we begin our day—with breakfast. Once upon a time, the only reason we used our microwaves in the morning was to zap our cooled-down mug of coffee.

Since then, we have come a long way. As you can see from the following collection, we like breakfast. But we especially like cooking up a bowl of hot cereal and thumbing our noses at that repulsive oatmeal-encrusted pot soaking in the sink, quickly cooking a strip or two of bacon without making a mess on the stovetop, or cooking an egg right in its little dish in less than 2 minutes. All these are things we can attribute to the tidiness and efficiency of our microwaves—and all without sacrificing taste and with the added plus, thanks to the clever technology of the microwave oven, of often having the serving dish and the cooking utensil one and the same.

One of the best ways to use your microwave is as a handy kitchen tool. For instance, when you are trying to fry bacon for a crowd and scramble a mess of eggs, follow our microwave instructions for Bacon for a Crowd while simultaneously scrambling eggs in your favorite skillet on top of the stove. Learning to use the microwave with intelligence, style, and good plain sense—and making life just a little easier without compromising our favorite meal—is, indeed, very possible.

Oh, we still zap our cooled-down mug of coffee in the microwave. But we also use it to heat up a mug of Hot Lemonade, Red Zinger with Ginger, or perhaps a Hot Chocolate before we dash off to work—or play.

RECIPES

EGGS

Lemon-Thyme Egg
Eggs with Sweet Butter and Black Pepper
Santa Fe Egg
Scrambled Egg, Bacon, Broccoli, and Cheddar Cheese Sandwiches
Red and Green Pepper and Sausage Frittata
Tomato, Basil, and Mozzarella Frittata

CEREALS

Wheatena with Pears and Golden Raisins*
Old-fashioned Oatmeal*
Irish Oatmeal with Fruit*
Quick-Cooking Oatmeal*
Fastest Cream of Wheat*

BRINGING HOME THE BACON

Bacon
Canadian Bacon
Link Sausages
Sausage Patties

HOT DRINKS FOR BREAKFAST, OR ANY TIME

Hot Spiced Cider*
Morning Mocha
Hot Chocolate
Hot Spiced Pineapple Juice*
Red Zinger with Ginger*
Hot Lemonade*

* Especially good for you.

EGGS

LEMON-THYME EGG

This dish couldn't be easier or more delicious; it has the flavor and texture of an egg poached in cream. There are the many possible seasoning variations—try orange zest and fresh parsley, or lime zest and cilantro, or use your own ideas.

▶ **PREPARATION TIME: 3 minutes**
COOKING TIME: 2 minutes

1 large egg
1 teaspoon heavy cream
Pinch **each** grated lemon zest, fresh thyme leaves, salt, and freshly ground pepper

Break the egg into a 4-ounce microwave-safe porcelain ramekin. Prick the yolk with a fork four or five times. Mix the remaining ingredients in a small bowl and pour over the egg. Microwave uncovered on medium power (50%) for 1½ to 2 minutes, turning the dish twice. If not cooked to desired doneness, continue to microwave; check at 5-second intervals.

SERVES 1

EGGS WITH SWEET BUTTER AND BLACK PEPPER

This is reminiscent of soft-cooked eggs without the shells. Serve with strips of lavishly buttered toast to complete the picture.

▶ **PREPARATION TIME: 30 seconds**
COOKING TIME: 2 minutes

2 large eggs
1 teaspoon unsalted butter, cut into 4 pieces
Freshly ground black pepper
A few grains salt

Break the eggs into an 8-ounce microwave-safe glass custard cup or small shallow bowl. Prick the yolks with a fork four or five times. Dot with the butter. Microwave uncovered on medium power (50%) for 1 minute; stir gently with a fork. Microwave 30 seconds longer, or until soft-cooked to your liking, increasing the time in 5-second increments if necessary. Top with a generous grinding of pepper and add a few grains of salt, or to taste.

SERVES 1

SANTA FE EGG

Try using an egg substitute for the egg if you need to watch your cholesterol intake closely—the dish will still have those wonderful Southwestern flavors.

▶ **PREPARATION TIME: 5 minutes**
COOKING TIME: 2 minutes

1 large egg
1 tablespoon finely minced seeded red bell pepper
1 tablespoon finely minced scallion
1/2 teaspoon minced cilantro
Pinch **each** salt, cayenne, ground cumin seed, and ground coriander seed

Whisk all the ingredients together in a small bowl and pour into a 4-ounce microwave-safe porcelain ramekin. Microwave uncovered on medium power (50%) for 1½ to 2 minutes, stirring with a fork three times. If not cooked to desired doneness, continue to microwave, checking at 5-second intervals.

SERVES 1

SCRAMBLED EGG, BACON, BROCCOLI, AND CHEDDAR SANDWICHES

This is a great brunch dish, but we bet you will never see it turned down at any time of day!

▶ **PREPARATION TIME: 5 minutes**
COOKING TIME: 8 minutes

3 slices bacon
1 cup small broccoli flowerets
   with tender stems
1 tablespoon water
4 large eggs
½ cup shredded Cheddar
   cheese
Freshly ground pepper
2 hard rolls, split and toasted

1. Fold two paper towels together and place in the bottom of a microwave-safe 11 × 7-inch baking dish. Place the bacon on the paper towels and cover with another folded paper towel. Microwave on high power 2 ½ minutes. Remove from the oven and let cool, then crumble and set aside.

2. Place the broccoli in a microwave-safe 2-quart glass casserole with a lid; sprinkle with the water. Microwave covered on high power for 3 minutes; drain off any water.

3. Whisk the eggs until blended and pour over the broccoli. Add the bacon and the cheese and pepper; stir to blend. Microwave 2½ minutes, or until eggs are soft-scrambled, stirring every 30 seconds. Spoon the eggs onto the split rolls and serve hot.

SERVES 2

RED AND GREEN PEPPER AND SAUSAGE FRITTATA

The microwave makes fast work of a frittata, which is a cross between an omelet and scrambled eggs. Try the flavorful and lowfat Italian-style turkey sausage, also available both sweet and hot, in this frittata recipe. Served with a mixed green salad and some crusty bread, a frittata makes a deliciously simple supper.

▶ **PREPARATION TIME:** 5
minutes
COOKING TIME: 14 minutes
STANDING TIME: 1 minute

*4 links (about 8 ounces)
Italian-style pork or turkey
sausage, removed from casings and crumbled
½ red bell pepper, seeded and
cut into ¼-inch strips
½ green bell pepper, seeded
and cut into ¼-inch strips
1 small red onion, quartered
and cut into ¼-inch strips
1 tablespoon olive oil
4 large eggs
Shavings of Parmigiano-
Reggiano cheese*

1. Place the sausage meat in a microwave-safe 9-inch glass pie plate. Microwave on high power, uncovered, for 4 minutes, stirring twice. Transfer the sausage to a sieve to drain off the fat; mince the sausage with kitchen shears; set aside.

2. Combine the red and green peppers, onion, and olive oil in the pie plate; microwave 5 minutes, stirring once. Stir in the reserved sausage; microwave 1 minute.

3. Whisk the eggs in a small bowl; stir into the hot sausage mixture. Microwave 3 minutes, stirring twice, or until the eggs are almost set. Arrange the cheese on top of the frittata, cover with an inverted plate, and microwave 1 minute. Let stand, covered, 1 minute before serving.

SERVES 4

TOMATO, BASIL, AND MOZZARELLA FRITTATA

▶ **PREPARATION TIME:** 10
minutes
COOKING TIME: 8 minutes
STANDING TIME: 1 minute

*1 small sweet red onion, cut
into ¼-inch vertical strips
1 tablespoon olive oil, preferably extra-virgin
3 or 4 ripe plum tomatoes, cored
and cut into ½-inch wedges*

*2 tablespoons torn fresh basil
leaves
1 tablespoon finely chopped
Italian parsley
½ teaspoon fresh thyme leaves,
stripped from stems
½ clove garlic, crushed
4 large eggs
Salt
½ cup coarsely shredded mozzarella cheese
Freshly ground pepper*

1. Combine the onion and olive oil in a microwave-safe 9-inch glass pie plate; cover with microwave-safe plastic wrap and vent one side. Microwave on high power for 2 minutes, stirring once. Stir in the tomatoes, basil, parsley, thyme, and garlic. Microwave covered for 2 minutes, or until the tomatoes are heated through.

2. Whisk the eggs with salt to taste in a small bowl; stir the eggs and mozzarella into the warm tomato mixture. Microwave uncovered for 4 minutes, stirring twice, or until the eggs are almost set. Cover with an inverted plate and let stand 1 minute before serving. Season with pepper, to taste.

SERVES 4

CEREALS

WHEATENA WITH PEARS AND GOLDEN RAISINS*

Textthis is a breakfast perfect for a winter morning—hearty and delicious. To vary the recipe, use your favorite dried fruit; try peaches, apricots, cherries, currants, dates, prunes, or figs, in any combination that pleases you.

▶ **PREPARATION TIME: 5 minutes**
COOKING TIME: 5 minutes
STANDING TIME: 1 minute

¾ cup water
¼ cup Wheatena cereal
Pinch salt
2 dried pears, diced
1 tablespoon golden raisins
2 teaspoons dark brown sugar (optional)
Hot milk for serving (lowfat or skim if desired)

Mix the water, Wheatena, and salt in a microwave-safe 1-quart glass measure. Microwave uncovered on high power for 1 minute. Stir in the dried pears and raisins and microwave 2 to 4 minutes longer, until almost all the liquid is absorbed. Remove from the oven, cover with a saucer, and let stand 1 minute. Transfer to a cereal bowl, sprinkle with brown sugar if desired, and top with hot milk.

SERVES 1

OLD-FASHIONED OATMEAL*

Oatmeal is a wonderful breakfast—not only does it stick to your ribs, but it's delicious and good for you. This one is even healthier and tastier than plain oatmeal, because of the added flavorful fruit.

▶ **PREPARATION TIME:** 5 minutes
COOKING TIME: 5 minutes
STANDING TIME: 1 minute

¾ cup water
⅓ cup old-fashioned oatmeal
1 teaspoon brown sugar or honey
Pinch salt
2 dried peaches or 4 dried apricots, thinly sliced
¼ cup fresh or thawed frozen blueberries
Hot milk for serving (lowfat or skim if desired)

Mix the water, oatmeal, brown sugar, and salt in a large microwave-safe cereal bowl. Microwave uncovered on medium power (50%) for 2½ minutes. Stir in the peaches and microwave 2½ minutes longer. Remove from the oven, cover with a saucer, and let stand 1 minute. Serve topped with blueberries and hot milk.

SERVES 1

IRISH OATMEAL WITH FRUIT*

Irish oatmeal is the greatest; it has loads of flavor and great texture. You may even find yourself wanting it every day, especially in the cool months. The little bit of butter in the oatmeal keeps it from boiling over while cooking. On top of the stove, Irish oatmeal can take up to an hour to cook, but in the microwave it takes only about 15 minutes—and you don't have a messy pot to clean.

▶ **PREPARATION TIME:** 5 minutes
COOKING TIME: 13 minutes
STANDING TIME: 2 minutes

1 cup water
¼ cup Irish oatmeal (steel-cut)
1 teaspoon unsalted butter
Pinch **each** salt and ground cinnamon

2 tablespoons raisins
1/2 medium apple, cored and
    diced
1 teaspoon honey, or to taste
Hot milk for serving (lowfat or
    skim if desired)

---

1. Mix the water, oatmeal, butter, salt, and cinnamon in a microwave-safe 3-quart casserole with a lid. Microwave covered on high power for 6 minutes, stirring three times. Stir in the raisins and microwave covered 5 to 7 minutes longer, stirring twice, until almost all the liquid is absorbed.

2. Remove from the oven and stir in the apple. Cover and let stand for about 2 minutes. Transfer to a cereal bowl and top with the honey and hot milk.

SERVES 1

QUICK-COOKING OATMEAL*

This is really quick! In 5 minutes you can have a nutritious breakfast on the table—without additives, chemicals, or excessive sugar. Try topping the cooked oatmeal with bananas instead of the berries if it is more appealing.

▶ **PREPARATION TIME: 3
    minutes
COOKING TIME: 1 1/2 minutes
STANDING TIME: 1 minute**

2/3 cup water
1/3 cup quick-cooking oatmeal
1 teaspoon honey or brown
    sugar
Pinch salt
1/4 cup fresh raspberries or blueberries, or a fruit of your
    choice
Hot milk for serving (lowfat or
    skim if desired)

Mix the water, oatmeal, honey, and salt in a large microwave-safe cereal bowl. Microwave uncovered on high power for 1 1/2 minutes. Remove from the oven, cover with a saucer, and let stand 1 minute. Remove saucer and top with the berries and hot milk.

SERVES 1

FASTEST CREAM OF WHEAT*

Use lowfat or skim milk if you'd like to reduce the fat and calories—it will taste just as good. You might also want to try using honey instead of brown sugar, and any other berries that suit you.

▸ **PREPARATION TIME:** 5
minutes
COOKING TIME: 2 minutes
STANDING TIME: 2 minutes

¾ cup milk (lowfat or skim if
desired)
3 tablespoons Cream of Wheat
cereal
Pinch salt
2 teaspoons dark brown sugar,
or to taste
3 fresh strawberries, hulled and
sliced
Hot milk for serving (lowfat or
skim if desired)

Mix the ¾ cup milk, Cream of Wheat, and salt in a microwave-safe 1-quart glass measure. Microwave uncovered on high power for 1½ minutes, stirring once. Remove from the oven and stir again. Cover with a saucer and let stand 2 minutes. Transfer the cereal to a bowl and top with the brown sugar, fresh strawberries, and hot milk.

SERVES 1

BRINGING HOME THE BACON

BACON

Standing over a hot stove cooking bacon with its fiery spattering fat is no fun in the winter, and truly miserable in the summer. If you begin cooking bacon in your microwave, you'll be out of the heat, the bacon will be ready much faster, it will shrink less, and there will be no spattering fat or greasy skillet to clean. Bacon cooked in the microwave stays in long flat straight strips and looks great. The high fat content of bacon allows it to brown and crisp even though it has a short cooking time. Bacon continues to cook and brown as it stands, so be careful not to overcook it.

The timing for cooking bacon will vary according to the fat, sugar, and salt content, the thickness of the slices, and whether it's just out of the refrigerator or at room temperature; also the wattage and the size of your oven will make a big difference in the cooking time, so watch it carefully and don't overcook it. Lay the slices out flat between layers of paper towels, and don't let the slices overlap. Here are some timing guidelines:

2 slices—*1 to 2½ minutes*
4 slices—*2½ to 4½ minutes*
6 slices—*4 to 7 minutes*

To defrost frozen bacon, remove from package, put on large microwave-safe plate, and microwave on high power for 30 seconds to 1 minute, or on defrost for 4 to 6 minutes per pound, turning halfway through, just until strips can be separated.

BACON FOR ONE

3 slices bacon

Fold two paper towels together and place in the bottom of a microwave-safe 11 x 7-inch baking dish. Place the bacon on folded paper towels and cover with another folded paper towel. Microwave on high power for 2 minutes. If crisper bacon is desired, continue to microwave, checking at 20-second intervals.

BACON FOR A CROWD

If you'd like to cook a larger amount of bacon (up to a pound) all at once, layer it in a microwave-safe 13 x 9 x 2-inch glass baking dish. Use 5 strips of bacon per layer, and separate each layer with a folded paper towel. Microwave on high power about 4 minutes (or longer, for crisper bacon) for each layer; a pound will take about 15 minutes.

CANADIAN BACON

Canadian bacon is much lower in fat than most breakfast meats. Bacon and sausage are both about 80 percent fat; Canadian bacon is only 40 percent fat. Not only is it really wonderful for breakfast, but it's great to add as a garnish to salads, soups, and stews.

▶ **PREPARATION TIME: 2 minutes**
COOKING TIME: 1 minute

3 thin slices Canadian bacon

Place the Canadian bacon in a microwave-safe 9-inch glass pie plate. Cover with microwave-safe plastic wrap and vent one side. Microwave on high power for 30 seconds to 1 minute. Serve hot.

SERVES 1

LINK SAUSAGES

▶ **PREPARATION TIME: 7 minutes**
COOKING TIME: 3 minutes

4 breakfast link sausages

Heat a browning tray in the microwave according to manufacturer's directions, approximately 4 to 7 minutes. Place the sausages on the tray and immediately turn them. Microwave on high power for 2 to 3 minutes, turning every 30 seconds to brown all sides. Drain briefly on paper towels.

SERVES 1

SAUSAGE PATTIES

Cook sausage this no-muss, no-fuss way for breakfast or to add to soups or casseroles.

▸ **PREPARATION TIME: 7 minutes**
COOKING TIME: 2 minutes

3 breakfast sausage patties (½ inch thick)

Heat the browning tray according to the manufacturer's directions, approximately 4 to 7 minutes. Place the sausage on the tray and immediately flip the patties over. Microwave uncovered on high power for 2 minutes, turning the patties over halfway through.

SERVES 1

HOT DRINKS FOR BREAKFAST, OR ANY TIME

HOT SPICED CIDER*

This is a perfect fall or winter drink. Fresh cider makes a great brew, but apple juice will do just as well—pear cider or pear juice is terrific, too. Make this all for yourself and store it in the refrigerator, heating it up as you want it, or serve it to a cozy gathering of friends around the fire.

▶ **PREPARATION TIME:** 5
   minutes
COOKING TIME: 10 minutes
STANDING TIME: 2 minutes

4 cups apple cider or juice
2–4 tablespoons honey, depending on sweetness of
   cider
½ lemon, sliced thin
1 cinnamon stick, halved
1 tablespoon minced crystallized ginger
10 **each** whole cloves and
   allspice
2 whole cardamom pods,
   crushed

Place all the ingredients in a microwave-safe 2-quart glass measure, and whisk to mix completely. Microwave uncovered on high power for 10 minutes, stirring three times. Cover with a dinner plate and let stand for 2 minutes. Strain if desired and serve hot in cups or mugs.
SERVES 4

MORNING MOCHA

▶ **PREPARATION TIME:** 2
  minutes
COOKING TIME: 2 minutes

1 tablespoon unsweetened
   cocoa powder
2 tablespoons sugar
½ mug hot brewed coffee
½ mug milk
Pinch ground cinnamon
   (optional)

Stir the cocoa powder and sugar together in a microwave-safe mug. Gradually stir in the coffee and the milk until blended; add the cinnamon, if desired. Microwave uncovered on high power for 2 minutes, or until very hot.

SERVES 1

HOT CHOCOLATE

Hot cocoa is delicious, but real hot chocolate is where it's at. There are many ways to vary this recipe—try adding ½ teaspoon instant espresso powder, ⅛ teaspoon cinnamon sugar, or a 1-inch by ½-inch strip of orange zest, or come up with your own variations. This is a great way to start the day, and a terrific treat after work or school.

▶ **PREPARATION TIME:** 2
  minutes
COOKING TIME: 2 minutes

¾ cup milk
¼ cup half-and-half or milk
2 ounces bittersweet (not unsweetened) or semisweet
   chocolate, finely chopped

Place the milk, half-and-half, and chopped chocolate in a microwave-safe 1-quart glass measure. Microwave uncovered on high power for 2 minutes, whisking vigorously once. Pour into a mug and serve hot.

SERVES 1

HOT SPICED PINEAPPLE JUICE*

▶ **PREPARATION TIME:** 2
    minutes
COOKING TIME: 2 minutes

Approximately 6 ounces pine-
    apple juice
Hot tap water
1 tablespoon fresh lemon juice
1 tablespoon sugar
1 2-inch piece cinnamon stick
3 or 4 whole cloves
Grating of fresh nutmeg

Fill a microwave-safe mug about two-thirds full with pineapple juice. Add enough hot water to fill the mug almost to the top. Stir in the lemon juice and sugar; add the cinnamon stick and cloves. Microwave uncovered on high power for 2 minutes, or until very hot. Sprinkle the top with nutmeg.

SERVES 1

RED ZINGER
WITH GINGER*

▶ **PREPARATION TIME:** 3
    minutes
COOKING TIME: 3 minutes
STANDING TIME: 2 minutes

2 or 3 thin slices pared fresh
    ginger
Hot tap water
1 red zinger tea bag
Wedge of lemon

Place the ginger slices in a microwave-safe mug; crush with the tip of a spoon to extract some of the juices. Fill the mug almost to the top with hot tap water. Microwave uncovered on high power for 2 to 3 minutes, or until almost boiling. Add the red zinger tea bag; cover with a saucer and steep 1 to 2 minutes. Squeeze the lemon wedge into the hot tea.

SERVES 1

HOT LEMONADE

▶ *PREPARATION TIME: 2 minutes*
COOKING TIME: 2 minutes

Hot tap water
1 lemon, halved and seeded
2 tablespoons sugar

Fill a microwave-safe mug two-thirds full with hot tap water. Cut a thin slice from one lemon half and add to the hot water. Squeeze the juice from the rest of the lemon into the water; stir in the sugar. Microwave uncovered on high power for 2 minutes, or until very hot. Stir to mix.

SERVES 1

CHAPTER 2

SNACKS

There is a sense of immediacy about the word *snack* that jibes with our philosophy of microwave cooking—good and fast! So, if it is instant gratification you are after, more than a few of the following recipes are right on the mark.

We enter the 90s riding the coattails of a popcorn revival, and not the plain old movie theater variety that we all know and love. The single most successful grocery product of 1989 was popcorn packaged especially for the microwave. Unfortunately, microwavable popcorn is preseasoned (not very well) and full of chemicals and unhealthy fats, so it's not good for you and it doesn't taste good either. Instead of using it, why not try our just-as-easy, just-as-quick recipes that use regular popcorn you can flavor yourself. Caramel Corn for Grown-ups or Popcorn with Lemon Herb Butter is terrific, or try a batch plain, maybe with just a little salt.

The sandwich section is filled with appealing and creative combos to give the little bit of Dagwood in each of us something to rave about. Furthermore, the recipes are multi-appliance-friendly—toast the bread in the toaster, melt cheese in the microwave, whip up a mean red pepper spread in the food processor—all smart ways to position your microwave right up there with other indispensable kitchen tools.

For the more sophisticated "snacker," there are recipes for elegant Salmon Rillettes, an exotic Baba Ganoush, and trendy Sticky Chicken Wings, Shrimp in the Raw, and Caponata. For toasting to good health on a cold winter's night we offer four wonderful hot drinks spiced with a touch of spirits.

R E C I P E S

FLAVORS FOR POPPED CORN

Plain Popcorn*
Lemon-Parsley Popcorn
Popcorn with Nut Butter
Caramel Corn for Grown-ups
El Paso Popcorn

SANDWICHES

Cheddar, Bacon, and Tomato Melt
Mozzarella and Red Pepper Melt
Gouda and Pear Sandwich
Chicken and Roasted Red Pepper Sandwich*
Jalapeno-Avocado Tortilla Melt

SOPHISTICATED SPREADS

Salmon Rillettes
Baba Ganoush*

Caponata*
Garlic-Thyme Spread*

FINGER FOODS

Sticky Chicken Wings
Nachos
John's Toastitaritas
Spiced Shrimp in the Raw*

DRINKS WITH SPIRIT

Wassail
Glogg
Hot Buttered Rum
Athole Brose

* Especially good for you.

FLAVORS FOR POPPED CORN

PLAIN POPCORN

Your microwave is great for popping popcorn. There are many microwave popcorn poppers available on the market (Nordic Ware is our favorite). Follow the directions for your popper and you will have the quickest, easiest, and best popcorn ever—free of chemicals and preservatives. Experiment a few times with your microwave and popper to get the best results, but ⅓ cup popcorn kernels microwaved on high power for 3–4 minutes will usually make 2 quarts popped corn. Popcorn made especially for hot air poppers works well.

▶ **PREPARATION TIME:** 1 minute
COOKING TIME: 4 minutes

───────

⅓ *cup popcorn*

Place the popcorn in a microwave popcorn popper. Follow the manufacturer's directions to pop corn. Carefully remove the lid and serve as is, with a little salt and/or butter, or use it to make one of the varieties of flavored popcorn that follow.

SERVES 4

NOTE: To make caramel popcorn you need a candy thermometer. Acu-rite makes a great one that can be left right in your microwave while cooking.

LEMON-PARSLEY POPCORN

You can use this basic recipe just as it is—or try some variations like lime zest and cilantro or orange zest and rosemary.

▶ **PREPARATION TIME: 5 minutes**
COOKING TIME: 1 minute

3 tablespoons unsalted butter
2 teaspoons minced fresh parsley
¼ teaspoon grated lemon zest
¼ teaspoon salt, or to taste
Large pinch freshly ground pepper, or to taste

2 quarts hot popped corn

Microwave the butter, parsley, lemon zest, salt, and pepper uncovered in a small microwave-safe bowl on high power until the butter is melted, about 1 minute. Place the hot popped corn in a serving bowl and pour the butter mixture over it. Toss to blend and serve immediately.

SERVES 4

POPCORN WITH NUT BUTTER

Adapted from an American Indian recipe in *Native Harvest* by Barrie Kavasch (published by Random House), this is wonderful and very easy. You might also want to try it with almond or cashew butter.

▶ **PREPARATION TIME: 5 minutes**
COOKING TIME: 2 minutes

2 tablespoons unsalted butter
2 tablespoons chunky peanut butter
2 quarts hot popped corn
1 cup dry roasted peanuts
Salt to taste

Place the butter and peanut butter in a small microwave-safe bowl and microwave uncovered on high power for about 1 to 2 minutes, until melted. Place the hot popcorn in a serving bowl and pour the butter mixture over it. Add the peanuts and salt and toss to mix well. Serve hot.

SERVES 4

CARAMEL CORN FOR GROWN-UPS

Here's a sophisticated caramel corn that's delicious and really easy to make in your microwave. It's even easier to prepare if you have a microwave candy thermometer that can stay inside your microwave while you're cooking, so that you can watch the temperature closely. Use dark corn syrup if you'd like a darker colored caramel.

▸ **PREPARATION TIME:** 15 minutes
COOKING TIME: 11 minutes

6 cups popped corn
1 cup coarsely chopped toasted cashews, almonds, and/or peanuts
1/3 cup **each** minced crystallized ginger and golden raisins
2/3 cup sugar
6 tablespoons unsalted butter
1/3 cup light or dark corn syrup
Pinch salt
1 teaspoon vanilla extract
1/4 teaspoon baking soda

1. Lightly oil a microwave-safe 3-quart glass casserole. Add the popped corn, cashews, ginger, and raisins, and toss to mix well.

2. Combine the sugar, butter, corn syrup, and salt in a microwave-safe 2-quart glass measure. Microwave uncovered on high power for 3 to 4 minutes, until the mixture boils, stirring after each minute. Then microwave on high power for 4 to 5 minutes, or until the mixture reaches 300° on a candy thermometer.* Stir in the vanilla and baking soda.

3. Immediately pour the caramel over the popped corn and toss to blend completely. Microwave uncovered on high power for 2 minutes. Turn out onto a waxed-paper-lined baking sheet to cool. Break up and store in an airtight container.

SERVES 4–6

EL PASO POPCORN

This popcorn recipe packs a lot of flavor and takes only minutes to prepare.

▶ PREPARATION TIME: 5 minutes
COOKING TIME: 1 minute

3 tablespoons unsalted butter
2 teaspoons minced cilantro
1/4 teaspoon ground cumin seed
1/4 teaspoon salt, or to taste
1/8 teaspoon **each** cayenne and ground coriander seed
2 quarts hot popped corn

Place the butter, cilantro, ground cumin, salt, cayenne, and ground coriander in a small microwave-safe bowl. Microwave uncovered on high power for about 1 minute, until the butter is melted. Place the hot popcorn in a serving bowl, pour the melted butter mixture over it, and toss to blend completely. Taste and adjust the seasoning. Serve hot.

SERVES 4

SANDWICHES

GOUDA AND PEAR SANDWICH

The combination of the sweet chutney and the salty cheese in this sandwich is especially delicious.

▶ **PREPARATION TIME: 7 minutes**
COOKING TIME: 45 seconds

½ cup grated Gouda cheese
    (about 2 ounces)
2 teaspoons minced mango
    chutney
1 teaspoon minced fresh parsley
½ teaspoon Dijon mustard
1 slice rye bread, toasted
4 thin slices ripe pear or tart
    apple

Mix the cheese, chutney, parsley, and mustard in a small bowl, and spread on the rye toast. Microwave open-faced on a folded paper towel on a microwave-safe dinner plate on high power until the cheese melts, about 15 to 45 seconds. Top with pear slices and serve hot.

SERVES 1

CHEDDAR, BACON, AND TOMATO MELT

Use your favorite Cheddar—mild, medium, sharp, or extra-sharp. This sandwich melt works particularly well with low-salt bacon, a new product worth trying. You might also want to try one of the lowfat Cheddars on the market.

▸ *PREPARATION TIME: 5
minutes*
COOKING TIME: 4½ minutes

2 slices bacon, halved crosswise
2 slices whole wheat toast
*½ cup Cheddar cheese, grated
(about 2 ounces)*
*1 large plum tomato, sliced into
6 thin slices*
*1 teaspoon minced fresh pars-
ley (optional)*
Pinch freshly ground pepper

1. Place the bacon in a micro-wave-safe glass 8-inch cake dish on two folded paper towels and cover with two folded paper towels. Micro-wave on high power for 2 to 3 minutes, until cooked through and crisp.

2. Place the whole wheat toast on top of two folded paper towels and put them on a microwave-safe dinner plate. Divide the cheese evenly between the two slices of toast. Place the bacon crosswise on top of the cheese, two slices per sandwich. Top each sandwich with three slices of tomato in a lengthwise pattern.

3. Microwave the two melts uncovered on high power for 45 to 90 seconds, just until the cheese is melted. Sprinkle with parsley, if desired, and pepper. Serve hot.

SERVES 1

MOZZARELLA AND RED PEPPER MELT

Use red peppers that you've roasted yourself and stored in olive oil in your refrigerator, or fire-roasted peppers from the jar—Progresso makes good ones. Served with soup this makes a very satisfying lunch.

▸ *PREPARATION TIME: 5
minutes*
COOKING TIME: 1 minute
STANDING TIME: 1 minute

*1 piece Italian bread (6 inches
long × 3 inches wide),
preferably semolina bread,
halved lengthwise*

*3 ounces grated mozzarella,
preferably fresh (generous
½ cup)*
*1 small roasted red pepper, cut
into 6 ½-inch strips*
*1 tablespoon shredded fresh
basil leaves*
Freshly ground pepper

1. Remove some of the doughy center of bread if desired, and toast or broil the bread. When the bread has cooled slightly, top with grated mozzarella and lay three strips of roasted red pepper diagonally across each sandwich.

2. Fold two paper towels and place on a microwave-safe dinner plate. Place the bread and cheese on the paper towels. Microwave uncovered on high power for 1 minute, just until the cheese is melted. Remove from the oven and top with the fresh basil and pepper. Let stand 1 minute, then serve hot.

SERVES 1

CHICKEN AND ROASTED RED PEPPER SANDWICH

Intense Mediterranean flavors make this a great sandwich for a trip to the park or to the office for lunch.

▶ **PREPARATION TIME:** 10 minutes
COOKING TIME: 2 minutes

½ boneless, skinless chicken breast
1 tablespoon dry white wine or chicken broth
1 tablespoon coarsely chopped roasted red pepper
1 tablespoon olive oil, preferably extra-virgin
2 teaspoons minced fresh parsley
1 teaspoon balsamic or red wine vinegar
½ teaspoon fresh thyme leaves
½ teaspoon capers
Pinch **each** salt and freshly ground pepper

1 small baguette (about 10 inches long), split lengthwise

1. Place the chicken breast in a microwave-safe 9-inch glass pie plate and drizzle the wine over the top. Cover with microwave-safe plastic wrap and vent one side. Microwave on high power for 2 minutes, turning the dish after 1 minute. Let stand until cool enough to handle.

2. Meanwhile, process the remaining ingredients except the baguette in a food processor until blended. Tear the chicken into strips and place in a small bowl. Add the red pepper mixture and stir to combine. Spoon into the split baguette.

SERVES 1

JALAPENO-AVOCADO TORTILLA MELT

Jalapeno Jack lends a terrific touch, but if you can't find it, use plain Monterey Jack for a great quick snack or lunch.

▶ **PREPARATION TIME: 7 minutes**
COOKING TIME: 1½ minutes

1 flour tortilla (7–8 inches in diameter)
½ cup grated jalapeno Monterey Jack cheese, grated (about 2 ounces)
1 thin slice red onion, separated into rings
2 tablespoons fresh or thawed frozen corn kernels (optional)
¼ California avocado, peeled, pitted, and diced
1 teaspoon minced cilantro
Pinch crushed hot red pepper flakes

Place the tortilla on a microwave-safe dinner plate and sprinkle the cheese evenly over the top. Scatter the onion rings and the corn kernels over the cheese. Microwave uncovered on high power for 45 to 90 seconds, just until the cheese is melted. Toss the avocado cubes over the melted cheese and season with minced cilantro and hot red pepper flakes. Serve hot, either open-faced or folded over into a half-moon shape.

SERVES 1

SOPHISTICATED SPREADS

SALMON RILLETTES

A sophisticated hors d'oeuvre that's good to have on hand when friends drop in during the holiday season—or any season. You can make it even fancier by garnishing it with caviar, but it's certainly not necessary. It's a festive dish and would be great served with chilled champagne or white wine and a wide variety of crackers and breads or toasts. Use high-quality smoked salmon, and the freshest salmon available—the quality of the dish depends on it. If you're especially fond of Dijon mustard, capers, or lemon, try adding more after you've assembled the dish, if you think it still needs it.

▶ **PREPARATION TIME:** 15
   minutes
COOKING TIME: 3 minutes
STANDING TIME: 2 minutes
CHILLING TIME: 1 hour

---

8 ounces fresh salmon fillet or
   steak (1 inch thick)
8 ounces smoked salmon, diced
1 shallot, finely minced
½ cup (1 stick) unsalted butter,
   at room temperature
¼ cup chopped fresh parsley
   leaves
1 tablespoon fresh lemon juice
1 teaspoon **each** Dijon mustard, capers, Cognac, and
   grated lemon zest
Salt and freshly ground pepper

Parsley leaves, for garnish
Salmon caviar, for garnish
   (optional)
Thin slices pumpernickel, for
   serving

---

1. Place the fresh salmon in a microwave-safe 9-inch pie plate, cover with microwave-safe plastic wrap, and vent one side. Being careful not to overcook, microwave on high power for 2 to 3 minutes, until just done. Let stand 2 minutes, then let cool slightly.

2. Remove the skin and bones from the cooked salmon and place the fish in a mixing bowl. Using a wooden spoon, work to an almost smooth paste. Add the smoked salmon, shallot, butter, parsley, lemon juice, mustard, capers, Cognac, and lemon zest and combine thoroughly. Season to taste with salt and pepper.

3. Spoon the salmon mixture into a small crock or serving bowl and refrigerate covered at least 1 hour. Garnish with parsley leaves and caviar, and serve with thin slices of pumpernickel.

SERVES 8

BABA GANOUSH*

The microwave is a great tool for making this Middle Eastern appetizer; it's quick, easy, and very tasty. (Cooking eggplant in a conventional oven could take anywhere from 30 minutes to an hour.)

▶ **PREPARATION TIME: 10 minutes**
COOKING TIME: 10 minutes
CHILLING TIME: 30 minutes

1 medium eggplant (about 1 pound), pricked several times with a fork
2 tablespoons tahini (sesame seed paste)
2 tablespoons fresh lemon juice
2 scallions, minced
2 tablespoons minced cilantro
1 tablespoon olive oil, preferably extra-virgin
1 clove garlic, minced
½ teaspoon sugar
Salt and freshly ground pepper

Microwave the eggplant uncovered in a microwave-safe 9-inch glass pie plate on high power until softened, 7 to 10 minutes. Let cool slightly, then trim and remove peel. Using a fork, mash the pulp to a paste in a mixing bowl. Add the remaining ingredients and mix well. Refrigerate covered for 30 minutes. Serve chilled with crudités or toasted pita bread.

SERVES 6

CAPONATA*

This Sicilian dish is served cold or at room temperature, as a spread on crostini (see page 173) or crackers, or sometimes as a vegetable side dish. The microwave manages to capture the fresh, tangy taste of the eggplant. Make it in the summer when eggplants are firm and the skins are a glossy, unblemished deep purple. Caponata is best when the flavors have been allowed to mellow 24 hours before serving.

▶ **PREPARATION TIME:** 15 minutes
DRAINING TIME (for eggplant): 1 to 2 hours
COOKING TIME: 25 minutes

---

1 medium firm unblemished eggplant (about 1 pound), trimmed, peeled, and cut into ½-inch-thick slices
Salt
½ cup diced trimmed celery
½ cup diced sweet red onion
¼ cup extra-virgin olive oil
1 clove garlic, crushed
1 cup diced raw tomato
1 tablespoon flavorful red wine vinegar
1 teaspoon balsamic vinegar
1 tablespoon rinsed and drained capers
1 tablespoon pitted and chopped brine-cured black olives
1 tablespoon finely chopped Italian parsley
Freshly ground pepper

1. Layer the eggplant slices in a large colander, sprinkling each layer lightly with salt. Place a plate on the top so that it rests on the eggplant and weight it with something heavy. Place the colander over a shallow bowl; let stand from 1 to 2 hours to drain the excess moisture.

2. Blot the eggplant dry between double layers of paper towels and cut into ½-inch cubes. Combine the eggplant, celery, onion, oil, and garlic in a microwave-safe 3-quart glass casserole. Microwave uncovered on high power for 10 minutes, stirring once halfway through cooking. Stir in the tomato. Microwave uncovered for 10 minutes. Stir in the red wine vinegar and balsamic vinegar. Microwave uncovered for 5 minutes. Stir in the capers, olives, parsley, and black pepper. Cool at room temperature.

MAKES ABOUT 2 CUPS

GARLIC-THYME SPREAD*

The garlic in this dish becomes really sweet when cooked with the chicken stock and shallots—just like garlic roasted in the oven for an hour, but this only takes 12 minutes. This is a perfect spread for Tuscan whole grain bread or your favorite crackers. Wonderful served with grapes.

▶ **PREPARATION TIME:** 15 minutes
COOKING TIME: 12 minutes

20 cloves garlic
2 shallots
1 cup homemade or canned chicken broth
1 bay leaf
½ cup part-skim or whole milk ricotta cheese
1 teaspoon fresh thyme leaves
1 teaspoon olive oil, preferably extra-virgin
Salt
Lots of freshly ground pepper

1. Peel the garlic cloves and shallots, and split them in half lengthwise. Remove the inner green section of the garlic if necessary; it will cause the dish to be bitter.

2. Place the garlic, shallots, broth, and bay leaf in a microwave-safe 2-quart glass measure. Cover with a microwave-safe dinner plate and microwave on high power for 12 minutes, until very soft. Remove the garlic and shallots from the liquid with a slotted spoon and puree in a food processor with 1 teaspoon of the chicken broth. Save the remaining broth for another use.

3. Add the ricotta, thyme, olive oil, and salt and pepper to taste to the food processor and process until smooth, about 2 minutes, scraping the sides. Taste and adjust seasonings. Serve at room temperature.

MAKES 1 CUP

FINGER FOODS

STICKY CHICKEN WINGS

No one will ever guess that these were prepared in the microwave. They have great "Chinese restaurant" flavor—and a beautiful dark sheen. Serve them hot or at room temperature as an appetizer or keep them chilled for snacking. Cold rice wine is a good accompaniment.

▶ **PREPARATION TIME:** 20
   minutes
MARINATING TIME: 30
   minutes
COOKING TIME: 12 minutes

¼ cup soy sauce, preferably
   low-sodium
2 tablespoons honey
2 teaspoons dry sherry
1 small clove garlic, minced
½ teaspoon minced fresh ginger
½ teaspoon Oriental sesame oil
Large pinch Chinese five-spice
   powder
6 chicken wings, tips removed
   and discarded, separated at
   joint
1 teaspoon toasted sesame
   seeds
1 scallion, finely minced
2 teaspoons minced cilantro

1. Stir together the soy sauce, honey, sherry, garlic, ginger, sesame oil, and five-spice powder in a microwave-safe 9-inch glass pie plate. Add the chicken wings and turn to coat. Let stand, turning frequently, for at least 30 minutes.

2. Rearrange the wing pieces in the pie plate with the thickest pieces toward the outer edge of the plate. Cover the dish with microwave-safe plastic wrap and vent one side. Microwave on high power for 5 minutes. Turn the plate and microwave 5 minutes longer.

3. Remove the wings from the pie plate. Microwave the remaining marinade uncovered on high power for 1 to 2 minutes, until very thick. Return the wings to the plate and turn to coat with sauce. Transfer to a serving plate and sprinkle with sesame seeds, scallion, and cilantro.

MAKE 12 PIECES

NACHOS

Perfect for unexpected guests, Nachos take very little time to make and offer lots of flavor.

▶ **PREPARATION TIME:** 5
   minutes
COOKING TIME: 30 seconds

10 round tortilla chips
½ cup grated Monterey Jack
   cheese (about 2 ounces)
1 small fresh jalapeno pepper,
   thinly sliced and seeded
Salsa (optional)

Layer three folded paper towels on a microwave-safe dinner plate. Arrange the tortilla chips on the towels and top with the cheese and jalapeno pepper. Microwave on high power until cheese melts, about 30 seconds. Transfer to serving dish, top with a little salsa, if desired, and serve hot.

MAKES 10 PIECES

JOHN'S TOASTITARITAS

Toastitaritas are tortillas filled with cheese and chunky salsa. Add whatever vegetables suit your whim when you put these together—corn kernels, diced jicama, or minced jalapenos, for example. This dish, while really fast, is not at all short on flavor—and the cleanup is almost nonexistent.

▶ **PREPARATION TIME:** 15
   minutes
COOKING TIME: 8 minutes

20 cherry tomatoes, halved,
   seeded, if desired
1 ripe medium California avocado, peeled, pitted, and
   diced
4 scallions, minced

1 tablespoon fresh lime juice
1 tablespoon minced cilantro
¼ teaspoon grated lime zest
¼ teaspoon salt, or to taste
⅛ teaspoon ground cumin
Pinch cayenne, or to taste
8 flour tortillas (6-inch)
8 ounces Monterey Jack cheese,
   grated (about 2 cups)

1. Stir together the tomatoes, avocado, scallions, lime juice, cilantro, lime zest, salt, cumin seed, and cayenne in a medium bowl, mixing completely. You will have about 3 cups salsa.

2. Place 1 tortilla on a dinner plate and sprinkle with about ¼ cup grated Monterey Jack. Microwave uncovered on high power for about 1 minute, until the cheese is melted. Fold the tortilla over into a half-circle and top with a generous ⅓ cup salsa. Serve immediately. Repeat with the remaining ingredients.

MAKES 8

SPICED SHRIMP IN THE RAW*

S erve these shrimp warm or chilled with frosty glasses of beer. Have a basket of dampened towels or cloth napkins handy for wiping juicy fingertips between feasting and sipping.

▶ **PREPARATION TIME: 5 minutes**
COOKING TIME: 3 minutes
STANDING TIME: 5 minutes

1 pound large shrimp (about 20)
2 tablespoons olive oil
2 cloves garlic, crushed
½ teaspoon crushed hot red pepper flakes
1 tablespoon shredded fresh basil or cilantro
1 tablespoon fresh lemon or lime juice

Place the shrimp in a microwave-safe 10-inch glass pie plate. Top with the olive oil, garlic, and red pepper flakes. Stir to combine, then spread the shrimp in an even layer. Cover with microwave-safe plastic wrap and vent one side. Microwave on high power for 3 minutes. Uncover and stir. Cover and let stand 5 minutes to continue cooking. Serve warm, or refrigerate until cold and serve chilled. Drain the liquid off just before serving. Sprinkle with basil or cilantro and lemon or lime juice.

SERVES 2 TO 4

DRINKS WITH SPIRIT

WASSAIL

This classic traditional holiday drink from the British Isles adds its own seasonal cheer.

PREPARATION TIME: 10 minutes
COOKING TIME: 9 minutes

12 whole cloves
4 thick slices red-skinned apple
1½ cups ale
1½ cups dry sherry
Zest from 1 lemon, cut in thin strips
Juice from 1 lemon
3 tablespoons sugar, or to taste
1 tablespoon minced fresh ginger
3 whole cardamom pods, crushed
⅛ teaspoon freshly grated nutmeg

Stick 3 cloves into the peel side of each apple slice. Pour the ale into a microwave-safe 2-quart glass measure and add the apples. Microwave uncovered on high power for 2 minutes, until hot but not boiling. Add the remaining ingredients and microwave uncovered on high power for about 6 to 7 minutes, until very hot but not boiling. Strain, reserving the apple slices. Serve hot or chilled, garnished with the apple slices.

SERVES 4

GLOGG

Serve glogg with your favorite ginger cookies, and keep warm and happy like the Scandinavians do.

▸ **PREPARATION TIME:** 7
   minutes
COOKING TIME: 8 minutes

3 cups dry red wine
2 pieces lemon zest, 3 inches x
   1 inch
1 cinnamon stick
2 tablespoons light brown
   sugar
2 tablespoons dried currants
2 tablespoons toasted slivered
   almonds
1/2 teaspoon ground ginger
4 whole cloves

1/4 cup vodka (optional)

Combine the red wine, lemon
zest, cinnamon stick, brown sugar,
currants, almonds, ginger, and cloves
in a microwave-safe 2-quart glass
measure. Microwave uncovered on
high power for about 6 to 8 minutes,
until very hot but not boiling. Remove
and discard the lemon zest. Add the
vodka, if desired. Serve hot in sturdy
wine glasses.

SERVES 4

HOT BUTTERED RUM

The perfect drink for sitting around the fire on a very cold winter
evening.

▸ **PREPARATION TIME:** 5
   minutes
COOKING TIME: 10 minutes

2 cups apple or pear cider or
   juice, at room temperature
1 1/2 cups water, at room
   temperature
2 tablespoons dark brown
   sugar
1 tablespoon minced crystallized ginger
1/2 cup dark rum
1/2 teaspoon vanilla extract
1/4 cup unsalted butter, at room
   temperature

4 cinnamon sticks, for garnish

Stir the cider, water, brown
sugar, and crystallized ginger together in a microwave-safe 2-quart
glass measure. Microwave uncovered
on high power until the sugar has dissolved and it begins to bubble, about
8 to 10 minutes. Stir in the rum and
vanilla extract. Swirl in the butter and
stir until mixed. Pour into mugs;
serve hot, garnished with cinnamon
sticks.

SERVES 4

ATHOLE BROSE

A classic drink in Scotland. The honey and milk soften the flavor of the whiskey, pleasing even those who aren't big Scotch lovers.

▸ **PREPARATION TIME:** 3 minutes
COOKING TIME: 6 minutes

1½ cups milk
1 cup half-and-half
½ cup mild honey
1 cup Scotch whiskey
Freshly grated nutmeg, for garnish (optional)

Whisk the milk, half-and-half, and honey together in a microwave-safe 2-quart glass measure. Microwave uncovered on high power for about 6 to 8 minutes, until very hot. Whisk in the Scotch and serve hot or chilled, sprinkled with nutmeg if desired.

SERVES 4

CHAPTER 3

SOUPS

As you can tell from the length of this chapter, we are both hard-core soup-makers. Although there are some favorite soups we wouldn't think of making in the microwave—a traditional minestrone comes to mind immediately—there are many soups that are naturals for it.

Making broth in the microwave is a simple thing to do regularly—once you get into the swing of it. To begin, take inspiration from Lori's habit of making small batches of chicken broth to use in cooking. Collect the wing tips, backbones, and ribs from fresh chickens in a plastic bag in the freezer, then whip up a batch of stock. Homemade broth is always so much more flavorful than canned. (Of course, for those who don't want to bother making their own chicken broth, the convenient canned variety, now available both unsalted and with less salt, can be used in any of our recipes.)

Besides cooking soups fast—most of our soups take well under 25 minutes—the microwave heats them evenly, a real advantage over conventional cooking because you don't have to worry about scorching the bottom of the saucepan—especially with the milk-based soups.

Our hearty soups and chowders are delicious and make a wonderful centerpiece main course for a Sunday supper or easy dinner. The light soups and cold soups make stylish and flavorful lunches or first courses. All our soups are delightfully simple, but simplest of all are the cups of soup. Keep the ingredients for these on hand and you can have a very healthful—and good-tasting— lunch or first course in a matter of minutes.

Leftover soups are a natural for reheating in the microwave. Heat uncovered on high power approximately 2 minutes per cup; stir well and continue to heat in 30-second increments until heated to taste.

R E C I P E S

Chicken Broth*

HEARTY SOUPS

Acorn Squash and Carrot Soup
Sweet Potato and Orange Soup
Hearty Lentil and Mushroom Soup
Cream of Two Mushrooms
Cannellini Bean and Escarole Soup with Italian Sausage
Pastina, Broccoli, and Parmesan Cheese Soup
More Than Just Lentil Soup*
Curried Cauliflower and Cannellini Bean Soup
Curried Butternut Squash Soup with Peanuts

LIGHTER SOUPS

Tomato, Green Chile, and Lime Soup*
Avgolemono (Greek Egg and Lemon Soup)
Thai Chicken Coconut Soup
Lemon Borscht*
Tomato-Fennel Soup*
Carrot-Parsnip Soup

CHOWDERS

Salmon, Bacon, and Corn Chowder
Shrimp, Corn, and Potato Chowder
New England Fish Chowder

CHILLED SOUPS

Chilled Fresh Tomato and Leek Soup*
Chilled Curried Spinach Soup*
Creamy Carrot and Cilantro Soup

CUPS OF SOUP

Curried Tomato Soup
Chinese-style Broth*
Spinach, Beef, and Mushroom Soup*

* Especially good for you.

CHICKEN BROTH*

Making chicken broth in the microwave is a great idea; it takes much less time than on the stove and you can pretty much ignore it while it's cooking. You can serve it as broth, use it as a soup base, or keep it on hand to use whenever stock is needed in cooking. It will keep in the refrigerator for several days; or freeze it in small batches that approximate the amounts used in your favorite recipes.

Try cooking some fresh ginger in the broth if you'll be using it for an Oriental dish—or you just want to add some zing. The broth can be reduced to a glaze for sauce-making if you cook it uncovered on high power after it's been strained until it's reduced to about a cup. If possible, refrigerate broth before using it so you can skim off the fat.

▶ **PREPARATION TIME:** 10 minutes
COOKING TIME: 1 hour
STANDING TIME: 10 minutes

---

4 cups cool water
2 pounds chicken wings, backs, and/or bones, cut into smaller pieces
1 large leek (white part only), chopped and washed
2 small carrots, trimmed and chopped
1 rib celery, trimmed and chopped
4 sprigs parsley
1 bay leaf
1 teaspoon dried thyme
5 whole black peppercorns
Salt and freshly ground pepper

---

1. Combine all the ingredients except the salt and pepper in a mi-crowave-safe 3-quart glass casserole with a lid. Microwave covered on high power for about 20 minutes, until the broth comes to a boil. Stir and cook covered on medium power (50%) for 35 to 40 minutes, until the broth is highly flavored. Let stand covered 10 minutes.

2. Strain completely. Season to taste with salt and freshly ground pepper.

MAKES 1 QUART

NOTE: Canned chicken broth, preferably unsalted or reduced salt variety, can be used instead of homemade in any of our recipes if desired. To defat canned broth, skim fat off the top with a spoon.

HEARTY SOUPS

ACORN SQUASH AND CARROT SOUP

This bright orange soup adds a colorful note and is especially good in fall or winter.

> **PREPARATION TIME:** 15 minutes
> **COOKING TIME:** 17 minutes

½ acorn squash (about 12 ounces), seeded
3 carrots, pared and cut in 1-inch lengths
1 tablespoon water
1 tablespoon unsalted butter
2 fresh mushrooms, minced
1 shallot, minced
1 cup milk
¾ cup homemade or canned chicken broth
½ cup heavy cream
Salt and freshly ground pepper
1 tablespoon snipped fresh chives

1. Place the acorn squash cut-side down in a microwave-safe 9-inch glass pie plate. Microwave uncovered on high power for 5 minutes. Turn cut-side up and microwave for 1 minute longer.

2. Place the carrots and water in a microwave-safe 2-quart glass casserole with a lid. Microwave covered on high power until fully cooked, 3 to 4 minutes, stirring once.

3. Melt the butter in a microwave-safe 9-inch glass pie plate on high power about 30 seconds. Add the mushrooms and shallot and stir well. Cover with microwave-safe plastic wrap and vent one side. Microwave until softened, 1 to 2 minutes.

4. Scoop the squash from the rind into the food processor. Add the carrots, the mushroom mixture, and ¼ cup milk. Process until very smooth, then transfer to a clean 2-quart casserole, straining if desired for a smoother soup. Add all the remaining ingredients except the chives and stir until blended. Microwave covered until hot, 2 to 4 minutes. Top with chives and serve hot.

SERVES 2

SWEET POTATO AND ORANGE SOUP

Sweet potato and orange are a wonderful flavor combination, and one you'll enjoy in this silky soup.

▶ *PREPARATION TIME: 12 minutes*
COOKING TIME: 18 minutes

---

2 tablespoons unsalted butter
2 medium onions, chopped
1 medium sweet potato (8 ounces), pared and grated
1½ cups homemade or canned chicken broth
1 carrot, pared and grated
¼ teaspoon salt, or to taste
Pinch grated orange zest (optional)
¾ cup half-and-half
¾ cup orange juice, preferably fresh-squeezed
Dash hot red pepper sauce, or to taste
1 tablespoon minced fresh parsley, for garnish

1. Microwave the butter uncovered in a microwave-safe 2-quart glass casserole with a lid on high power until melted, about 1 minute. Add the onions and stir to coat well. Microwave covered on high power for 2 minutes.

2. Add the sweet potatoes, broth, carrot, salt, and orange zest if desired. Microwave covered for 10 minutes. Puree, in batches, in a food processor or blender.

3. Place the sweet potato mixture in the same clean glass casserole and add the half-and-half, orange juice, and red pepper sauce. Stir to mix. Microwave covered on high power until heated through, about 3 to 5 minutes. Serve hot, sprinkled with minced fresh parsley.

SERVES 4

HEARTY LENTIL AND MUSHROOM SOUP

Although this soup isn't exactly quick-cooking, it takes less time than when it is made conventionally. Furthermore, the flavor is excellent—which is reason enough to include it here.

▸ *PREPARATION TIME: 10 minutes*
COOKING TIME: 40 minutes
STANDING TIME: 5 minutes

2 slices bacon, diced
2 cups chopped fresh
    mushrooms
½ cup chopped onion
2 cloves garlic, crushed
2 cups very hot tap water
1½ cups homemade or canned
    chicken broth
1 cup dried lentils, rinsed
1 bay leaf
1 cup heavy cream
Salt and freshly ground pepper
1 tablespoon chopped fresh
    parsley, for garnish

1. Microwave the bacon in a microwave-safe 3-quart glass casserole with a lid, uncovered, on high power until crisp, about 2 minutes. Remove with a slotted spoon to paper towel to drain; reserve the drippings in the casserole.

2. Stir the mushrooms, onion, and garlic into the drippings. Microwave covered on high power for 8 to 10 minutes, stirring once. Stir in the water, chicken broth, lentils, and bay leaf. Microwave covered for 30 minutes, stirring twice during the cooking. Let stand, covered, for 5 minutes. Remove the bay leaf.

3. Transfer half of the lentil mixture to a food processor. Puree while gradually adding the heavy cream through the feed tube. Return the pureed mixture to the casserole; stir to blend. Reheat until hot, about 2 minutes. Season with salt and pepper to taste. Ladle into bowls; garnish each serving with the reserved bacon and fresh parsley.

SERVES 4

CREAM OF TWO MUSHROOMS

A potato sautéed along with the mushrooms thickens this hearty soup without requiring the richness of a butter and flour roux. But just in case that touch of real creaminess is missed, you can finish the soup off with a dash of cream or half-and-half. Dried porcini (wild mushrooms from Italy available in specialty food shops) add an intense, earthy mushroom flavor to this soup.

▶ *PREPARATION TIME: 20 minutes*
COOKING TIME: 22 minutes
STANDING TIME: 30 minutes

1 cup hot tap water
¼ cup crumbled dried porcini
    (about ½ ounce)
2 tablespoons unsalted butter
3 cups coarsely chopped white
    button mushrooms (about 8
    ounces)
1 cup diced peeled all-purpose
    potato
¼ cup finely chopped onion
2 cups unsalted beef broth or
    half water and half broth
Salt and freshly ground pepper

Sliced Mushroom Garnish:
1 tablespoon unsalted butter
1 cup thinly sliced mushrooms
    (about 3 ounces)
1 tablespoon chopped fresh
    parsley
Salt and freshly ground pepper

1. Combine the water and the porcini in a microwave-safe 1-quart glass measuring cup. Microwave uncovered on high power for 4 minutes. Cover and let stand 20 minutes.

2. Melt the butter in a microwave-safe 3-quart glass casserole with a lid, about 2 minutes. Stir in the chopped mushrooms, potato, and onion. Microwave covered for 5 minutes, stirring once. Stir in the broth; microwave covered for 5 minutes. Let stand covered for 10 minutes.

3. Using a slotted spoon, transfer the solids from the broth to the bowl of a food processor. Add about ½ cup of the broth to the solids. Process until very smooth, about 2 minutes. Stir back into the broth.

4. Drain the soaked porcini in a fine sieve set over a measuring cup. Add the porcini soaking liquid to the soup. Check the reconstituted porcini for any grit; rinse briefly with water. Finely chop the porcini and add to the soup.

5. *Make the Sliced Mushroom Garnish:* Melt the butter in a microwave-safe 9-inch glass pie plate, 1 minute. Stir in the mushrooms; microwave uncovered for 4 minutes, stirring once. Drain off any liquid and add it to the soup. Season the mushrooms with the parsley and salt and pepper.

6. Reheat the soup in the microwave, uncovered, for 2 minutes or until heated through. Season to taste with salt and pepper. Ladle into bowls and garnish each with the mushroom garnish, dividing evenly.

SERVES 4

CANNELLINI BEAN AND ESCAROLE SOUP WITH ITALIAN SAUSAGE

S erved with sesame breadsticks, this hearty soup becomes a satisfying and nourishing supper.

▸ **PREPARATION TIME:** 10 minutes
COOKING TIME: 22 minutes
STANDING TIME: 5 minutes

12 ounces sweet Italian sausage, casings removed, meat crumbled
1 cup coarsely chopped onion
1 clove garlic, minced
3 cups (packed) tender inside escarole leaves, rinsed, trimmed, and torn
1 19-ounce can cannellini (white kidney) beans, with liquid
1 14½-ounce can whole tomatoes, with liquid
1½ cups homemade or canned chicken broth
¼ teaspoon fennel seeds
Salt and freshly ground pepper

1. Crumble the sausage into a microwave-safe 3-quart glass casserole with a lid; add the onion and garlic. Microwave covered on high power until the sausage is cooked through, about 6 to 7 minutes.

2. Break up the sausage meat with a fork. Stir in the escarole leaves, the beans with their liquid, the tomatoes with their liquid, the chicken broth, and the fennel seeds. Break up the tomatoes with a fork. Microwave covered on high power for 15 minutes. Let stand covered for 5 minutes. Before serving, add salt and pepper to taste.

SERVES 4

PASTINA, BROCCOLI, AND CHEESE SOUP

W ith these few ingredients on hand you can serve this soup on a moment's notice with little or no effort. Parmigiano-Reggiano adds a salty flavor to the soup so you might prefer using lightly salted or unsalted chicken broth.

▸ **PREPARATION TIME:** 5
minutes
COOKING TIME: 18 minutes

1½ cups homemade or canned
    chicken broth, preferably
    unsalted
1 cup water
2 tablespoons pastina
1 cup chopped broccoli
    flowerets
1 large egg
1 tablespoon grated Parmigiano-
    Reggiano cheese, plus more
    for garnish

---

1. Pour the chicken broth and water into a microwave-safe 2-quart glass measuring cup. Add the pastina; microwave uncovered on high power for 10 minutes. Stir in the broccoli; microwave uncovered for 5 minutes.

2. Meanwhile, in a small bowl beat the egg and 1 tablespoon of cheese until blended. As soon as the broccoli has finished cooking, immediately pour the egg mixture in a slow, steady stream into the steaming hot soup, stirring constantly. Microwave uncovered for 3 minutes, or until the soup is thickened. Stir vigorously to break up any clumps of egg. Sprinkle each serving generously with additional grated cheese.

SERVES 2

MORE THAN JUST LENTIL SOUP*

This hearty, simple, comforting country soup is good for you—and uncomplicated. It will serve four as a main course (a satisfying dinner with whole grain bread and a salad), or six as a first course or lunch.

▸ **PREPARATION TIME:** 20
minutes
COOKING TIME: 34 minutes
STANDING TIME: 10 minutes

---

1 tablespoon safflower oil
2 cloves garlic, minced
1 teaspoon curry powder

½ teaspoon ground cumin
¼ teaspoon ground coriander
    seed
¼ teaspoon ground ginger
¼ teaspoon grated lemon zest
1 bunch scallions (6 medium)
    trimmed, finely minced
1 medium carrot, pared and
    finely diced

1 small zucchini, finely diced
1 small turnip (3 ounces),
    pared and finely diced
1 bay leaf
3 cups homemade or canned
    chicken broth
1 16-ounce can Italian crushed
    tomatoes
¾ cup dried lentils
2 cups shredded cooked
    chicken, turkey, or duck
¼ cup cilantro leaves
1 jalapeno pepper, seeded and
    minced
Salt (optional)

1. Stir together the oil, garlic, curry powder, cumin, ground coriander, ginger, and lemon zest in a microwave-safe 3-quart casserole with a lid. Microwave covered on high power for 2 minutes. Stir in the scallions, carrot, zucchini, turnip, and bay leaf. Cover and microwave on high power for 2 minutes longer.

2. Add the chicken broth, crushed tomatoes, and lentils and stir to mix well. Cover and microwave on high power for 30 minutes, stirring three times. Stir in the chicken, cilantro leaves, and jalapeno pepper. Let stand 10 minutes. Taste and add salt, if desired. Remove the bay leaf and serve hot.

SERVES 4–6

CURRIED CAULIFLOWER AND CANNELLINI BEAN SOUP

Served with a crusty loaf of whole grain bread and a mixed green salad, this is our idea of the perfect midwinter supper.

▶ **PREPARATION TIME:** 10
    minutes
COOKING TIME: 15 minutes
STANDING TIME: 5 minutes

½ cup chopped onion
1 tablespoon olive oil
2 teaspoons curry powder
½ teaspoon ground turmeric
1 small clove garlic, minced
¼ teaspoon **each** ground ginger and cumin

3 cups homemade or canned
    chicken broth
1 head cauliflower (about 1½
    pounds), trimmed and cut
    into small flowerets
1 29-ounce can cannellini
    beans, drained
1 cup frozen small green peas
½ teaspoon salt
Freshly ground pepper

1. Combine the onion, olive oil, curry powder, turmeric, garlic, ginger, and cumin, in a microwave-safe 3-quart glass casserole with a lid. Add the broth and the cauliflower. Cover and microwave on high power 10 minutes, or until the cauliflower is tender, stirring once. Let stand covered for 5 minutes.

2. Uncover; remove about 1 cup of the cooked cauliflower with a slotted spoon and reserve. Puree the remaining soup in a food processor, working in batches, if necessary. Return to the casserole. Add the reserved cooked cauliflower, the cannellini beans, and the peas. Cover and microwave 5 minutes, or until heated through. Season to taste with salt and pepper before serving.

SERVES 6

CURRIED BUTTERNUT SQUASH SOUP WITH PEANUTS

▶ *PREPARATION TIME: 10 minutes*
COOKING TIME: 12 minutes
STANDING TIME: 10 minutes

1 butternut squash (about 1¼ pounds)
½ cup finely chopped onion
1 tablespoon unsalted butter
1 clove garlic, crushed
1 teaspoon curry powder
½ teaspoon ground cumin
1 16-ounce can whole tomatoes, with liquid
1 cup half-and-half
1 cup homemade or canned chicken broth
Salt and freshly ground pepper (optional)
¼ cup coarsely chopped unsalted dry roasted peanuts

1. Using a heavy knife, make four evenly spaced, deep slashes in the squash. Microwave on high power 6 minutes. Wrap in a towel and let stand on counter 10 minutes to continue cooking.

2. Meanwhile, combine the onion, butter, garlic, curry powder, and cumin in a microwave-safe 3-quart glass casserole with a lid; microwave covered on high power for 3 minutes.

3. When the squash is cool, cut in half lengthwise; discard the seeds. Scoop out the pulp and discard the skin. Combine the squash, the onion mixture, and the tomatoes with their liquid in a food processor. Puree in batches if necessary in the food processor; slowly add the half-and-half through the feed tube until blended.

4. Pour the mixture back into the

casserole; stir in the chicken broth. Taste and add salt and pepper, if needed. Reheat in the microwave, covered, for 2 to 3 minutes, stirring once, or until very hot. Do not boil. Ladle into bowls and sprinkle with the peanuts.

SERVES 4

LIGHTER SOUPS

TOMATO, GREEN CHILE, AND LIME SOUP*

▶ **PREPARATION TIME:** 10 minutes
COOKING TIME: 8 minutes

½ cup finely chopped onion
1 tablespoon olive oil
1 clove garlic, crushed
½ teaspoon ground cumin
½ teaspoon chili powder
1 14½-ounce can whole tomatoes, with liquid
½ cup homemade or canned chicken broth
1 tablespoon chopped hot or mild canned chiles
1 fresh lime
1 tablespoon chopped cilantro leaves
1 tablespoon sour cream

1. Combine the onion, olive oil, and garlic in a microwave-safe 2-quart glass casserole with a lid. Microwave uncovered on high power for 3 minutes, stirring once. Stir in the cumin and chili powder. Add the tomatoes with liquid, chicken broth, and chopped chiles; break up and mash the tomatoes with a fork. Microwave uncovered for 5 minutes, or until almost boiling.

2. Cut two thin slices from the center of the lime and reserve for garnish. Squeeze the juice from the remaining lime and stir into the hot soup. Ladle into bowls, divide the cilantro between the bowls, and garnish each bowl with a lime slice and a dollop of sour cream.

SERVES 2

AVGOLEMONO (GREEK EGG AND LEMON SOUP)

Avgolemono is the queen of Greek soups. Served in ancient times, its golden color and piquant lemon flavor are every bit as appealing today. *Lemono* obviously means lemon and *avgo* is Greek for egg, so you'll sometimes see this on menus as egg and lemon soup. Some Greek peasants make a loud kissing sound when they add the lemon to keep the soup from curdling, but you won't need to resort to that superstition if you follow these simple directions. Serve Avgolemono hot or chilled; and if you're looking for a variation try using orzo or vermicelli instead of rice, use part beef broth, or add a little cream or lemon zest. But first try this pale, elegant low-calorie soup just the way it is.

▶ **PREPARATION TIME:** 10 minutes
COOKING TIME: 16 minutes

4 cups homemade or canned chicken broth
½ cup long-grain rice, well rinsed and drained
2 large egg yolks
Juice of 1 lemon
Salt and freshly ground pepper
Very thin lemon slices, for garnish
2 tablespoons minced fresh mint, for garnish

1. Place the broth and rice in a microwave-safe 2-quart glass casserole with a lid. Cover and microwave on high power until the rice is cooked, about 15 minutes.

2. Whisk the egg yolks and lemon juice in a medium bowl until blended. Gradually whisk 1 cup hot broth from the casserole into the egg mixture, then return to casserole and stir to blend. Microwave covered on high power until heated through, about 1 minute. Season to taste with salt and pepper. Ladle into serving bowls, float lemon slices on top, and sprinkle with fresh mint.

SERVES 4

THAI CHICKEN COCONUT SOUP

Known in Thailand as Gai Tom Ka, this simple country-style soup, bursting with exciting Thai flavors, is among the most often requested dishes in Thai restaurants. Soups are included in almost every meal in Thailand, and are served with the entrée, not before as here in the West. Great for entertaining, this soup can be served as a first course or a main course. The lemon grass, lime leaves, and fish sauce can be found in Oriental markets and specialty stores.

▶ **PREPARATION TIME:** 15 minutes
COOKING TIME: 14 minutes

1 14-ounce can unsweetened coconut milk (see Note)
1½ cups homemade or canned chicken broth
¼ cup fresh lime juice
1 stalk fresh lemon grass, trimmed and cut into 1-inch lengths (optional)
4–5 Thai lime leaves (optional) or 1 piece lime zest, 1 inch × 3 inches
2 tablespoons nam pla (Oriental fish sauce)
2 tablespoons minced fresh ginger
2 chicken thighs, skinned, boned, trimmed, and cut into ½-inch strips
¼ cup **each** minced seeded red bell pepper and cilantro
⅛ teaspoon crushed hot red pepper flakes, or to taste

Stir together the coconut milk, chicken broth, lime juice, lemon grass, lime leaves or lime zest, nam pla, ginger, and chicken in a microwave-safe 2-quart glass measure until blended. Cover with microwave-safe plastic wrap and vent one side. Microwave on high power until the chicken is cooked through, about 12 to 14 minutes. Remove the lime zest and stir in the red bell pepper, cilantro, and crushed hot red pepper flakes. Serve immediately.

SERVES 4

NOTE: *If you want to make your own* coconut milk, process 2 cups shredded unsweetened coconut and 3 cups very hot water in 2 batches in the blender. Let stand for 5 minutes and strain.

LEMON BORSCHT*

A great, fast, lowfat and low-calorie soup, *if* you use yogurt—the addition of sour cream changes everything.

▸ **PREPARATION TIME:** 15
minutes
COOKING TIME: 11 minutes

3 cups homemade or canned
chicken and/or beef broth
2 cups shredded fresh beets
(about 2 large beets, 5–6
ounces without greens)
1/2 cup very finely shredded red
cabbage
6 scallions, trimmed and
minced
2 tablespoons fresh lemon juice,
or to taste
1 tablespoon minced fresh dill
1/2 teaspoon grated lemon zest
Salt and cayenne pepper to
taste
1/2 cup lowfat or nonfat yogurt
(or sour cream if you prefer)
Julienne lemon zest, for garnish
Dill sprigs, for garnish

Place the broth, beets, cabbage, and half of the scallions in a microwave-safe 3-quart glass casserole with a lid. Microwave covered on high power for 7 to 10 minutes, until the vegetables are desired doneness. Stir in the remaining scallions and the lemon juice, dill, grated lemon zest, and salt to taste. Microwave covered for 1 minute longer. Stir in cayenne pepper to taste. Serve chilled or hot, topped with yogurt, and garnished with lemon zest and dill sprigs.

SERVES 4

TOMATO-FENNEL SOUP*

The best tomatoes for this soup come in aseptic packages and are called strained fresh tomatoes; they have great texture and no seeds. You can find them in a box in any supermarket. Pomi is a good brand.

▶ *PREPARATION TIME: 8 minutes*
COOKING TIME: 11 minutes

---

2 scallions, finely minced
2 tablespoons safflower oil
½ teaspoon fennel seeds
2 cups strained fresh tomatoes
1½ cups homemade or canned
　　chicken broth
2 tablespoons ouzo or Pernod,
　　or to taste
1 teaspoon sugar (optional)
¼ teaspoon salt, or to taste
3 dashes hot red pepper sauce,
　　or to taste
¼ cup shredded fresh basil

---

1. Stir together the scallions, oil, and fennel seeds in a microwave-safe 2-quart glass casserole with a lid. Microwave covered on high power for 3 minutes, stirring once.

2. Add the tomatoes, broth, ouzo, sugar, and salt. Microwave covered on high power for 8 minutes, stirring once. Season with hot red pepper sauce. Taste and adjust seasoning. Ladle into bowls and garnish with shredded basil.

SERVES 4

CARROT-PARSNIP SOUP

Celebrate root vegetables with this soup, and enjoy the rich, deep flavor. To save time, grate the vegetables in the food processor.

▶ *PREPARATION TIME: 15 minutes*
COOKING TIME: 16 minutes

½ cup minced onion
2 tablespoons unsalted butter
2 cups grated pared carrots
1½ cups homemade or canned
　　chicken broth
1 medium all-purpose potato,
　　pared and grated, liquid
　　reserved

½ cup grated pared parsnip
1 teaspoon fresh thyme leaves
½ teaspoon grated orange zest
½ cup half-and-half
¼ teaspoon **each** salt and
　　freshly ground pepper, or to
　　taste
Fresh thyme sprigs, for garnish
　　(optional)

---

1. Place the onion and butter in a microwave-safe 2-quart glass casserole with a lid. Microwave covered on high power for 3 minutes, stirring once. Stir in the carrots, chicken broth, potato with liquid, parsnip, thyme, and orange zest. Microwave covered on high power for 9 to 11 minutes, until the vegetables are soft, stirring twice.

2. Puree the soup in batches in a blender or food processor, and strain into a clean casserole.

3. Stir the half-and-half into the soup. Microwave covered until hot, about 2 minutes. Season with salt and pepper. Ladle into serving bowls, garnish with thyme sprigs if desired, and serve hot.

SERVES 4

CHOWDERS

SALMON, BACON, AND CORN CHOWDER

This soothing chowder is a great way to use up leftover cooked salmon, but if you have a yearning for salmon chowder and no leftovers, you can always buy a fillet or steak at the fish market. This is filling enough to be a main course; round out the menu with a basket of corn sticks and a crisp green salad.

▸ **PREPARATION TIME:** 10 minutes
COOKING TIME: 13 minutes

---

2 strips bacon, diced
¼ cup finely chopped onion
¼ cup finely chopped celery
    plus 1 celery leaf, chopped
1 17-ounce can cream-style
    corn
1 cup milk or half-and-half
½ teaspoon fresh thyme leaves,
    or a pinch dried thyme
1 12-ounce piece fresh salmon
    fillet or steak, skin and
    bones removed, cut into ½-
    inch pieces, or leftover
    grilled or broiled salmon
2 teaspoons fresh lemon juice
Salt

Cayenne
2 tablespoons finely chopped
    seeded green bell pepper,
    for garnish

---

1. Place the diced bacon in a microwave-safe 2-quart glass casserole with a lid. Microwave uncovered on high power for 3 minutes, stirring once. Remove the bacon with a slotted spoon; set aside. Reserve the bacon drippings in the casserole.

2. Stir the onion and celery into the bacon drippings; microwave covered for 3 minutes, or until tender, stirring once. Add the creamed corn, milk, and thyme. Microwave covered for 4 minutes, or until very hot, stirring once.

3. *If using raw salmon,* stir into the hot chowder mixture and microwave covered for 3 minutes, stirring once. *If using leftover cooked salmon,* stir into the hot chowder and microwave covered for 1 minute. Stir in the lemon juice and salt to taste. Ladle into bowls and sprinkle generously with cayenne. Garnish each with the reserved bacon and minced green pepper, dividing evenly.

SERVES 4

SHRIMP, CORN, AND POTATO CHOWDER

Save this recipe for a cool summer or early fall supper, when fresh corn is still in season.

▶ **PREPARATION TIME:** *15 minutes*
COOKING TIME: *17 minutes*
STANDING TIME: *2 minutes*

2 thick slices bacon, diced
2 medium-sized russet potatoes, peeled, halved lengthwise, and cut into thin slices (about 2 cups)
½ cup finely chopped onion
1 clove garlic, crushed
2 ears of corn, husks removed, kernels cut from cobs (about 2 cups)
1 cup heavy cream
2 cups milk
1 bay leaf
½ teaspoon salt
Pinch dried thyme, or a sprig fresh thyme

8 ounces shrimp, shelled, deveined, and coarsely chopped
2 tablespoons finely chopped seeded green or red bell pepper, for garnish

1. Place the bacon in a microwave-safe 3-quart glass casserole with a lid. Microwave uncovered on high power for 2 minutes. Stir in the potatoes, onion, and garlic. Microwave covered for 5 to 6 minutes, or until the potatoes are evenly tender; stir once.

2. Meanwhile, combine 1 cup of the corn kernels and the heavy cream in the food processor. Process just until the corn is finely chopped. Stir into the cooked potatoes. Add the milk, bay leaf, salt, and thyme. Microwave covered for 6 to 8 minutes, or until the milk is almost boiling, stirring once. Stir in the remaining 1 cup corn kernels and the shrimp. Microwave covered for 1 minute. Let stand 2 minutes covered before serving. Ladle into bowls and sprinkle each with a little chopped red or green bell pepper.

SERVES 5

NEW ENGLAND FISH CHOWDER

Some say a true New England fish chowder is comprised of just bacon or salt pork, onion, cream, and fish, which is what this recipe calls for. But if you would like a heartier chowder, add ¼ cup each finely diced potatoes and carrots or celery when the onions are added to the recipe below, and increase the cooking time by 1-minute increments until the vegetables are tender. Accompanied by a basket of warm bread and a crisp green salad, this is a perfect dish for a simple but satisfying supper.

▶ **PREPARATION TIME:** 5
  minutes
COOKING TIME: 17 minutes
STANDING TIME: 2 minutes

2 thick slices bacon, diced
½ cup finely chopped onion
1 pint half-and-half
½ teaspoon salt
Pinch dried thyme
1 pound cod fillet, cut into 1- to
  1½-inch cubes
Salt
Cayenne

1. Place the bacon in a microwave-safe 3-quart glass casserole with a lid. Microwave uncovered on high power for 2 minutes, or until the bacon is lightly browned. Stir in the onion. Microwave covered until the onion is tender, 4 to 5 minutes. Add the half-and-half, salt, and thyme. Microwave uncovered 4 to 5 minutes, or until the half-and-half is very hot.

2. Add the fish. Microwave covered for 4 to 5 minutes, until the fish is opaque, turning a half-turn once during cooking. Let stand 2 minutes before serving. Taste and add salt if desired. Ladle into bowls, dividing fish and broth evenly. Sprinkle each serving generously with cayenne.

SERVES 4

CHILLED SOUPS

CHILLED FRESH TOMATO AND LEEK SOUP*

Make this soup when fresh local tomatoes are in season. It is wonderful served chilled on a warm, humid summer day, but if you aren't in the mood for a cold soup, you can heat it up. It is just as delicious served hot. Always defat chicken broth when used in a chilled soup; cold chicken fat will solidify on the surface.

▶ **PREPARATION TIME:** 15 minutes
COOKING TIME: 8 minutes
CHILLING TIME: 2 hours

1 small slender leek (white part only), well rinsed and trimmed, coarsely chopped
1 tender inside rib celery including green leafy top, chopped
1 tablespoon olive oil, preferably extra-virgin
2 cups coarsely chopped fresh ripe tomatoes
1½ cups homemade or canned chicken broth, defatted
2 large leaves fresh basil
1 sprig Italian parsley
½ clove garlic
1 strip orange zest, 3 inches × ½ inch, coarsely chopped

Salt and freshly ground black pepper

1. Combine the leek, celery, and olive oil in a microwave-safe 1½-quart glass casserole with a lid. Microwave on high power for 3 minutes. Stir in tomatoes and chicken broth; microwave covered for 5 minutes. Let cool slightly, then puree the tomato mixture in a food processor or press through a food mill. (If a smoother soup is preferred, the pureed soup can be pressed through a sieve.)

2. Finely chop the basil leaves, parsley, garlic, and orange zest together. Stir into the warm soup. Season to taste with salt and pepper. Refrigerate until well chilled, about 2 hours, or chill in the freezer for 1 hour.

SERVES 4

CHILLED CURRIED SPINACH SOUP*

The refreshing tang of buttermilk lends a perfect touch to a chilled summer soup. Despite its name buttermilk is very low in fat and calories.

▸ **PREPARATION TIME:** 5 minutes
COOKING TIME: 7 minutes
CHILLING TIME: 2 hours (1 hour in freezer)

¼ cup chopped scallions
1 to 2 teaspoons curry powder
1 10-ounce package frozen chopped spinach
2 cups buttermilk
1 teaspoon fresh lemon juice
½ teaspoon salt
Freshly ground black pepper
2 tablespoons finely chopped tomato, for garnish

1. Stir the scallion and curry powder together in a microwave-safe 2-quart glass casserole with a lid; place the frozen spinach on top. Microwave covered on high power until the spinach is thawed and the mixture is hot, 5 to 7 minutes.

2. Transfer the spinach and cooking liquid to the bowl of a food processor; add the buttermilk. Process the spinach mixture until pureed. Transfer to a large bowl; add the lemon juice, salt, and a grinding of black pepper to taste. Refrigerate until mixture is thoroughly chilled, about 2 hours, or chill in the freezer for 1 hour. Ladle into bowls and garnish each with chopped tomato.

SERVES 2

CREAMY CARROT AND CILANTRO SOUP

▸ **PREPARATION TIME:** 10 minutes
COOKING TIME: 10 minutes
STANDING TIME: 5 minutes
CHILLING TIME: 2 hours

1½ cups homemade or canned chicken broth
1½ cups finely diced pared carrots

½ cup finely diced pared all-
  purpose potato
1 scallion, trimmed, white part
  chopped, green sliced thin
1½ teaspoons ground coriander
¾ cup half-and-half or milk
1 tablespoon chopped cilantro
2–3 teaspoons minced fresh
  chili pepper (to taste, depending on heat of pepper)
1 teaspoon fresh lemon juice
Salt to taste
Whole cilantro leaves, for
  garnish

1. Combine the broth, carrots, potato, white part of scallion, and coriander in a microwave-safe 2-quart glass casserole with a lid. Microwave covered on high power for 10 minutes, stirring once. Let stand, covered, for 5 minutes.

2. Using a slotted spoon, transfer the cooked carrots and potatoes to a food processor; add about ½ cup of the hot broth from the casserole and process until pureed. With the motor running, add the half-and-half through the feed tube just until blended. (For a smoother texture, strain the soup through a fine sieve after processing.) Stir back into the casserole.

3. Stir in the cilantro and chili pepper. Refrigerate until well chilled, about 2 hours, or chill in the freezer for 1 hour.

4. Add the lemon juice and salt to taste if desired to the chilled soup, ladle into bowls, and garnish each with a few whole leaves of cilantro and slices of green scallion tops.

SERVES 2

CUPS OF SOUP

CURRIED TOMATO SOUP

▶ **PREPARATION TIME:** 5 minutes
COOKING TIME: 5 minutes

---

1 tablespoon unsalted butter, cut into small pieces
1 tablespoon minced onion
1 teaspoon curry powder, or to taste
1/4 teaspoon ground cumin
1 1/2 cups tomato juice
1 tablespoon lowfat plain yogurt

Cilantro leaves or thin slices of scallion tops

Combine the butter, onion, curry powder, and cumin in a microwave-safe 2-cup glass measure. Microwave uncovered on high power for 2 minutes, stirring once. Add the tomato juice. Microwave uncovered for 3 minutes, or until mixture is very hot, stirring once. Pour into a mug; top with the yogurt and cilantro or scallion.

SERVES 1

CHINESE-STYLE BROTH*

▶ **PREPARATION TIME:** 10 minutes
COOKING TIME: 4 minutes

---

1 1/2 cups homemade or canned chicken broth, preferably unsalted

1–1 1/2 teaspoons tamari or low-sodium soy sauce
1 teaspoon rice vinegar
6 Chinese snow peas, trimmed and cut into 1/4-inch diagonals

6 thin slices carrot, cut from the
  fat end of the carrot
1/2 cup diced tofu (1/4-inch dice)
1 small inside leaf bok choy,
  rinsed, white part diced (1/4-
  inch), leafy part cut into
  thin shreds
1/2 teaspoon Oriental sesame oil
Thin diagonal slices scallion, for
  garnish

Combine the chicken broth, tamari, rice vinegar, snow peas, and
carrot slices in a microwave-safe 1-
quart glass measure. Microwave, covered with a saucer, on high power for
3 minutes, or until very hot. Uncover
and stir in the tofu, bok choy, and
sesame oil. Cover with the saucer and
microwave 1 minute, or until heated
through. Pour into a large mug and
garnish with the scallion slices.

SERVES 1

SPINACH, BEEF, AND MUSHROOM SOUP*

Tubes of imported tomato paste, available in many specialty stores, are convenient for recipes like this one that call for just a few teaspoons. Or you can freeze small blobs of canned tomato paste on a cookie sheet until firm and store them in the freezer.

▶ **PREPARATION TIME:** 5
  minutes
COOKING TIME: 6 minutes
STANDING TIME: 2 minutes

1 13¾-ounce can beef broth,
  preferably unsalted
1 tablespoon tomato paste
1/4 cup chopped fresh
  mushrooms
2 tablespoons instant couscous
1/2 cup (packed) rinsed shredded fresh spinach leaves
2 cherry tomatoes, coarsely
  chopped

Whisk the beef broth and tomato
paste in a microwave-safe 1-quart
glass measure until blended. Stir in
the mushrooms and coucous. Microwave, covered with a saucer, on high
power for 5 minutes, or until boiling,
stirring once. Stir in the spinach,
cover with the saucer, and microwave
1 minute. Let stand covered for 2 minutes before serving. Pour into a mug
and garnish with the chopped tomato.

SERVES 1

CHAPTER 4

SAUCES

The ability of a microwave to cook small amounts of food quickly and efficiently makes it the perfect tool for preparing sauces using less than two cups of liquid.

Béchamel Sauce is a good example of the microwave at its best. The entire process takes about five minutes, so although you will have to keep your eye on the timer, you won't have to struggle with getting a stirrer's cramp in your hand.

Both of us are fresh applesauce aficionados, and cooking apples down to sauce in the microwave quickly became a habit with us. Here was a great microwave technique: fast, simple, tidy, labor-saving, and even more important—at least to us—retaining the excellent fresh-picked apple flavor! In fact, we were so enamored, you will find two savory applesauces—a delectable Applesauce with Onion, Garlic, and Thyme and an Apple-Horseradish Sauce—in this chapter, and a whole section devoted entirely to sweet applesauce in the dessert chapter.

But the real tour de force in the sauce-making category is what one can do when pasta is on the menu. Cooking pasta—at least the pasta we know and love—is not within the realm of microwave powers. But cooking the sauce in the microwave while the pasta boils away merrily on the stovetop is a collaboration worth talking about. If you get the water on to boil early enough, and get to work on the sauce right away—pronto!—the pasta and sauce will be ready at just about the same time. Another example of how the microwave integrates successfully with traditional cooking methods.

R E C I P E S

SAUCES IN A SNAP

Béchamel Sauce and Variations
Peanut Sauce
Apricot, Ginger, and Cranberry Sauce
Beurre Rouge
Beurre Blanc
Apple-Horseradish Sauce*
Applesauce with Onion, Garlic, and Thyme*
Barbecue Sauce

PUSH-BUTTON PASTA, PRONTO

Garden Pasta Sauce*
Creamy Lemon Pasta Sauce
Bacon and Broccoli Pasta Sauce
Chunky Tomato Sauce* and Variations

Tomato Sauce with Porcini*
Sauce of Cooked Fresh Tomatoes*
Spicy Sausage, Mushroom, and Red and Green Pepper Sauce
Tomato-Ginger Pasta Sauce*
Red Clam Sauce for Linguine*
Carrot-Butter Sauce

* Especially good for you.

SAUCES IN A SNAP

BÉCHAMEL SAUCE

Béchamel is a classic sauce with many uses. It will keep refrigerated for several days. Reheat it gently.

▶ **PREPARATION TIME:** 5 minutes
COOKING TIME: 6 minutes

2 tablespoons unsalted butter
2 tablespoons all-purpose flour
Pinch salt, or to taste
1 cup milk, half-and-half, or
    lowfat milk
Dash hot red pepper sauce, or
    to taste
Pinch freshly grated nutmeg
    (optional)

1. Place the butter in a microwave-safe 1-quart glass measure. Microwave uncovered on high power until melted, about 1 minute.
2. Whisk in the flour and salt until smooth, and microwave uncovered on high power for 30 seconds. Gradually pour in the milk, whisking until smooth, scraping the bottom of the measure with a spoon if necessary. Microwave uncovered on high power for 4 minutes, whisking once. Whisk until smooth and stir in the hot red pepper sauce, and nutmeg if desired. Strain if desired and serve hot.
MAKES 1¼ CUPS (Serves 4 to 6)

V A R I A T I O N S

Cheese Sauce: Proceed as in the recipe above, omitting the nutmeg. Whisk in 1 cup (4 ounces) grated Cheddar cheese at room temperature with the hot red pepper sauce. Makes about 1⅓ cups. Terrific for macaroni and cheese or as a sauce for vegetables, especially broccoli.

Mustard Sauce: Proceed as in the recipe above, omitting the nutmeg.

Whisk in 4 teaspoons Dijon mustard and 2 teaspoons imported grainy mustard with the hot red pepper sauce. Makes a generous 1 cup. Terrific served with fish or pork chops.

Horseradish Sauce: Proceed as in the main recipe, omitting the nutmeg. Whisk in 2 tablespoons prepared horseradish and 1 teaspoon Dijon mustard with the hot red pepper sauce. Stir in or top with 1 tablespoon fresh-snipped or freeze-dried chives.

Makes a generous 1 cup. A great sauce for braised or corned beef.

Lemon-Herb: Proceed as in the main recipe, omitting the nutmeg. Add 3 strips (2 inches × ½ inch) lemon zest with the milk. When the sauce is done, strain and stir in 2 teaspoons minced fresh parsley and ½ teaspoon fresh lemon juice, or to taste, with the hot red pepper sauce. Makes a generous 1 cup. Serve with vegetables or fish.

PEANUT SAUCE

A versatile sauce, this can be served warm or at room temperature with crisp cooked or raw vegetables, grilled chicken or pork, or as a sauce for satay. Using the coconut extract gives you the flavor of coconut without the fat.

▶ **PREPARATION TIME: 10 minutes**
COOKING TIME: 5 minutes

2 shallots, minced
1 tablespoon unsalted butter
1 cup chunky peanut butter
1 cup water
6 tablespoons fresh lime juice
1 tablespoon minced fresh ginger
1 teaspoon chili paste with garlic

¼ teaspoon coconut extract
2 teaspoons Oriental sesame oil

Stir together the shallots and butter in a microwave-safe 2-quart glass casserole with a lid. Microwave covered on high power for 1 minute. Stir in all the remaining ingredients except the sesame oil until blended. Microwave covered on high power for 4 minutes. Stir in the sesame oil. If sauce is too thick, thin with water.

MAKES 1¼ CUPS (Serves 4)

APRICOT, GINGER, AND CRANBERRY SAUCE

Fresh or frozen cranberries can be used, but if you use frozen, don't thaw them before cooking and cook them for 2 to 3 minutes longer than the fresh berries. This sauce can be served with a traditional Thanksgiving turkey, with grilled poultry, or with pork.

▸ **PREPARATION TIME:** 10 minutes
COOKING TIME: 11 minutes
COOLING TIME: 20 minutes
CHILLING TIME: 1 hour

15 dried apricots, each cut into 3 strips
½ cup cranberry juice
1 12-ounce package fresh or frozen cranberries
½ cup sugar
1 tablespoon minced fresh ginger

1. Place the apricots in a microwave-safe 2-quart glass casserole with a lid and pour the cranberry juice over them. Microwave covered on high power for 2 minutes. Let stand covered 2 minutes.

2. Pick over and stem the cranberries. Stir together the apricot mixture, the cranberries, sugar, and ginger. Microwave covered on high power for 5 to 7 minutes, stirring once, until the cranberry skins begin to pop and the syrup begins to thicken.

3. Let stand to come to room temperature, then refrigerate at least 1 hour before serving. Serve chilled.

MAKES 2 CUPS (Serves 4 to 6)

BEURRE ROUGE

The name of this sauce in English is red butter, and that's what it is— a red butter sauce. It's not only a beautiful color, it's really delicious, especially on lamb, beef, or fish, and it's very easy to make.

▸ **PREPARATION TIME:** 8 minutes
COOKING TIME: 9 minutes

6 tablespoons dry red wine
2 tablespoons balsamic or red wine vinegar

2 tablespoons minced shallot
6 tablespoons unsalted butter,
    at room temperature, cut
    into 6 pieces
Salt and freshly ground pepper

1. Place the red wine, vinegar, and shallot in a microwave-safe 2-cup glass measure. Microwave uncovered on high power for 7 to 9 minutes, until reduced to ¼ cup.

2. While whisking vigorously and constantly, add the butter a piece at a time, adding the next piece only when the previous one is incorporated. Strain, and season to taste with salt and pepper. Serve immediately.

**MAKES ABOUT ½ CUP
(Serves 2)**

BEURRE BLANC

A classic French sauce that is terrific on fish. For variety, you can add flavored vinegar, fresh ginger, lemon grass, or fresh herbs—but it's excellent just the way it is.

▶ **PREPARATION TIME: 8
   minutes
COOKING TIME: 9 minutes**

6 tablespoons dry white wine
2 tablespoons white wine
    vinegar
2 tablespoons minced shallot
6 tablespoons unsalted butter,
    at room temperature, cut
    into 6 pieces
Salt and freshly ground white
    pepper

1. Place the white wine, vinegar, and shallot in a microwave-safe 2-cup glass measure. Microwave uncovered on high power for 7 to 9 minutes, until reduced to ¼ cup.

2. While whisking vigorously and constantly, add the butter a piece at a time, adding the next piece only when the previous one is incorporated. Strain, and season to taste with salt and white pepper. Serve immediately.

**MAKES ABOUT ½ CUP
(Serves 2)**

APPLE-HORSERADISH SAUCE*

A classic combination that is a perfect addition to a homey autumn dinner of roast pork or poultry. Luckily, apples and horseradish are both at their best during fall.

▶ *PREPARATION TIME: 10 minutes*
COOKING TIME: 18 minutes

---

2 tablespoons unsalted butter
1 medium onion, diced
1 clove garlic, halved
4 large Rome Beauty apples (about 10 ounces each), cored and coarsely chopped
½ cup homemade or canned chicken broth
1 tablespoon fresh lemon juice
2 strips lemon zest, 2½ inches x ¾ inch each
3 tablespoons very finely grated fresh horseradish, or to taste

Salt and freshly ground pepper
1 tablespoon minced fresh parsley

Melt the butter uncovered on high power in a microwave-safe 3-quart glass casserole with a lid, about 1 minute. Add the onion and garlic and stir to coat. Microwave covered for 2 minutes. Add the apples, chicken broth, lemon juice, and lemon zest and microwave covered for 15 minutes, stirring twice. Stir in the horseradish and salt and pepper to taste. Remove the lemon zest. Serve warm topped with parsley.

MAKES 4 CUPS (Serves 6)

APPLESAUCE WITH ONION, GARLIC, AND THYME*

H ere's another wonderful accompaniment for roast pork or poultry—an unusual, refreshing, and very tasty savory applesauce.

▶ *PREPARATION TIME: 8 minutes*
COOKING TIME: 15 minutes

4 large red cooking apples (about 2 pounds), cored and coarsely chopped

1 medium red onion, coarsely
chopped
1/3 cup homemade or canned
chicken broth
4 cloves garlic, left whole
1 tablespoon balsamic vinegar
1 teaspoon fresh thyme leaves
1/4 teaspoon **each** salt and
freshly ground pepper
2 tablespoons unsalted butter,
cut in pieces

1. Stir together the apples, onion, chicken broth, garlic, vinegar,
thyme, and salt in a microwave-safe
2-quart glass casserole with a lid.
Cover and microwave on high power
for 15 minutes, stirring three times.

2. Remove from the oven and
puree in a food mill or food processor.
Stir in the pepper and butter. Taste
and adjust seasonings. Serve warm.

MAKES 4 CUPS (Serves 6)

BARBECUE SAUCE

It's just not summertime without a barbecue. You can have summer all
year round by using this irresistible microwave sauce on steaks, chicken,
or ribs in your oven. Don't brush the sauce on too early—wait until the
meat is about one third done so the sauce won't burn. Basting with barbecue
sauce provides excellent aroma and flavor. Use about 1/3 to 1/2 cup sauce
per pound of meat. It will keep in the refrigerator for a couple of weeks,
or for several months in the freezer.

▶ **PREPARATION TIME:** 20
minutes
COOKING TIME: 11 minutes

1 medium onion, chopped
4 tablespoons (1/2 stick) unsalted butter
1 clove garlic, minced
1/2 cup diced celery
1 cup water
1 cup ketchup
1 red bell pepper, seeded and
diced

1/4 cup fresh lime juice
2 tablespoons apple cider
vinegar
1 tablespoon Worcestershire
sauce
1 slice lime
1/2 teaspoon ground cumin seed
1/4 teaspoon chili powder
3 dashes hot red pepper sauce,
or to taste
Salt
1/4 cup minced cilantro

1. Stir together the onion, butter, and garlic in a microwave-safe 2-quart glass casserole. Cover with microwave-safe plastic wrap and vent one side. Microwave on high power for 2 minutes. Stir in the celery; microwave covered and vented 2 minutes longer.

2. Stir in the water, ketchup, bell pepper, lime juice, vinegar, Worcestershire sauce, lime slice, cumin, chili powder, red pepper sauce, and salt until blended. Microwave covered and vented for 7 minutes, stirring once.

3. Puree the sauce in a food processor or blender. Transfer to a bowl and stir in the cilantro.

MAKES 2½ CUPS

PUSH-BUTTON PASTA, PRONTO– SAUCES WHILE THE PASTA COOKS

It doesn't make sense to cook pasta in the microwave. It's not any faster, it doesn't make any less of a mess, it doesn't save any steps, and there's a bigger chance of uneven cooking and the pasta sticking together. So don't.

But *do* use the microwave for pasta sauces. If you get the water on to boil early enough, the sauce will be ready at about the same time that the pasta is ready for the sauce. Using the microwave to make pasta sauce not only will save you lots of cooking time, but will cut down on the amount of fat and calories too.

It's a good idea to make sauces ahead and reheat them just when you need them. It's also possible to reheat cooked pasta in the microwave. Just toss the pasta with oil after cooking, and place 1 cup of cooked pasta in a small bowl and microwave on high power for 1 minute. Or, reheat sauced pasta right on the serving plate, covered with waxed paper, on high power— 1 minute for 1 cup or 3 minutes for 4 cups.

GARDEN PASTA SAUCE*

Preparing a pasta sauce richly flavored with herbs and vegetables can take hours on top of the stove. But thanks to modern technology, the sauce below spends only sixteen minutes in the microwave. It can be stored in portion-sized containers for days in the refrigerator—or for months in the freezer. To serve four, defrost about 2 cups of sauce for a pound of spaghetti, linguine, or long fusilli.

▸ *PREPARATION TIME: 20 minutes*
COOKING TIME: 16 minutes

2 small onions, diced
3 cloves garlic, minced
1 tablespoon olive oil, prefera-
    bly extra-virgin
1 **each** red and yellow bell pep-
    per, trimmed, seeded, and
    diced
1 small zucchini, trimmed and
    diced
6 medium mushrooms, trimmed
    and sliced
1 28-ounce can crushed
    tomatoes
1 bay leaf
1 teaspoon **each** dried oregano,
    sugar, and salt
1 7-ounce jar roasted red pep-
    pers, drained and diced
½ cup minced fresh parsley
¼ cup shredded fresh basil
¼ teaspoon crushed hot red
    pepper flakes, or to taste

1. Stir together the onions, garlic, and olive oil in a microwave-safe 2-quart glass measure. Cover with microwave-safe plastic wrap and vent one side. Microwave on high power for 3 minutes, stirring once. Stir in the bell peppers, zucchini, and mushrooms. Cover with plastic wrap and vent one side. Microwave on high power for 3 minutes, stirring once.

2. Stir in the crushed tomatoes, bay leaf, oregano, sugar, and salt. Cover with plastic wrap and vent one side. Microwave on high power for 10 minutes, stirring twice. Remove and discard bay leaf. Stir in the remaining ingredients. Taste and adjust seasonings.

MAKES 6 CUPS

VARIATIONS

1. Stir in a pinch each of fennel seed and grated orange zest with the crushed tomatoes.

2. Add 1 tablespoon capers with the fresh herbs.

3. After cooking the onions, cook a pound of lean ground beef on high power for 3 to 5 minutes, just until pinkness disappears.

4. Stir in a handful of pitted olives of your choice with the fresh herbs.

5. Dice 10 sun-dried tomatoes (packed in oil) and add with the fresh herbs.

CREAMY LEMON PASTA SAUCE

Lite, part skim, or whole milk ricotta will all work well for this dish. The food processor is perfect for shredding the squash, although hand grating on the coarse side of a grater will work fine, too.

▸ **PREPARATION TIME:** 15 minutes
COOKING TIME: 9 minutes
STANDING TIME: 5 minutes

1 cup heavy cream
2 shallots, minced
1 clove garlic, peeled and left whole
2 teaspoons grated lemon zest
1 cup ricotta cheese
1 small zucchini (4 ounces), coarsely grated
1 small yellow squash (4 ounces), coarsely grated
½ teaspoon **each** salt and freshly ground pepper, or to taste
2 tablespoons minced fresh parsley
1 tablespoon fresh lemon juice, or to taste

1. Stir together the heavy cream, shallots, garlic, and lemon zest in a microwave-safe 2-quart glass casserole. Microwave uncovered on high power for 5 minutes. Let stand for 5 minutes.

2. Meanwhile, puree the ricotta in a food processor, scraping the sides, until completely smooth, about 1 to 2 minutes. Set aside at room temperature.

3. Remove the garlic clove and whisk in the ricotta, zucchini, yellow squash, salt, and pepper. Microwave uncovered for 4 minutes. Stir in the parsley and lemon juice. Taste and adjust seasonings.

MAKES 3 CUPS (Serves 4 as a main course with 1 pound dry pasta)

V A R I A T I O N

Creamy Goat Cheese and Lemon Pasta Sauce: Add 2 ounces (¼ cup) mild goat cheese to the ricotta cheese and puree until smooth. Reduce the heavy cream to ¾ cup and proceed as above.

BACON AND BROCCOLI PASTA SAUCE

A good simple pasta sauce with a lot of flavor. If you're concerned about saturated fat in your diet, try using 1 tablespoon of olive oil instead of the bacon fat to cook the broccoli.

▶ **PREPARATION TIME: 12 minutes**
COOKING TIME: 8 minutes

2 slices bacon, diced
4 large scallions, trimmed and thinly sliced on diagonal
2 cloves garlic, minced
1 stalk broccoli, cut into flowerets (3 cups)
2 tablespoons olive oil, preferably extra-virgin
1 teaspoon fresh oregano leaves, or ½ teaspoon dried
½ small red bell pepper, seeded and diced
Generous pinch **each** salt and crushed red pepper flakes, or to taste
1 tablespoon toasted pine nuts
Freshly grated Parmigiano-Reggiano cheese, for serving (optional)

1. Place the bacon in a microwave-safe 2-quart glass casserole with a lid, and separate the bacon pieces with a fork. Microwave covered on high power, stirring every 45 seconds, for about 2½ to 3½ minutes, until browned and crisp. Carefully remove the bacon from the fat with a slotted spoon and set aside.

2. Add the scallions and garlic to the bacon fat in the dish and microwave covered on high power for 1 minute. Stir in the broccoli, olive oil, and oregano and microwave covered on high power for 3 minutes. Stir in the bell pepper, salt, and crushed pepper flakes and microwave on high power for 30 seconds. Taste and adjust seasonings.

3. Toss with hot cooked pasta and serve garnished with bacon and pine nuts. Sprinkle with grated cheese, if desired.

SERVES 4 AS A FIRST COURSE OR 2 AS A MAIN COURSE (with ½ pound dry pasta)

CHUNKY TOMATO SAUCE*

The secret to a good tomato sauce is a robust and flavorful extra-virgin olive oil to help balance the acidity of the tomato—and, of course, good-quality tomatoes. Make this simple recipe in large batches and freeze in one-cup portions for a quick supper. Try the easy and unusual variations, too.

▶ **PREPARATION TIME:** 5 minutes
COOKING TIME: 17 minutes
STANDING TIME: 5 minutes

2 tablespoons minced onion
2 tablespoons olive oil, preferably extra-virgin
1 14-ounce can Italian-style plum tomatoes, with juice
1 clove garlic, crushed
2 tablespoons chopped fresh basil
Salt and freshly ground pepper

1. Combine the onion and olive oil in a microwave-safe 10-inch glass pie plate. Microwave uncovered on high power for 2 minutes, or until the onion is tender, stirring once.
2. Add the tomatoes and juice; break the tomatoes into small pieces with the side of a fork or cut them up with kitchen shears. Microwave uncovered for 12 to 15 minutes, or until the sauce is thickened slightly, stirring twice.
3. Stir in the garlic and basil.

Cover and let stand 5 minutes. Season with salt and pepper, and add an extra dash of olive oil if desired.

MAKES 1 CUP (Serves 2 as a main course with ½ pound dry pasta)

V A R I A T I O N S

Chunky Tomato Sauce with Fresh Basil and Cream: In Step 2: Microwave the tomatoes uncovered on high power for 10 minutes, stirring once. Stir in 2 tablespoons heavy cream until blended. Microwave 5 minutes, or until slightly thickened. Stir in 1 tablespoon torn fresh basil leaves and complete the recipe as directed above, omitting the last dash of olive oil.

Chunky Tomato Sauce with Sun-dried Tomatoes*: In Step 2: Microwave the tomatoes with their juices and 1 tablespoon sun-dried tomato bits uncovered on high power for 12 to 15 minutes, or until the sauce is slightly thickened, stirring twice. Complete the recipe as directed above.

TOMATO SAUCE WITH PORCINI*

Dried porcini, a wild mushroom harvested in Italy, adds a rich meaty flavor to this simple tomato sauce.

▶ **PREPARATION TIME: 8 minutes**
COOKING TIME: 19 minutes
STANDING TIME: 25 minutes

½ cup hot tap water
2 tablespoons crumbled dried porcini mushrooms
2 tablespoons olive oil, preferably extra-virgin
2 tablespoons minced onion
1 14-ounce can Italian-style plum tomatoes, drained
2 tablespoons chopped Italian parsley
Salt and freshly ground pepper

1. Combine the water and porcini in a microwave-safe 1-quart glass measure. Microwave on high power for 2 minutes. Cover and let stand 20 minutes.

2. Meanwhile, combine the oil and onion in a microwave-safe 10-inch glass pie plate. Microwave uncovered on high power for 2 minutes, or until onion is tender.

3. Drain the soaked porcini in a fine sieve set over a measuring cup. Add the porcini liquid and the drained tomatoes to the cooked onion. Break up the tomatoes with the side of a fork or cut into small pieces with kitchen shears. Check the porcini for any grit and rinse briefly; chop fine and add to the tomatoes.

4. Microwave uncovered for 12 to 15 minutes, or until the sauce is slightly thickened, stirring twice. Stir in the parsley. Cover with plastic wrap and let stand 5 minutes. Season to taste with salt and pepper.

MAKES 1 CUP (Serves 2 with ½ pound dry pasta)

SAUCE OF COOKED FRESH TOMATOES*

When local tomatoes are in season, nothing beats the fresh flavor of a sauce made with them. Fortunately, basil, a favorite and perfect herb with tomatoes, is in season at the same time. One has three choices when deciding on the consistency of the sauce. For a smoother sauce you might consider peeling the tomatoes before cooking them; or you can use unpeeled tomatoes and enjoy the extra texture the peels add to the sauce; or for a very smooth texture, pass the cooked sauce of unpeeled tomatoes through a food mill.

▶ **PREPARATION TIME:** *10 minutes*
COOKING TIME: *13 minutes*
STANDING TIME: *10 minutes*

¼ cup minced onion
2 tablespoons olive oil, preferably extra-virgin
3 cups cored, diced fresh tomatoes (see headnote)
2 tablespoons chopped fresh basil leaves
½ clove garlic, crushed
Salt and freshly ground pepper

---

1. Combine the onion and oil in a microwave-safe 10-inch glass pie plate. Microwave uncovered on high power for 3 minutes, or until the onions are soft, stirring once.

2. Stir in the tomatoes; cover with microwave-safe plastic wrap and vent one side; microwave for 5 minutes, or until the tomatoes are very soft. Uncover and microwave 5 minutes, or until the sauce is slightly thickened. Stir in the basil and garlic. Cover with plastic wrap and let stand 10 minutes. Season to taste with salt and pepper. Serve as is, or press through a food mill for a smooth sauce.

MAKES 2 CUPS CHUNKY SAUCE; 1¼ CUPS SIEVED SAUCE (Serves 4 with 1 pound dry pasta)

SPICY SAUSAGE, MUSHROOM, AND RED AND GREEN PEPPER SAUCE

For best results, serve this chunky sauce with a thick pasta like radiatore, shells, or rotelle.

▸ **PREPARATION TIME:** 10 minutes
COOKING TIME: 17 minutes

2 links (about 4 ounces) Italian sweet sausage, casings removed
1 cup sliced fresh mushrooms
½ **each** red and green bell pepper, seeded and cut into ¼-inch strips
½ sweet red onion (cut lengthwise), cut into ¼-inch vertical strips
2 tablespoons olive oil, preferably extra-virgin
1 clove garlic, crushed
1 cup canned crushed tomatoes
1 teaspoon fresh minced oregano leaves, or pinch dried oregano
¼ teaspoon crushed hot red pepper flakes
2 tablespoons chopped Italian parsley
Salt and freshly ground pepper

1. Crumble the sausage into a microwave-safe 10-inch glass pie plate. Microwave uncovered on high power for 4 minutes, stirring once. Transfer to a sieve and drain off the fat; crumble the sausage meat with a fork or cut into smaller pieces with kitchen shears; set aside.

2. Wipe out the pie plate; add the mushrooms, green and red pepper strips, onion, olive oil, and garlic. Cover with microwave-safe plastic wrap and vent one side. Microwave 5 minutes, stirring once. Add the crushed tomatoes, oregano, crushed red pepper flakes, and the reserved sausage; microwave uncovered for 8 minutes, or until the sauce is thickened slightly, stirring once. Add the parsley, and salt and pepper to taste.

MAKES 2 CUPS (Serves 4 as a main course with 1 pound dry pasta)

TOMATO-GINGER PASTA SAUCE*

This unusual and delicious sauce is very good served on pasta that has been tossed with freshly grated Parmigiano-Reggiano cheese and topped with chopped fresh herbs. You might also want to add a bit of cream if that appeals to you. It's a good sauce to make ahead and reheat when you need a really quick meal.

▶ *PREPARATION TIME: 10 minutes*
COOKING TIME: 21 minutes

2 tablespoons unsalted butter
2 medium onions, diced
2 tablespoons minced fresh
  ginger
2 cloves garlic, minced
1 28-ounce can Italian crushed
  tomatoes
Pinch sugar (optional)
Salt and freshly ground pepper
  to taste

1. Melt the butter in a microwave-safe 2-quart glass casserole with a lid about 1 minute. Stir in the onion and microwave covered on high power for 4 minutes. Stir in ginger and garlic and microwave covered for 2 minutes longer.

2. Stir in the tomatoes and the sugar if desired and cook covered for 10 minutes. Puree in the food processor or blender until smooth. Season with salt and pepper. Reheat for 2 to 4 minutes, if necessary, before serving.

MAKES 4 CUPS (2 cups per pound dry pasta serves 4)

RED CLAM SAUCE FOR LINGUINE*

We prefer the tiny West Coast Manilla Bay clams for this sauce. About the size of your thumb, they are tossed—shell and all—with the pasta. The smallest littleneck clams can also be tossed with shells in the sauce.

▸ **SOAKING TIME:** *10 minutes*
PREPARATION TIME: *10 minutes*
COOKING TIME: *16 minutes*

---

*2 pounds Manilla Bay clams, or
3 dozen very small littleneck
clams, scrubbed, soaked,
and rinsed*
*½ cup onion slivers, cut
lengthwise*
*5 tablespoons olive oil, prefera-
bly extra-virgin*
1 clove garlic, thinly sliced
*1 14-ounce can Italian-style
plum tomatoes, with liquid*
Pinch dried thyme or oregano
*2 tablespoons chopped Italian
parsley*
Salt and freshly ground pepper

---

1. Combine the onion, olive oil, and garlic in a microwave-safe 3-quart glass casserole with a lid. Microwave covered on high power for 5 minutes. Stir in the tomatoes and thyme; break up tomatoes with a fork or cut with kitchen shears. Microwave uncovered for 5 minutes, or until the sauce is boiling, stirring once.

2. Stir in the clams; microwave covered for 5 minutes, or until the clams are opened, turning the dish a half-turn and shaking to redistribute the clams halfway through cooking. Remove and reserve any unopened clams.

3. Toss the clam sauce and parsley with hot cooked pasta. Add salt and pepper to taste. Return any unopened clams to the casserole, cover, and microwave 30 to 60 seconds, or until opened. (Discard any that do not open.)

SERVES 4 AS A MAIN COURSE (with 1 pound dry pasta)

CARROT-BUTTER SAUCE

This unusual sauce is golden and sweet from the carrots and rich and creamy from the butter. Add a handful of chopped fresh herbs and a sprinkle of grated Parmigiano-Reggiano cheese to each serving and you'll have a perfect sauce for spaghetti.

▶ **PREPARATION TIME:** 10
minutes
COOKING TIME: 6 minutes
STANDING TIME: 5 minutes

6 tablespoons unsalted butter,
cut into ½-inch pieces
1⅓ cup grated carrots, about 2
large (use hand grater or
finely mince with steel blade
in food processor)
1 clove garlic, crushed
Salt and freshly ground pepper
1–2 tablespoons coarsely
chopped Italian parsley
1 teaspoon minced fresh chives,
thyme leaves, or oregano
leaves
Freshly grated Parmigiano-
Reggiano cheese, for serving
(use sparingly)

1. Microwave the butter in a microwave-safe 3-quart glass casserole with a lid on high power for 1½ minutes. Stir in the grated carrots and garlic. Cover and microwave 4 minutes, stirring once. Let stand, covered, for 5 minutes.

2. Add salt, pepper, a sprinkling of parsley, and the fresh chives, thyme, or oregano after tossing with hot cooked pasta. Sprinkle each serving with a little grated cheese.

SERVES 4 AS A FIRST COURSE (with 12 ounces dry pasta)

CHAPTER 5

MAIN DISHES: WITH MEAT AND WITHOUT

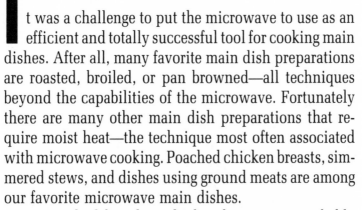

It was a challenge to put the microwave to use as an efficient and totally successful tool for cooking main dishes. After all, many favorite main dish preparations are roasted, broiled, or pan browned—all techniques beyond the capabilities of the microwave. Fortunately there are many other main dish preparations that require moist heat—the technique most often associated with microwave cooking. Poached chicken breasts, simmered stews, and dishes using ground meats are among our favorite microwave main dishes.

Poached boneless chicken breasts are probably right up there with the top five best microwaved foods. In three to four minutes you can have moist, flavorful, perfectly poached chicken—and as a bonus, a few tablespoons of pure chicken essence (collect this broth in a small container and keep frozen until you need it). Talk about efficiency—this is one recipe that can't be beat.

The chicken section is divided into two categories. The first category consists of imaginative ways to flavor the poached breasts and the second actually uses strips, pieces, or halved boneless chicken breasts in enticing ways as in Enchiladas Suizas, or Chicken and Shiitake Stew.

Speaking of stew, the microwave is capable of cooking some very nicely flavored, simple stews, based on small pieces of tender cuts of meat. Veal works best. The two veal stews given here, although not necessarily especially time-saving recipes, are both very delicious.

Typically, microwaves do not brown meat. Rather than ignore this deficiency and sacrifice that browned-meat flavor, we have incorporated conventional browning techniques into several of the recipes in this section. For instance, in the Pork Chops with Sauerkraut and Fruit the meat is browned in a cast iron skillet and finished off in the microwave.

Ground meats are especially successful in the microwave because they cook quickly and the meat juices have a chance to mingle with the other flavors as you cook and stir. The Lamb and Black Bean Chili and Spicy Picadillo are just two examples of the good things that follow.

As a tribute to pasta—one of our favorite foods, which, as we explained in Chapter 4, we don't cook in the microwave—we have included three dynamite pasta entrées that combine conventional cooking (the pasta) with microwave (the other elements of the dish), another excellent example of microwave and conventional cooking successfully combined.

R E C I P E S

CHICKEN BREASTS, PERFECTLY POACHED

Chicken Breasts with Niçoise Sauce*
Chicken Tonnato
Chicken Breasts with Tomato Salsa*

CHICKEN BREASTS, OTHER WAYS

Chicken Quesadillas
Enchiladas Suizas
Chicken-Shiitake Stew
Tangier Chicken Stew*
Sliced Chicken Breast with Roasted Red Pepper Puree*

VEAL STEWS

Veal Stew with Sage Potatoes and Gremolata*
Veal-Tarragon Stew

PORK

Baked Potatoes Picadillo
Pork Chops with Sauerkraut and Fruit

GROUND MEAT

Spaghetti Squash with Ground Beef and Eggplant Sauce*
Middle Eastern Meatballs*
Moussaka
Lamb and Black Bean Chili*
Simple Stuffed Cabbage Leaves*
Spicy Picadillo
Fastest Tex-Mex Tamale Pie

SAUSAGE

Polenta and Two Cheeses with Sausage and Mushrooms
Sausage, Peppers, Potatoes, and Smothered Onions, Vinaigrette

PASTA

Stuffed Pasta Shells
Lasagne Primavera
Macaroni and Cheese for Grown-ups

MEATLESS MAIN DISHES

Welsh Rabbit
Vegetable-stuffed Potatoes with Creamy Cottage Cheese
Black Bean Burritos*

* Especially good for you.

CHICKEN BREASTS, PERFECTLY POACHED

CHICKEN BREASTS WITH NIÇOISE SAUCE*

Here's an unusual and interesting version of tomato sauce—and one that has endless uses. It's perfect with chicken breasts, but also excellent with pasta, veal, lamb, or fish. It has the deep flavors typical of sunny southern French cuisine, and it's low in fat and calories. For a different taste, top with crumbled goat cheese before serving.

▶ **PREPARATION TIME: 20 minutes**
COOKING TIME: 18 minutes

2 whole chicken breasts, skinned, boned, and split
1 tablespoon homemade or canned chicken broth, white wine, citrus juice, or water
4 cups (packed) fresh spinach leaves, well washed
1 slice bacon, diced
1 medium onion, sliced
1 clove garlic, minced
1 cup canned crushed tomatoes
1 tablespoon minced fresh basil leaves
¼ teaspoon fennel seeds

⅛ teaspoon **each** dried thyme and oregano
Pinch grated orange zest
2 tablespoons chopped Niçoise olives
1 tablespoon drained capers
Pinch crushed hot red pepper flakes, or to taste

1. Trim the chicken breasts and place them in a microwave-safe 9-inch glass pie plate, arranging them with the thicker portions toward the outside of the dish. Drizzle with the chicken broth. Cover with microwave-safe plastic wrap and vent one side. Microwave on high power for 6

to 8 minutes, turning after 4 minutes. Let stand, covered, until ready to serve.

2. Microwave the spinach uncovered in a microwave-safe 2-quart glass casserole with a lid for 1½ minutes, stirring once. Let cool, squeeze as dry as possible, and finely chop.

3. Dry the casserole and place the bacon in it. Cover with the lid and microwave for 3 minutes, stirring once. Stir in the onion and garlic. Microwave covered for 3 minutes.

4. Add the tomatoes, basil, fennel seeds, thyme, oregano, orange zest, and reserved chopped spinach. Microwave uncovered on high power for 2 minutes. Remove from the oven and stir in the olives, capers, and red pepper flakes. Taste and adjust seasonings. Keep warm.

5. Place chicken on serving plates and top with warm Niçoise sauce. Serve immediately.

SERVES 4

CHICKEN TONNATO

Vitello tonnato is a fabulous classic Italian dish that takes hours to prepare; this version uses the same delicious sauce for fast, succulent microwaved chicken breasts.

▸ *PREPARATION TIME: 20 minutes*
COOKING TIME: 12 minutes

---

3 whole chicken breasts, skinned, boned, and split
1 tablespoon homemade or canned chicken broth, white wine, citrus juice, or water
1 6½-ounce can tuna (preferably packed in olive oil), drained
1 cup mayonnaise
2 tablespoons fresh lemon juice, or to taste
1 teaspoon Dijon mustard

2 dashes hot red pepper sauce
8–10 romaine lettuce leaves
1 ripe large tomato, peeled, seeded, and diced
1 tablespoon capers, drained
1 tablespoon minced fresh mint leaves
Mint sprigs for garnish

---

1. Trim the chicken breasts and place them in a microwave-safe 10-inch glass pie plate, arranging them with the thicker portions toward the outside of the dish. Drizzle with the chicken broth. Cover with microwave-safe plastic wrap and vent one side. Microwave on high power for 8 to 12 minutes, turning after 5 minutes. Let stand, uncovered, until cool.

2. Process the tuna and mayonnaise in a food processor until completely smooth. Transfer the tuna mixture to a small bowl and stir in the lemon juice, mustard, and pepper sauce. Refrigerate until ready to serve.

3. When ready to serve, line a large serving platter with the lettuce leaves. Arrange the cooled chicken breasts on the lettuce. Taste and adjust the seasonings in the tuna sauce and pour about half the sauce over the chicken breasts, dividing evenly; sprinkle with the tomato, capers, and minced mint. Garnish with mint sprigs and serve at once. Pass the remaining sauce.

SERVES 6

CHICKEN BREASTS WITH TOMATO SALSA*

Serve this chicken dish with a green salad and warm flour tortillas or crusty bread, and Mexican beer or seltzer with a squeeze of lime. You can easily halve or double the recipe by dividing the ingredients in two or multiplying by two.

▶ **PREPARATION TIME:** 15 minutes
COOKING TIME: 4 minutes

½ California avocado, peeled, seeded, and diced
4 cherry tomatoes, quartered
1 scallion, minced
½–1 jalapeno pepper, seeded and minced
1 tablespoon minced cilantro
¼ teaspoon fresh lime juice, or to taste
¼ teaspoon ground cumin seed
⅛ teaspoon chili powder, or to taste

Pinch salt
1 whole chicken breast, skinned, boned, and split
1 tablespoon homemade or canned chicken broth, white wine, citrus juice, or water

1. Combine all the ingredients except the chicken breast and broth in a small bowl. Set aside at room temperature.

2. Trim the chicken breast and place in a microwave-safe 9-inch glass pie plate, arranging with the thicker portions toward the outside of the dish. Drizzle with the chicken broth. Cover with microwave-safe plastic wrap and vent one side. Microwave on high power for 3 to 4 minutes, turning after 2 minutes. Let stand, covered, until ready to serve.

3. Add the juices from the cooked chicken to the salsa. Place the warm chicken on plates and top with the salsa. Serve immediately.

SERVES 2

CHICKEN BREASTS, OTHER WAYS

CHICKEN QUESADILLAS

An interesting, fast ethnic dinner from the microwave that you can have on the table in less than 30 minutes, while you and your kitchen keep cool! This recipe can easily be doubled.

▶ **PREPARATION TIME:** 15 minutes
MARINATING TIME: 15 minutes
COOKING TIME: 5 minutes

3 tablespoons fresh lime juice
1 tablespoon minced onion
¼ teaspoon ground cumin seed
¼ teaspoon chili powder
1 whole chicken breast, skinned, boned, and split, each half cut into 12 strips
2 small plum tomatoes, diced
½ small yellow bell pepper, seeded and diced
½ ripe California avocado, peeled, pitted, and diced
2 tablespoons minced cilantro
1 jalapeno pepper, seeded and minced
Pinch salt
2 flour tortillas

1 cup grated Monterey Jack cheese (4 ounces)
2 tablespoons sour cream

1. Mix 2 tablespoons of the lime juice and the onion, cumin, and chili powder in a mixing bowl. Add the chicken and toss to coat. Let stand, stirring occasionally, at least 15 minutes.

2. Meanwhile, combine the tomatoes, bell pepper, avocado, cilantro, jalapeno, salt, and the remaining 1 tablespoon lime juice in a small bowl and set aside.

3. Place the chicken slices in a microwave-safe 9-inch glass pie plate. Cover with microwave-safe plastic wrap and vent one side. Microwave on high power until cooked through, about 2 to 4 minutes.

4. Place one tortilla on a micro-

wave-safe dinner plate. Sprinkle with half of the cheese. Microwave until the cheese is melted, about 30 seconds. Arrange half the chicken on the tortilla and fold in half to cover it.

Top with half of the tomato mixture and then a dollop of sour cream. Repeat with the remaining ingredients.

SERVES 2

ENCHILADAS SUIZAS

You've had these delicious enchiladas in Mexican restaurants, and now you can make them yourself.

▶ *PREPARATION TIME: 15 minutes*
COOKING TIME: 38 minutes
STANDING TIME: 3 minutes

2 whole chicken breasts, skinned, boned, and split
1 tablespoon fresh lime juice
2 pounds fresh tomatillos, husks removed
1 jalapeno pepper, halved and seeded
1/3 cup minced onion
2 tablespoons corn oil
2 cloves garlic, minced
2 teaspoons sugar
1/2 teaspoon salt, or to taste
Freshly ground pepper
12 corn tortillas
1 cup shredded Monterey Jack cheese (about 4 ounces)
1 cup sour cream
2 tablespoons minced cilantro

1. Arrange the chicken in a microwave-safe 9-inch glass pie plate with the thickest sides at the edge of the plate; sprinkle with the lime juice. Cover with microwave-safe plastic wrap and vent one side. Microwave on high power for 6 to 8 minutes, turning after 4 minutes. Cool slightly, then shred the meat.

2. Meanwhile, place the tomatillos, stems down, and jalapeno in a microwave-safe 13 × 9-inch glass baking dish. Cover with microwave-safe plastic wrap and vent one side. Microwave for 8 minutes.

3. Microwave the onion, oil, and garlic in a covered and vented microwave-safe glass pie plate for 2 minutes.

4. Puree the tomatillos and jalapeno in a food processor or blender. Add the onion mixture and the sugar and puree until smooth. Return the sauce to the baking dish and microwave, covered and vented, for 5 minutes. Transfer to a medium mixing bowl; season to taste with salt and pepper.

5. Soak one tortilla at a time in the tomatillo sauce for 1 minute each; fill each with chicken and 1 generous tablespoon each cheese and sour cream, and roll up. Arrange in a microwave-safe 13 × 9-inch glass baking dish. Mix the remaining sauce with the remaining sour cream and pour over the top. Sprinkle with the remaining cheese and then with the cilantro. Microwave uncovered on high power for 12 to 15 minutes. Let stand 3 minutes. Serve hot.

SERVES 6

CHICKEN-SHIITAKE STEW

When cool weather is on the way try making this bone-warming stew, excellent accompanied by a glass of chilled Chardonnay. If possible let stand for 1 hour or refrigerate up to 24 hours after Step 2 to allow the stew to thicken and the flavors to blend.

▶ *PREPARATION TIME: 20 minutes*
STANDING TIME (OPTIONAL): 1 hour
COOKING TIME: 36 minutes

---

6 tablespoons unsalted butter
2 leeks, minced, rinsed well
4 shallots, minced
4 carrots, pared and diced
2 ribs celery, trimmed and diced
2 whole chicken breasts, skinned, boned, and cut into 1-inch chunks
½ cup all-purpose flour
1½ cups homemade or canned chicken broth
½ cup dry white wine

4 ounces shiitake mushrooms, stemmed and sliced
¼ cup minced fresh parsley
½ cup crème fraîche or sour cream, room temperature
1 tablespoon snipped fresh chives
Salt and freshly ground pepper to taste

---

1. Melt 4 tablespoons of the butter in a microwave-safe 3-quart glass casserole with a lid on high power for 30 to 60 seconds. Add the leeks and shallots and stir to coat. Microwave covered for 2 minutes. Stir in carrots and celery and microwave covered for 4 minutes.

2. Coat the chicken with the flour and shake off excess; add to the vegetables. Microwave covered 4 minutes, stirring once. Pour in broth and wine; microwave for 8 minutes, stirring once. Remove the cover and microwave 14 minutes, stirring three times. Remove from the oven. If possible, allow the stew to stand for 1 hour at room temperature or in the refrigerator up to 24 hours at this point.

3. Just before serving, melt the remaining 2 tablespoons butter in a microwave-safe 9-inch glass pie plate for 30 to 60 seconds. Add the mushrooms and toss to coat. Microwave 1½ minutes, stirring once, then stir in the parsley.

4. Stir the mushrooms, crème fraîche, and chives into the stew. Taste and adjust seasoning. Reheat gently until hot.

SERVES 4

TANGIER CHICKEN STEW*

S erved with hot or iced mint tea this is a wonderful and soothing supper, yet another example of how you and your microwave can prepare interesting *real* food, not reheated frozen dishes.

▶ **PREPARATION TIME:** 25 minutes
MARINATING TIME: 30 minutes
COOKING TIME: 20 minutes

1 tablespoon safflower oil
1 jalapeno pepper, seeded and minced
¼ teaspoon **each** ground coriander seed, ground cumin seed, and ground cinnamon
2 whole chicken breasts, skinned, boned, and cut into ½-inch chunks

½ acorn squash, seeded, pared, and cut into ½-inch chunks
2 small carrots, sliced diagonally ¼-inch thick
1 small onion, cut in ½-inch dice
3½ cups homemade or canned chicken broth
1 medium zucchini, cut in ½-inch dice
1 14-ounce can whole tomatoes, coarsely chopped, liquid reserved
⅓ cup raisins
½ cup cooked chick-peas (rinsed canned ones are fine)
¼ teaspoon salt, or to taste

3 tablespoons unsalted butter
2 cups quick-cooking couscous
1/4 cup slivered toasted almonds
1 tablespoon minced fresh mint

---

1. Mix the oil, jalapeno, and spices in a mixing bowl. Add the chicken and toss to coat. Let stand, stirring frequently, for 30 minutes.

2. Combine the acorn squash, carrots, and onions in a microwave-safe 3-quart glass casserole with a lid. Microwave covered on high power for 5 minutes. Add 1 cup of the broth and the zucchini, tomatoes with liquid, and raisins; microwave covered for 8 minutes, stirring three times. Stir in the chicken with the marinade; microwave covered for 3 minutes. Stir in the chick-peas, 1/2 cup of the broth, and the salt; microwave covered 2 minutes longer.

3. Meanwhile, heat the remaining 2 cups broth and the butter to boiling in a medium saucepan on top of the stove. Stir in the couscous, cover the pan, and remove from the heat. Let stand covered 5 minutes.

4. To serve, spoon the couscous onto a serving platter. Top with the chicken stew and sprinkle with almonds and mint.

SERVES 6

SLICED CHICKEN BREAST WITH ROASTED RED PEPPER PUREE*

Incredibly simple, this recipe makes an elegant presentation served with spinach noodles and a garnish of bright green steamed vegetables like broccoli flowerets.

▶ **PREPARATION TIME:** 10 minutes
COOKING TIME: 13 minutes

---

2 tablespoons olive oil
1/2 clove garlic, crushed
1 teaspoon minced fresh oregano leaves, or pinch dried oregano

2 whole chicken breasts, skinned, boned, split, and trimmed of fat
1 7-ounce jar roasted red peppers, rinsed and drained
1/4 cup minced onion
2 tablespoons finely chopped fresh parsley

1. Combine 1 tablespoon of the oil, garlic, and oregano on a saucer. Coat the pieces of chicken with the oil mixture and arrange in a microwave-safe 10-inch glass pie plate, placing the narrow end of the breasts toward the center and the thicker ends toward the outside rim. Cover with microwave-safe plastic wrap and vent one side. Microwave on high power for 6 to 8 minutes, turning the plate a half-turn and checking doneness after every minute. If the chicken facing toward the outside edges looks done, turn the pieces toward the center so the less cooked section is toward the outside edges. Drain off and reserve the flavored broth. Let the chicken stand, covered (remember it will continue cooking during standing time), while preparing the sauce.

2. Cut enough peppers to make 12 thin (about ⅛-inch) strips; place in a microwave-safe 2-cup glass measure. Place the remaining peppers in the bowl of a food processor fitted with the steel blade. Add the reserved chicken broth mixture.

3. Wipe out the glass pie plate and combine the remaining 1 tablespoon olive oil and the onion. Microwave uncovered for 3 minutes, or until the onion is tender. Transfer to the bowl of the food processor with the red peppers. Puree until smooth.

4. Pour back into the glass pie plate and add the reserved red pepper strips; microwave uncovered for 1 to 1½ minutes, or until very hot.

5. Carefully cut the chicken breasts, across the grain, into ¼-inch-thick diagonal slices. Spoon the sauce onto the center of four dinner plates, dividing evenly (reserve some of the strips of red pepper for a garnish). Arrange the chicken slices slightly overlapping in a row down the center of the plates and sprinkle with the chopped parsley. If using the spinach noodles and broccoli as suggested, spoon the noodles around the edges of the dish and add a few cooked broccoli flowerets to finish the presentation.

SERVES 4

VEAL STEWS

VEAL STEW WITH SAGE, POTATOES, AND GREMOLATA*

Traditionally Gremolata, a mixture of finely chopped fresh parsley, lemon zest, and garlic, is stirred into the classic Italian veal shank dish called osso buco. The pure, clean flavors of this raw seasoning also add a fresh taste to rich stews and soups.

PREPARATION TIME: 15 minutes
COOKING TIME: 35 minutes
STANDING TIME: 5 minutes

2 tablespoons olive oil
½ cup chopped onion
¼ cup finely chopped celery
1¼ pounds boneless veal leg or shoulder, well trimmed, cut into ½-inch pieces
1 15-ounce can peeled Italian-style plum tomatoes, cut up, with liquid
½ cup very hot water
½ teaspoon crumbled dried sage
4 medium-sized new potatoes, cut into ½-inch cubes
½ teaspoon salt
Freshly ground pepper
1 sprig Italian parsley
1 strip lemon zest, about 3 inches × ½ inch
1 small clove garlic, coarsely chopped

1. Combine the oil, onion, and celery in a microwave-safe 3-quart casserole with a lid; cover and microwave on high power for 5 minutes. Add the veal, tomatoes, hot water, and sage. Microwave covered for 15 minutes, stirring once. Stir in the potatoes; microwave covered for 15 minutes, or until the potatoes are tender, stirring twice. Season with salt and pepper.

2. Finely chop the parsley, lemon zest, and garlic together; stir the gremolata into the veal stew and let stand, covered, for 5 minutes before serving.

SERVES 4

VEAL-TARRAGON STEW

Like conventional stews, those prepared in the microwave can benefit from standing before serving—for an hour at room temperature to up to 24 hours in the refrigerator. They'll get thicker and the flavors will blend even more. Try serving this stew with a chilled Tavel rosé.

▸ **PREPARATION TIME:** 15 minutes
COOKING TIME: 55 minutes
STANDING TIME: 3 minutes

¼ cup (½ stick) unsalted butter
2 medium onions, diced
2 shallots, minced
2 pounds boneless veal leg or shoulder, cut into 1-inch cubes
½ cup all-purpose flour
1½ cups homemade or canned chicken broth
½ cup dry white wine
4 small carrots, pared and thinly sliced on the diagonal
2 teaspoons minced fresh tarragon leaves
2 teaspoons Dijon mustard
Salt and freshly ground black pepper

1. Melt the butter in a microwave-safe 3-quart glass casserole with a lid on high power for 30 to 60 seconds. Add the onions and shallots and stir to coat. Microwave covered for 4 minutes, stirring once.

2. Coat the veal with the flour; shake off excess; add veal to the onions. Microwave covered for 9 minutes, stirring twice. Pour in the chicken broth and wine. Reduce to medium power (50%) and microwave covered for 30 minutes. Stir in the carrots and microwave, covered, on medium power (50%) 10 minutes longer.

3. Stir in the tarragon and mustard. Let stand covered for 3 minutes. Season to taste with salt and pepper and serve hot.

SERVES 4

PORK

BAKED POTATOES PICADILLO

▶ **PREPARATION TIME:** *5 minutes*
COOKING TIME: *24 minutes*

4 medium-sized russet potatoes, scrubbed and pierced twice on each side with the tines of a fork
1 pound lean ground pork, or use half pork and half beef
1 8-ounce jar mild or hot taco sauce
½ cup chopped onion
¼ cup rinsed and drained pimiento-stuffed green olives (if possible, use salad olives), coarsely chopped
2 tablespoons raisins
½ teaspoon ground cinnamon
¼ cup **each** chopped seeded green and red bell pepper
¼ cup thinly sliced scallions
Salt and freshly ground pepper
1 cup shredded Monterey Jack cheese (about 4 ounces)

1. Arrange the potatoes in the microwave, leaving at least 1 inch of space between them. Microwave on high power for 12 to 13 minutes, or until almost tender when pierced with a skewer. Wrap in a kitchen towel and let stand before serving.

2. Crumble the ground pork into a microwave-safe 10-inch glass pie plate; add the taco sauce, onion, olives, raisins, and cinnamon. Cover with microwave-safe plastic wrap and vent one side. Microwave on high power for 8 to 10 minutes, stirring once halfway through the cooking to break up any clumps and mix the ingredients.

3. Cut a slit in the top of each potato and press the ends toward the center to open the slit. Stir the green and red pepper and the scallions into the sauce. Season to taste with salt and pepper. Arrange the potatoes like the spokes of a wheel on a large microwave-safe glass serving plate or shallow bowl. Spoon the Picadillo Sauce into and on top of the potatoes, dividing evenly; sprinkle the tops with the shredded cheese. Microwave just until the cheese melts, about 45 seconds.

SERVES 4

PORK CHOPS WITH SAUERKRAUT AND FRUIT

H ere's a good example of combination cooking. Browning the chops on top of the stove first and finishing the cooking in the microwave give you the best of both.

▶ **PREPARATION TIME:** 10 minutes
COOKING TIME: 11 minutes

2 slices bacon, diced
1 cup best-quality sauerkraut
1/2 cup pared, cored, and diced Granny Smith apple
1/2 pear, pared, cored, and diced
2 tablespoons dry white wine
2 tablespoons apple cider or juice
1/2 teaspoon fresh thyme leaves
1/8 teaspoon caraway seeds
1/8 teaspoon **each** salt and freshly ground pepper, or to taste
1/2 teaspoon Dijon mustard
1 teaspoon safflower oil
2 1-inch-thick pork loin chops (about 8 ounces each)

1. Spread the bacon in a microwave-safe 9-inch glass pie plate; microwave on high power for 1 minute. Using a slotted spoon, transfer the bacon to paper towels to drain. Pour off all but 1 teaspoon of fat from the dish. Return the bacon to the dish; add the sauerkraut, apple, pear, wine, apple cider, thyme, caraway seeds, salt, and pepper and combine well. Cover the dish with microwave-safe plastic wrap and vent one side. Microwave on high power for 3 minutes. Remove from the oven and stir in the mustard.

2. Heat the oil in a heavy medium skillet, preferably cast iron, over medium-high heat. Add the pork chops and cook, turning once, until browned, 4 to 5 minutes. Arrange the pork chops in a second glass pie plate or dinner plate; cover with plastic wrap and vent one side. Microwave on high power until cooked through, about 2 minutes. Stir the juices from the pork into the sauerkraut.

3. Spoon some sauerkraut onto each of two serving plates. Top with the pork chops and the remaining sauerkraut. Serve hot.

SERVES 2

GROUND MEAT

SPAGHETTI SQUASH WITH GROUND BEEF AND EGGPLANT SAUCE*

▶ **PREPARATION TIME: 10 minutes**
COOKING TIME: 33 minutes

1 spaghetti squash (3–3½ pounds)
1 pound lean ground beef
2 cups cored cubed pared eggplant (½-inch cubes)
2 cups cored cubed tomatoes (1-inch cubes; about 3 medium tomatoes)
½ cup chopped onion
3 tablespoons olive oil
1 clove garlic, crushed
½ teaspoon salt
¼ teaspoon freshly ground pepper
2 tablespoons chopped seeded green bell pepper
¼ cup grated Parmigiano-Reggiano cheese, plus more for serving

1. Pierce the squash completely through the hard flesh with a large fork or the tip of a paring knife at least six times at evenly spaced intervals. Place in the microwave on a piece of paper towel. Microwave on high power for 7 minutes. Turn the squash over and microwave for another 7 minutes. Remove from the oven, wrap in a kitchen towel, and let stand while cooking the sauce.

2. Crumble the meat into a microwave-safe 3-quart glass casserole with a lid. Microwave on high for 3 minutes. Spoon off any fat; break up the meat with a fork. Add the eggplant, half of the tomatoes, and the onion, oil, garlic, salt, and pepper; stir to blend. Microwave covered for 15 to 16 minutes, stirring twice.

3. Meanwhile, cut the squash in half lengthwise. Using a fork, pull out the pulp in long spaghetti-like strands. Place a bed of squash on a large platter. Spoon the sauce into the center, sprinkle with the remaining chopped tomatoes, the bell pepper, and the cheese. Using two forks, give the squash and sauce a few tosses to partially combine. Serve hot, and pass the grated cheese.

SERVES 4

MIDDLE EASTERN MEATBALLS*

These meatballs are especially good served in pita bread with lettuce, tomato, and minted yogurt, or serve on rice or couscous. In terms of flavor it's a tasty microwave variation on the classic shish kebab.

▸ *PREPARATION TIME: 10 minutes*
COOKING TIME: 7 minutes

1 pound lean ground beef
2 scallions, minced
1 large egg
1/4 cup dry bread crumbs
*3/4 teaspoon **each** ground cumin seed and sweet paprika*
1/2 teaspoon salt
*1/4 teaspoon **each** ground coriander seed and cinnamon*
Pinch cayenne pepper
1/2 cup minced mixed fresh herbs (parsley, cilantro, and mint)

Mix together the beef, scallions, egg, bread crumbs, cumin, sweet paprika, salt, ground coriander, cinnamon, and cayenne. Shape the mixture into twelve meatballs, about 1½ inches in diameter. Place the meatballs in a 13 × 9-inch microwave-safe glass baking dish and cover loosely with waxed paper. Microwave on high power for 5 to 7 minutes, stirring twice until the meatballs are cooked through, just until the pinkness almost disappears. Drain completely and roll in the mixed fresh herbs. Serve hot.

SERVES 4

MOUSSAKA

This classic Greek dish is made much more quickly and easily in the microwave, without any sacrifice of flavor.

▸ *PREPARATION TIME: 25 minutes*
COOKING TIME: 40 minutes
STANDING TIME: 3 minutes

1 pound lean ground lamb

6 tablespoons olive oil
1 medium eggplant (about 12 ounces), cut crosswise into 1/2-inch slices and then into thin strips
Salt and freshly ground pepper

2 medium onions, finely diced
1 clove garlic, minced
4 ounces fresh mushrooms,
    trimmed and sliced
2 medium zucchini (about 5
    ounces each), cut into 1 ×
    ¼-inch strips
6 canned Italian plum toma-
    toes, drained and chopped
¼ cup dry red wine
2 tablespoons tomato paste
4 tablespoons minced fresh
    parsley
1 bay leaf
½ teaspoon **each** dried thyme
    and oregano
Pinch ground cinnamon
3 tablespoons unsalted butter
3 tablespoons all-purpose flour
1 cup milk
½ cup **each** ricotta and Parmi-
    giano-Reggiano cheese
3 large eggs, lightly beaten
1 tablespoon dry bread crumbs

1. Preheat the microwave browning tray according to manufacturer's directions. Microwave the lamb uncovered on the browning tray on high power for 3 minutes, stirring twice.

2. Pour 4 tablespoons of the olive oil over the eggplant in a microwave-safe 13 × 9-inch glass baking dish. Cover with microwave-safe plastic wrap and vent one side. Microwave on high power for 5 minutes, stirring twice. Season with salt and pepper; transfer to a side dish and reserve.

3. Pour the remaining 2 tablespoons oil over the onions and garlic in a microwave-safe 10-inch glass pie plate and stir to blend completely. Microwave, covered and vented, for 2 minutes. Stir in the mushrooms and microwave, covered and vented, 2 more minutes. Stir in the zucchini; microwave covered for 6 minutes, stirring twice. Season with salt and pepper.

4. Combine the lamb, tomatoes, wine, tomato paste, 2 tablespoons of the minced parsley, and the bay leaf, thyme, oregano, and cinnamon in the 13 × 9-inch glass baking dish. Microwave, covered and vented, for 6 minutes, stirring twice. Remove the bay leaf; transfer lamb mixture to side dish.

5. Melt the butter uncovered on high power in a microwave-safe 2-quart glass measure, about 1 minute. Add the flour and whisk to blend. Microwave 1 minute. Whisk in the milk; microwave uncovered for 2 minutes, whisking once. Season with salt and pepper.

6. Process the ricotta in a food processor until smooth and season to taste with salt and pepper. Combine the white sauce, ricotta, and Parmigiano-Reggiano.

7. Stir the eggs and bread crumbs into the lamb mixture.

8. Spread eggplant in the 13 × 9-inch glass baking dish and top with half of the lamb mixture. Spoon the zucchini mixture over the lamb, then add the remaining lamb. Cover with the cheese mixture.

9. Microwave the moussaka uncovered until cooked through, about 10 minutes. Broil in preheated broiler 5 inches from the heat until the top is browned, about 2 minutes. Let stand 3 minutes. Sprinkle with the remaining 2 tablespoons parsley and serve hot.

SERVES 6

LAMB AND BLACK BEAN CHILI

Here is a great dish for feeding a crowd. The only accompaniments needed are a basket of cornbread and an enormous green salad. The interesting flavors in this dish deepen and intensify on standing, so make it a day or two before serving. Set out bowls of sour cream, sliced scallion, chopped tomato, diced avocado, and chopped cilantro—everyone can add the flavors they like best. When chopping the cilantro, don't forget to include the flavorful stems.

▶ **PREPARATION TIME:** 15 minutes
COOKING TIME: 35 minutes
STANDING TIME: 5 minutes

1 pound lean ground lamb
1 cup chopped seeded green
    bell pepper
1 cup chopped onion
2 tablespoons olive oil
1 clove garlic, minced
2–3 teaspoons good-quality
    chili powder, or more to
    taste
1 teaspoon ground cumin seed
1/4 teaspoon cayenne, or more
    to taste
2 15-ounce cans black beans,
    with juices
1 15-ounce can whole toma-
    toes, with juice

1 tablespoon finely chopped
    cilantro
1 tablespoon minced seeded
    fresh green chili pepper, or
    more to taste
Salt and freshly ground pepper
Sour cream
Chopped tomato
Thinly sliced scallions
Diced avocado
Torn cilantro leaves

1. Crumble the ground lamb into a microwave-safe 3-quart glass casserole with a lid. Microwave uncovered on high power for 5 minutes, stirring once to break up pieces; transfer to a strainer and drain off the juices. Wipe out the casserole.

2. Combine the green pepper, onion, oil, and garlic in the casserole.

Microwave covered on high power for 5 minutes, stirring once. Stir in the chili powder, cumin, and cayenne until blended. Add the reserved drained lamb and the black beans and tomatoes. Microwave covered for 15 minutes, stirring once, until the chili is very hot. Microwave uncovered for 10 minutes, stirring once, until chili boils and thickens slightly.

3. Stir in the chopped cilantro and minced chili pepper. Let stand covered for 5 minutes before serving. Season with salt and pepper, to taste. Serve with separate bowls of sour cream, chopped tomato, sliced scallion, diced avocado, and cilantro leaves to sprinkle on top.

SERVES 6–8

SIMPLE STUFFED CABBAGE LEAVES*

Fresh herbs and yogurt add a clean fresh taste to these stuffed cabbage leaves with a great Middle Eastern flavor.

▶ **PREPARATION TIME:** 15 minutes
COOKING TIME: 36 minutes

3/4 cup lowfat or nonfat plain yogurt
4 scallions, minced
1 small cucumber, peeled, seeded, and diced
1/4 cup minced fresh mint
1 cup water
1/3 cup long-grain rice
8 ounces lean ground beef
2 medium onions, finely chopped
3 tablespoons **each** olive oil and lemon juice
2 tablespoons **each** minced fresh parsley and dill
2 tablespoons **each** dried currants and pine nuts

1/2 teaspoon **each** salt and freshly ground pepper
1 large green cabbage

1. Stir together the yogurt, scallions, cucumber, and mint in a small bowl and set aside at room temperature.

2. Place the water and rice in a microwave-safe 1-quart glass measure, and cover loosely with microwave-safe plastic wrap. Microwave on high power for 7 minutes. Drain, rinse, and reserve.

3. Place the beef in a microwave-safe 13 × 9-inch glass baking dish, and break up the large pieces with a fork. Cover with microwave-safe plastic wrap and vent one side. Microwave on high power for 2 to 3 minutes, until cooked through and pinkness has disappeared. Drain completely. Add the beef to the rice in a bowl.

4. To the rice-beef mixture add ¼ cup of the yogurt mixture and the onions, 2 tablespoons each of the olive oil and lemon juice, parsley, dill, currants, pine nuts, and the salt and pepper. Combine thoroughly.

5. Core the cabbage, and remove and discard the tough outer leaves. Carefully remove 12 large leaves. Arrange the leaves in the same clean 13 × 9-inch glass baking dish. Cover and vent with plastic wrap. Microwave on high power for 5 to 8 min-

utes, or until softened.

6. Cut the hard rib end off each cabbage leaf with a V-shaped cut. Lay a leaf flat on a work surface and place a heaping ¼ cup of the beef mixture near the cut end. Fold over the sides and tightly roll the leaf around the beef mixture. Repeat with the remaining 11 leaves. Place the stuffed leaves seam-side down in the same baking dish. Drizzle with the remaining olive oil and lemon juice. Cover with plastic wrap and vent one side. Microwave on high power for 15 to 18 minutes. Serve hot, with yogurt sauce over the top.

SERVES 4

SPICY PICADILLO

A fantastic mixture for tacos or tostadas in crisp corn tortillas, or burritos in flour tortillas, served with sour cream, chopped tomatoes, cilantro, shredded lettuce, and grated Monterey Jack or mild Cheddar cheese.

▶ *PREPARATION TIME: 15 minutes*
COOKING TIME: 13 minutes

1 medium onion, diced
1 tablespoon olive oil
1 clove garlic, minced
1 pound lean ground beef
1 8-ounce can tomato sauce
1 apple, pared and grated
¼ cup golden raisins
1 jalapeno pepper, seeded and minced

1 tablespoon apple cider vinegar
2 teaspoons hot or mild chili powder
1 teaspoon **each** ground cumin seed and dried oregano
½ teaspoon salt, or to taste
Pinch ground cinnamon
¼ cup stuffed Spanish olives, sliced
3 scallions, trimmed and minced

1. Stir together the onion, oil, and garlic in a microwave-safe 8-inch-square glass baking dish. Cover with microwave-safe plastic wrap and vent one side. Microwave on high power for 3 to 4 minutes, or until soft, stirring once. Add the beef, stirring to break up the large pieces. Microwave, covered and vented, on high power for 4 to 5 minutes, stirring once, until the pinkness has almost disappeared.

Spoon off as much liquid as possible. Break up the beef with a wooden spoon.

2. Stir in all the remaining ingredients except the olives and scallions and microwave, covered and vented, for 4 minutes, stirring once. Stir in the olives and scallions and serve hot.

MAKES 4 CUPS (Serves 4)

FASTEST TEX-MEX TAMALE PIE

This easy microwave tamale pie takes about half the time of one prepared in a conventional oven, and there will be no loss of flavor. It's also great with Pepper Jack (Monterey Jack cheese with minced jalapenos).

▸ *PREPARATION TIME: 5 minutes*
COOKING TIME: 22 minutes
STANDING TIME: 3 minutes

1 ½ cups water
½ cup yellow cornmeal
½ teaspoon salt
1 cup shredded Monterey Jack or mild Cheddar cheese (about 4 ounces)
¼ cup minced cilantro
Freshly ground pepper to taste
1 recipe Spicy Picadillo (page 128)

1. Combine the water, cornmeal, and salt in a microwave-safe 2-quart glass measure. Microwave uncovered on high power for 10 minutes, or until all the water is absorbed, stirring twice to break up the lumps. Stir in the cheese, cilantro, and pepper.

2. Place the Spicy Picadillo in a microwave-safe 8-inch-square glass baking dish and spread the cornmeal mixture evenly over the top. Microwave uncovered on high power for 10 to 12 minutes, or until heated through. Let stand 3 minutes. Serve hot.

SERVES 4

SAUSAGE

POLENTA AND TWO CHEESES WITH SAUSAGE AND MUSHROOMS

Polenta prepared the conventional way requires constant stirring—unlike this microwave version which produces polenta that is just as smooth and creamy with minimal stirring.

▶ **PREPARATION TIME:** 15 minutes
COOKING TIME: 23 minutes

Sausage and Mushrooms:
1 pound sweet Italian sausage, casings removed, meat crumbled
1/2 cup chopped onion
1 tablespoon olive oil
2 cups sliced fresh mushrooms
1 clove garlic, crushed
1 teaspoon minced fresh oregano, or pinch dried oregano
1/2 teaspoon fresh thyme leaves, or pinch dried thyme
Salt and freshly ground pepper

Polenta:
2 cups homemade or canned unsalted chicken broth
1 cup water
1 cup yellow cornmeal

1/2 teaspoon salt
1/2 cup diced mozzarella cheese
1/4 cup freshly grated Parmigiano-Reggiano cheese
1 tablespoon softened unsalted butter (optional)
Salt and freshly ground pepper

1. Crumble the sausage into a microwave-safe 10-inch glass pie plate; microwave on high power for 5 to 6 minutes, or until the sausage is cooked through, stirring twice and breaking up the sausage meat with a fork. Transfer to a sieve to drain off the fat; set aside.

2. Add the onion and olive oil to the pie plate; microwave uncovered for 3 minutes; stir in the mushrooms; microwave uncovered for 3 minutes. Stir in the reserved sausage and the garlic, oregano, and thyme; cover

with microwave-safe plastic wrap and vent one side. Let stand until ready to reheat.

3. Microwave the chicken broth in a microwave-safe 3-quart glass casserole with a lid, covered, for 3 minutes, or until very hot. In a separate bowl, stir the water and cornmeal together until smooth. Gradually stir into the hot broth until smooth. Microwave uncovered for 6 minutes, stirring thoroughly with a spoon or whisk until smooth twice during the cooking time. Stir in the mozza-

rella and Parmigiano-Reggiano until blended. Stir in the butter if desired. Add salt and freshly ground pepper to taste.

4. Microwave the covered and vented sausage and mushroom mixture until hot, about 2 minutes. Season with salt and freshly ground pepper to taste. To serve, spoon the cornmeal mixture onto dinner plates and top with the sausage and mushroom mixture.

SERVES 4

SAUSAGE, PEPPERS, POTATOES, AND SMOTHERED ONIONS, VINAIGRETTE

▶ *PREPARATION TIME: 15 minutes*
COOKING TIME: 15 minutes

1 pound sweet Italian sausage, casings removed, meat crumbled
12 ounces all-purpose potatoes (3 medium-sized), peeled, halved lengthwise, and cut into 1/4-inch slices
1 large onion, halved lengthwise, cut into 1/4-inch slices (about 1 1/2 cups)
3 tablespoons olive oil, preferably extra-virgin

1 clove garlic, crushed
1 red or green bell pepper, halved, seeded, and cut into 1/4-inch strips
1 tablespoon red wine vinegar
1 tablespoon chopped Italian parsley
1 teaspoon minced fresh oregano leaves
Salt and freshly ground pepper

1. Place the sausage in a microwave-safe 10-inch glass pie plate. Microwave uncovered on high power for 5 minutes, stirring twice to break up sausage meat. Drain in a sieve; set aside.

2. Combine the potatoes, onion, 1 tablespoon of the olive oil, and garlic in the pie plate; cover with microwave-safe plastic wrap and vent one side. Microwave 5 minutes, stirring once. Stir the reserved sausage and the pepper strips into the potato mixture; cover and microwave for 5 minutes, or until the potatoes are evenly tender, stirring once.

3. Whisk the remaining 2 tablespoons olive oil and the vinegar, parsley, and oregano together and add to the potato mixture; season with salt and pepper and toss to blend.

SERVES 4

PASTA

LASAGNE PRIMAVERA

A dapted from a recipe by Julia Child, this lasagne is delicious as well as unusual.

> ▶ **PREPARATION TIME:** 30 minutes
> **COOKING TIME:** 46 minutes
> **STANDING TIME:** 3 minutes

1 onion, finely diced
1 tablespoon olive oil
1 clove garlic, minced
1 35-ounce can Italian plum tomatoes, drained and chopped
1/2 bay leaf
1/8 teaspoon **each** dried thyme, fennel seeds, crushed red pepper flakes, and grated orange zest
Large pinch saffron threads
Salt and freshly ground pepper to taste
9 lasagne noodles (8 ounces)
2 whole chicken breasts, skinned, boned, and split
1 cup broccoli flowerets
1/2 cup fresh or thawed frozen peas
3 tablespoons unsalted butter

4 ounces shiitake mushrooms, sliced
1 medium zucchini, scrubbed, cut into matchsticks
1 pound ricotta cheese
4 tablespoons minced fresh parsley
1/2 cup **each** grated mozzarella, Gruyère, and Parmigiano-Reggiano cheese

1. Combine the onion, oil, and garlic in a microwave-safe 10-inch glass pie plate. Cover with micro-wave-safe plastic wrap and vent one side. Microwave on high power for 2 minutes. Stir in the tomatoes, bay leaf, thyme, fennel seeds, red pepper flakes, orange zest, saffron, and salt and pepper to taste. Microwave on high power, covered and vented, 4 minutes, stirring once.

2. Cook the noodles in a large pot of salted boiling water until tender but firm to the bite. Drain and rinse.

3. Arrange the chicken in a microwave-safe 10-inch glass pie plate with the thickest sides at edge of the plate. Microwave, covered and vented, 6 to 8 minutes, turning the chicken pieces after 4 minutes. Cool slightly, shred the chicken, and season with salt and pepper.

4. Microwave the broccoli loosely covered with plastic wrap on a microwave-safe 9-inch pie plate until crisp-tender, 1 to 2 minutes. Add peas and season.

5. Melt the butter in a 10-inch pie plate, about 1 minute. Stir in the mushrooms. Microwave, covered and vented, 4 minutes, stirring once. Season lightly.

6. Place the zucchini on a 9-inch pie plate. Microwave, covered and vented, 2 minutes. Season with salt and pepper and combine with the broccoli and peas.

7. Puree the ricotta in a food processor. Season and stir in 3 tablespoons of the parsley.

8. Combine the mozzarella and Gruyère cheese.

9. Coat bottom of a microwave-safe 13 × 9-inch glass baking dish with olive oil. Arrange three lasagne noodles in the dish. Top with one third of the ricotta mixture; add half the vegetables and one third of the tomato sauce. Sprinkle with half the combined cheeses. Repeat layers once and cover with the last three lasagne noodles. Mix the remaining ricotta, tomato sauce, parsley, and Parmigiano-Reggiano; spread over noodles.

10. Microwave uncovered until heated through, 12 to 15 minutes. Let stand 3 minutes. Serve hot.

SERVES 6

STUFFED PASTA SHELLS

H ere's another delicious example of "real" food made in the microwave. The lively Provence-style tomato sauce takes less than 15 minutes to cook. If the sauce and the cheese mixture are made ahead of time, you can have dinner on the table in just a few minutes.

▸ **PREPARATION TIME:** 35 minutes
COOKING TIME: 10 minutes

1 small onion, diced
1 tablespoon olive oil, preferably extra-virgin

2 cloves garlic, minced
1/3 cup minced seeded red bell
    pepper
1/2 cup canned crushed
    tomatoes
1 bay leaf
1 teaspoon fresh thyme leaves
20 Niçoise olives, pitted and
    chopped
2 sun-dried tomatoes (packed
    in oil), diced
2 teaspoons capers
Pinch **each** grated orange zest
    and fennel seeds
Pinch **each** salt and freshly
    ground pepper
1 1/3 cups ricotta cheese
1/2 cup shredded mozzarella
    cheese, preferably fresh
1/4 cup minced fresh basil leaves
1/4 cup freshly grated Parmigi-
    ano-Reggiano cheese
1/3 cup **each** minced seeded red
    and yellow bell pepper
1/4 cup minced fresh parsley
16 jumbo pasta shells, cooked,
    rinsed, and drained well

---

1. Stir the onion and oil together in a microwave-safe 9-inch glass pie plate. Cover with plastic wrap and vent one side. Microwave on high power for 1 minute. Stir in the garlic; microwave, covered and vented, 2 minutes longer.

2. Stir in the red bell pepper; microwave, covered and vented, 2 minutes. Stir in the crushed tomatoes, bay leaf, thyme, olives, sun-dried tomatoes, capers, orange zest, fennel seeds, and a pinch each salt and pepper.

3. Combine the remaining ingredients except 1 tablespoon of the parsley and the pasta shells in a mixing bowl. Season to taste with salt and pepper. Spoon the cheese mixture into the pasta shells. Arrange the shells in a microwave-safe dish just large enough to hold them in a single layer. Spoon the sauce over the shells and sprinkle with the remaining 1 tablespoon parsley. Microwave uncovered until hot, about 5 minutes. Serve hot.

SERVES 4

MACARONI AND CHEESE FOR GROWN-UPS

Macaroni and cheese is the ultimate comfort food—for those times when you want to feel cozy and taken care of. It's so quick and easy in the microwave, it's almost as if someone *is* taking care of you and has prepared it for you. It'll be on the table in less than a half hour—about the same amount of time it takes to make the packaged kind—and it's so much better. Serve it with a green salad for a great dinner.

▶ **PREPARATION TIME:** 20 minutes
COOKING TIME: 9 minutes
STANDING TIME: 2 minutes

1 tablespoon unsalted butter
1 tablespoon all-purpose flour
¾ cup milk
¼ teaspoon grated lemon zest
⅛ teaspoon **each** salt and freshly ground pepper
6 ounces small shells, fusilli, or penne pasta, cooked and drained
½ cup grated mozzarella cheese (about 2 ounces)
½ cup freshly grated Parmigi-ano-Reggiano cheese
¼ cup diced Italian fontina cheese
¼ cup **each** minced seeded red bell pepper and minced fresh parsley
2 tablespoons crumbled blue cheese, preferably Gorgon-zola (optional)
1 tablespoon snipped fresh chives

1. Microwave the butter uncovered in a microwave-safe 2-quart glass measure on high power until melted, about 30 seconds. Add the flour and whisk until smooth. Microwave uncovered on high power for 20 seconds. Gradually whisk in the milk. Microwave until thickened, about 2 minutes, then whisk until smooth.

2. Stir the white sauce and all the remaining ingredients except the chives in same glass measure. Transfer to a microwave-safe 2-quart gratin dish or shallow casserole and cover with microwave-safe plastic wrap, venting one side. Microwave on high power for 5 minutes. Sprinkle with chives and microwave 1 minute longer. Let stand 2 minutes. Serve hot.

SERVES 2

MEATLESS MAINS

WELSH RABBIT

This can be a really quick and satisfying dinner. If you like the flavor, use a dark ale such as Bass Ale; for a milder flavor use any domestic beer. You can also choose the type of Cheddar to use—mild, medium, sharp, or extra-sharp.

▶ **PREPARATION TIME:** 15 minutes
COOKING TIME: 4 minutes

½ cup beer or ale at room temperature
2¼ cups grated Cheddar cheese (about 8 ounces)
1 teaspoon Worcestershire sauce
½ teaspoon Dijon mustard
⅛ teaspoon cayenne pepper, or to taste
Salt to taste, if necessary
4 slices whole wheat toast
6 cherry tomatoes, halved, seeded, and sliced
1 teaspoon minced fresh parsley

1. Microwave the beer in a 2-quart microwave-safe glass measure for 1½ to 2 minutes, until very hot. Gradually whisk in the grated cheese, whisking constantly. Place in a food processor and puree until smooth. Add the Worcestershire sauce, mustard, cayenne, and salt if needed. Process to blend completely.

2. Wipe out the glass measure and return the Welsh Rabbit to it. Reheat for 1 to 2 minutes uncovered on high power, until heated through. Taste and adjust seasonings.

3. Divide the toast between two dinner plates. Pour the thick Welsh Rabbit over the toast and top with the cherry tomato and the minced fresh parsley. Serve immediately.

SERVES 2

VEGETABLE-STUFFED POTATOES WITH CREAMY COTTAGE CHEESE

Serve this dish for lunch. To complete the menu begin with a mug of tomato soup and serve a basket of assorted crackers on the side.

▸ **PREPARATION TIME:** 15 minutes
COOKING TIME: 20 minutes
STANDING TIME: 2 minutes

---

2 large baking potatoes (about 6 ounces each)
1 zucchini (about 4 ounces), scrubbed, trimmed, cut in ¼-inch slices
1 yellow summer squash (about 4 ounces), scrubbed, trimmed, cut in ¼-inch slices
1 medium carrot, trimmed, pared, cut in ¼-inch slices
1 cup broccoli flowerets (1-inch pieces)
¼ cup finely chopped sweet red onion
1 tablespoon unsalted butter
2 tablespoons fresh lemon juice
½ teaspoon grated lemon zest
¼ teaspoon freshly ground pepper
8 ounces small-curd creamed cottage cheese, at room temperature

---

1. Scrub the potatoes and pierce at least twice on each side with the tines of a fork. Microwave on high power for 7 to 9 minutes, or until the potatoes feel almost tender when pierced with a fork; wrap in a kitchen towel and let stand until ready to serve.

2. Combine the zucchini, yellow squash, carrot, broccoli, and onion in a microwave-safe 2-quart glass casserole with a lid. Microwave covered for 5 to 6 minutes, or until the vegetables are tender, stirring once. Add the butter, 1 tablespoon of the lemon juice, ¼ teaspoon of the lemon zest, and ⅛ teaspoon of the pepper; toss to blend. Cover and let stand 2 minutes.

3. Whisk the cottage cheese with the remaining 1 tablespoon lemon juice, ¼ teaspoon lemon zest, and ⅛ teaspoon pepper.

4. To serve, place each potato on a dinner plate; carefully cut the potatoes down the center and press in on the ends to open. Divide the cottage cheese mixture evenly between the potatoes and top with the steaming vegetables. Serve immediately.

SERVES 2

M A I N   D I S H E S   W I T H O U T   M E A T

BLACK BEAN BURRITOS*

Black bean burritos are not only delicious, they are also a nutritionally balanced meal. They fit the most recent dietary recommendations: low in fat (less than 30 percent), moderate protein (15 percent), and high in carbohydrates (55 percent), and they contain no cholesterol (but go easy on the cheese and sour cream garnishes for they do contain cholesterol). Burritos are a complete meal—you don't need to serve anything else, a long cool drink rounds it out perfectly.

▶ **PREPARATION TIME:** 20 minutes
COOKING TIME: 7 minutes

1 small onion, finely diced
2 teaspoons safflower oil
1 jalapeno pepper, seeded and diced
1 clove garlic, minced
¼ teaspoon **each** ground cumin seed, dried oregano, ground coriander seed, and chili powder
1 16-ounce can black beans, drained and rinsed
3 tablespoons water
Salt and freshly ground pepper
½ ripe California avocado, peeled, pitted, and diced
1 plum tomato, diced
1 scallion, trimmed and minced
1 tablespoon minced cilantro
2 teaspoons fresh lime juice
Pinch grated lime zest, or to taste
4 flour tortillas, warmed

Optional Garnishes:
Shredded romaine lettuce
Diced red onion
Grated Monterey Jack cheese
Sour cream

1. Stir together the onion, oil, jalapeno, and garlic in a microwave-safe 9-inch glass pie plate. Cover with microwave-safe plastic wrap and vent one side. Microwave on high power for 1 minute. Stir in the cumin, oregano, coriander, and chili powder and microwave covered and vented for 1 minute. Stir in the beans and water; microwave, covered and vented, 2 minutes. Transfer ½ cup of the bean mixture to a food processor or blender and puree. Stir back into the remaining beans. Season to taste with salt and pepper.

2. Combine the avocado, tomato, scallion, cilantro, lime juice, and zest in a small bowl. Season the salsa to taste with salt and pepper.

3. When ready to serve, microwave the beans, covered and vented, until very hot, 1 to 3 minutes. Divide the beans among the warm tortillas and serve with salsa and garnishes.

SERVES 2

CHAPTER 6

MAIN DISHES WITH SEAFOOD

Fish is one of the foods the microwave does best. The moist heat cooks it to perfection quickly with little risk of drying out, and the minimal cooking time preserves its delicate flavor and texture.

In the section called Fish Fillets, Oriental Style, we take advantage of the mildly sweet flavor of fish fillets and use them as the perfect foil for the spicy, salty, pungent flavors of Oriental ingredients like fresh ginger, scallions, garlic, sesame oil, soy sauce, fermented black beans, and cilantro.

Fish steaks are one of our favorite cuts of fish for microwave cooking. The uniformity of size guarantees an evenly and perfectly cooked piece of fish every time. The pretty pale pink color, flaky texture, and mild flavor of the salmon steak provide a great canvas for the creative cook. The number of salmon steak recipes—and the broad range of flavors used—are all living testimony to our enthusiasm for this particular fish. Firmer textured swordfish, stands up to more robust flavors; for example the spices of India as in the Bengali Swordfish or the mango and ginger flavoring in the Tropical Fish recipe.

Speaking of robust flavors, because we are both passionate about flavors of the Mediterranean we decided to create a section of fish recipes dedicated to our favorite sun-drenched flavors of tomato, rosemary, black olives, oranges, basil, red peppers, garlic, and, of course, olive oil. What could be bad?

Shellfish cooked in the microwave—particularly clams and mussels—are another pleasant surprise. Our enthusiasm for Clams with Black Bean Sauce and Mussels with Red Onion and Parsley have made both of these recipes personal favorites. Inspired by our success with these two bivalves, we expanded our repertoire to include other shellfish with our recipes for Scallops with Bacon and Apple, Fresh Tomato and Seafood Stew with Orange and Basil, and Seafood in Saffron-Tomato Broth with Red Onion Gremolata.

For perfectly cooked fish and shellfish every time be sure to read and carefully follow the Microwave Tips for Fish Fillets and Steaks and the Microwave Tips for Shellfish that follow.

MICROWAVE TIPS FOR FISH FILLETS AND STEAKS

▶ Arrange fish fillets so that the thickest part is toward the outside rim of the dish and the narrow and thinnest section is in the center.

▶ If the fillets are very small and delicate, fold in half and arrange with center fold toward the outside rim of the dish and the ends toward the center.

▶ Turn the plate a half-turn halfway through the cooking time and check the fillets every 30 seconds to 1 minute once half the cooking time has elapsed.

▶ Arrange fish steaks with the thicker portions toward the outside of the dish. Sometimes the steaks are turned over halfway through cooking.

▶ Fish cooked "until it flakes with a fork" is a direction for overcooking fish.

▶ Fish is cooked when the flesh—except for a thin line in the center—changes appearance from translucent to opaque. Err on the side of undercooking and if undercooked return to the microwave for 30-second intervals. The fish will continue to cook while standing.

▶ Strictly observe the standing time—set your microwave digital timer.
▶ Serve the fish immediately after the standing time. If you allow it to stand longer (especially if it is covered) it may overcook.

HOW TO HANDLE CLAMS AND MUSSELS

▶ Buy all shellfish from a reputable store. Farm-raised (in carefully tested and monitored waters) clams and mussels are now readily available.
▶ Clams should be tightly closed; do not buy if they have chipped or cracked shells. If mussels are slightly opened (called gapers) they should close tightly when the shell is lightly tapped.
▶ If shellfish will not be used right away, store in the refrigerator in a shallow dish or paper or plastic bag poked with holes (so the shellfish can breathe). *Do not store mussels or clams in a bowl of water.*
▶ Just before cooking soak in a bowl of ice-cold water for at least 10 minutes; scrub the shells with a stiff brush under cold running water. Pull the beards off the mussels or cut off with a small knife or kitchen shears.

MICROWAVE TIPS FOR COOKING MUSSELS AND CLAMS

▶ Select a dish large enough to hold the shellfish in a single layer or overlapping double layers. If the dish is too full, it will be difficult to stir thoroughly, resulting in uneven cooking. A microwave-safe 9- or 10-inch glass pie plate or a broad microwave-safe 3- or 4-quart glass casserole with a cover are both good choices.
▶ Always cook shellfish covered with microwave-safe plastic wrap vented on one side or with a microwave-safe lid.
▶ When you stir, remove any clams or mussels that are wide open (they are done); set aside in a bowl, covered, as you continue to cook the remaining shellfish.

R E C I P E S

FISH FILLETS ORIENTAL STYLE

Black Fish with Oriental Black Bean Sauce and Scallions*
Fish Fillets with Oriental Flavors*
Sole with Tamari-scented Julienned Vegetables*

SALMON STEAKS

Salmon Steaks with Four-Onion Confit
Salmon Steaks Topped with Spinach and Red Onion*
Salmon Steaks with Salsa*
Salmon Steaks with Niçoise Sauce*
Salmon Steaks with Saffron-Scallop Cream Sauce
Salmon Steaks with Lime, Garlic, and Cilantro*

SWORDFISH STEAKS

Bengali Swordfish*
Swordfish Marinated in Olive Oil, Lemon, and Oregano*
Swordfish with Red Pepper Sauce*
Tropical Fish*

SEAFOOD MEDITERRANEAN STYLE

Moroccan Snapper in Parchment*
Flounder with Thyme and Red Bell Pepper Strips*
Flounder Roulades with Spinach, Tomatoes, and Fresh Basil*
Fish Steaks Provençal*
Red Snapper with Orange, Rosemary, and Olive Oil*

SHELLFISH

Mussels with Red Onion and Parsley*
Scallops with Bacon and Apple
Sea Scallops with White Wine and Saffron Butter
Clams with Black Bean Sauce*
Clams with Sausage and Saffron Rice

SHRIMP

Basic Cooked Shrimp*
Shrimp-stuffed Potatoes
Shrimp in Spicy Tomato Sauce*
Shrimp with Garlic and Wine Sauce*

FISH STEWS

Fresh Tomato and Seafood Stew with Orange and Basil*
Gulf Shore Seafood Stew*
Seafood in Saffron-Tomato Broth with Red Onion Gremolata*

* Especially good for you.

FISH FILLETS ORIENTAL STYLE

BLACK FISH WITH ORIENTAL BLACK BEAN SAUCE AND SCALLIONS*

Fermented black beans are widely used in Chinese cooking. Most Chinese restaurant menus feature at least one dish—often shellfish—with black bean sauce. The sauce is simple to make once you have gathered the ingredients. Shop in an Oriental market for the beans, and a liquor store in an Oriental neighborhood for the rice wine (dry sherry can be substituted for the wine). On your way home, pick up the fish. Black fish has a firm white flesh (almost like lobster); if it is not available, any firm-fleshed fish (scrod or snapper) can be used. Fermented black beans are pretty salty. Therefore you might want to use low-sodium soy sauce in place of traditional soy sauce.

▶ **PREPARATION TIME:** 5 minutes
COOKING TIME: 4 minutes

1 tablespoon soy sauce
1 tablespoon Chinese rice wine or dry sherry
2 teaspoons fermented black beans, finely chopped
1 teaspoon Oriental sesame oil
1/2 clove garlic, crushed
1–1 1/4 pounds black fish or other firm-fleshed fish fillets, divided evenly into 4 portions

Green tops from 1 scallion, rinsed and cut into julienne, for garnish

1. In a small bowl, combine the soy sauce, Chinese rice wine, beans, sesame oil, and garlic; stir to blend; set aside.

2. Arrange the black fish fillets in a single layer in a microwave-safe 10-inch glass pie plate with the thickest parts toward the outside. Spoon half the soy mixture over the tops of

the fillets, dividing evenly. Cover with microwave-safe plastic wrap and vent on one side. Microwave on high power for 3 minutes, turning the dish a quarter-turn twice. Uncover and brush the fillets with the remaining soy mixture; re-cover and micro-wave 30 seconds to 1 minute, or until the fish is opaque.

3. Arrange on a serving platter, spoon some of the juice over the fish, garnish with the thin strips of green scallion tops, and serve.

SERVES 4

FISH FILLETS WITH ORIENTAL FLAVORS*

▶ *PREPARATION TIME: 5 minutes*
COOKING TIME: 4 minutes
STANDING TIME: 1 minute

1½ *pounds flounder, sole, or other delicate skinless fish fillets, cut into 6–8-ounce serving pieces*
1 *tablespoon Oriental sesame oil*
2 *teaspoons grated fresh ginger*
1 *teaspoon soy sauce*
1 *small clove garlic, crushed*
1 *teaspoon toasted sesame seeds*
2 *scallions, trimmed and cut into thin diagonal slices, for garnish*

1. Arrange the fish fillets in a single layer in a microwave-safe 10-inch glass pie plate. In a small bowl, combine the sesame oil, ginger, soy sauce, and garlic; spread over the surface of the fillets, distributing evenly. Cover with microwave-safe plastic wrap and vent one side; microwave on high power for 2 minutes. Turn the plate a half-turn; microwave until the fish is opaque, 1 to 2 minutes longer. Let stand, covered, 1 minute.

2. Sprinkle sesame seeds on the fish. Garnish with slices of scallion and serve immediately.

SERVES 4

SOLE WITH TAMARI-SCENTED JULIENNED VEGETABLES*

PREPARATION TIME: 10 minutes
COOKING TIME: 7 minutes
STANDING TIME: 1 minute

2 ounces (about 12) slender green beans, stem ends trimmed, halved lengthwise
1 small carrot, trimmed, pared, and cut into julienne
2 tablespoons water
1/2 teaspoon tamari or soy sauce
1 teaspoon Oriental sesame oil
2 6-ounce pieces fillet of sole
2 teaspoons fresh lemon juice
Salt and freshly ground pepper
2 thin slices lemon
1 teaspoon toasted sesame seeds

1. Combine the green beans, carrot, water, and tamari in a microwave-safe 2-quart glass casserole with a lid. Microwave covered on high power until crisp tender, 2 to 3 minutes. Pour off the liquid. Add the sesame oil, toss to coat, and set aside.

2. Place the fish fillets in a microwave-safe 10-inch glass pie plate; sprinkle with the lemon juice, a pinch of salt, and a grinding of pepper. Divide the vegetables between the pieces of fillet, fold the fillets tip to tip over the vegetables, and top each folded fillet with a lemon slice. Cover loosely with waxed paper and microwave on high power for 2 minutes. Turn the plate a half-turn and microwave 2 minutes longer. Let stand, covered, 1 minute. Sprinkle with toasted sesame seeds and serve.

SERVES 2

SALMON STEAKS

SALMON STEAKS WITH FOUR-ONION CONFIT

The microwave's a perfect way to cook salmon steaks—the added bonus is that there is no messy broiler to clean.

▶ **PREPARATION TIME:** 15 minutes
COOKING TIME: 26 minutes
STANDING TIME: 4 minutes

3 tablespoons unsalted butter
1 medium red onion, thinly sliced
2 shallots, minced
2 leeks, dark green tops and roots trimmed, well rinsed, thinly sliced
3 scallions, trimmed and minced
¼ cup dry red wine
1 tablespoon brown sugar
1 teaspoon fresh thyme leaves
Pinch salt, or to taste
¼ teaspoon freshly ground pepper
2 ¾-inch-thick salmon steaks (about 6 ounces each)

1. Melt 2 tablespoons of the butter in a microwave-safe 10-inch glass pie plate on high power for 1 minute. Stir in the onion, shallots, leeks, scallions, and wine. Cover with microwave-safe plastic wrap and vent one side. Microwave on high power, stirring three times, until the onions are softened, about 15 minutes. Stir in the sugar and thyme. Microwave uncovered on high until the sugar is dissolved, about 2 minutes. Season with salt and pepper and set aside.

2. Melt the remaining 1 tablespoon butter in another microwave-safe 10-inch glass pie plate on high power for 1 minute. Place the salmon steaks in the pie plate and turn to coat with butter. Cover dish with plastic wrap and vent one side.

3. Microwave on medium power (50%) until a milky substance comes to the surface and the fish is slightly firm to the touch, 3 to 5 minutes. Turn

the steaks over and cover dish again. Microwave on medium power (50%) just until cooked through, about 3 minutes. Let stand covered 4 min-utes. Serve hot, topped with onion confit.

SERVES 2

SALMON STEAKS TOPPED WITH SPINACH AND RED ONION*

A delicious and good-for-you dish—try serving it with herbed rice and a glass of dry white wine.

▶ **PREPARATION TIME:** 10 minutes
COOKING TIME: 11 minutes
STANDING TIME: 4 minutes

---

1 tablespoon unsalted butter
2 ³/₄-inch-thick salmon steaks (about 6 ounces each)
1 teaspoon olive oil
1 small red onion, finely diced
1 small garlic clove, minced
4 ounces fresh spinach, stems removed, rinsed and dried
¹/₂ teaspoon fresh lemon juice
Lemon wedges, for garnish

---

1. Melt the butter in a microwave-safe 9-inch glass pie plate on high power for 1 minute. Place the salmon steaks in the pie plate and turn several times to coat with butter. Cover with microwave-safe plastic wrap and vent one side.

2. Microwave on medium power (50%) until a milky substance comes to the surface and the fish is slightly firm to the touch, 3 to 5 minutes. Turn the steaks over. Microwave, covered and vented, on medium power (50%) for 3 minutes. Let stand, covered, 4 minutes.

3. Meanwhile, place the olive oil, onion, and garlic in a microwave-safe 9-inch glass pie plate. Microwave, covered and vented, on high power until softened, about 30 seconds. Add the spinach leaves and stir well to combine. Microwave uncovered until the spinach is wilted, about 30 seconds. Stir in the lemon juice; microwave uncovered 30 seconds longer. Spoon the spinach mixture over the salmon steaks and serve at once, garnished with lemon wedges.

SERVES 2

SALMON STEAKS
WITH SALSA*

The southwestern flavors of the salsa complement the salmon deliciously.

▶ **PREPARATION TIME:** 15 minutes
COOKING TIME: 9 minutes
STANDING TIME: 4 minutes

---

1 tablespoon unsalted butter
2 ¾-inch-thick salmon steaks (about 6 ounces each)
½ cup fresh or thawed frozen corn kernels
8 cherry tomatoes, halved and seeded
2 tablespoons diced roasted red pepper
1 tablespoon minced cilantro
1 teaspoon minced scallion
1 teaspoon safflower oil
½ teaspoon fresh lime juice, or to taste
½ teaspoon minced jalapeno pepper
Pinch ground cumin seed

---

1. Melt the butter in a microwave-safe 10-inch glass pie plate on high power for 1 minute. Place the salmon steaks in the pie plate and turn to coat with butter. Cover with microwave-safe plastic wrap and vent one side.

2. Microwave on medium power (50%) until a milky substance comes to the surface and the fish is slightly firm to the touch, 3 to 5 minutes. Turn steaks over and cover and vent. Microwave on medium power (50%) until just cooked through, about 3 minutes. Let stand covered 4 minutes.

3. Meanwhile, combine all the remaining ingredients in a small bowl and serve at room temperature on the salmon.

SERVES 2

SALMON STEAKS WITH NIÇOISE SAUCE*

The sunny flavors typical of southern French cooking make a wonderful sauce that's perfect for topping fresh salmon steaks.

▸ **PREPARATION TIME:** 20 minutes
COOKING TIME: 11 minutes
STANDING TIME: 4 minutes

---

1 tablespoon unsalted butter
2 ¾-inch thick salmon steaks (about 6 ounces each)
1 clove garlic, minced
1 teaspoon olive oil
20 cherry tomatoes
⅛ teaspoon **each** crushed hot red pepper flakes, fennel seeds, and dried thyme
25 Niçoise olives, pitted
2 teaspoons drained capers
Pinch **each** grated orange zest and salt, or to taste
1 teaspoon minced fresh parsley

---

1. Melt the butter in a microwave-safe 10-inch glass pie plate on high power for about 1 minute. Place the salmon steaks in the pie plate and turn to coat with butter. Cover with microwave-safe plastic wrap and vent one side.

2. Microwave on medium power (50%) until a milky substance comes to the surface and the fish is slightly firm to the touch, 3 to 5 minutes. Turn steaks over and cover and vent dish again. Microwave on medium power (50%) just until cooked through, about 3 minutes. Let stand covered 4 minutes.

3. Meanwhile, stir the garlic and oil together in a microwave-safe 9-inch glass pie plate. Microwave uncovered on high power for 1 minute. Stir in the tomatoes, red pepper flakes, fennel, and thyme. Cover the dish with plastic wrap and vent one side. Microwave until heated through, about 1 minute.

4. Stir in the olives, capers, and orange zest and microwave uncovered for 30 seconds longer. Season with salt. Sprinkle the sauce with parsley and serve on the hot salmon.

SERVES 2

SALMON STEAKS WITH SAFFRON-SCALLOP CREAM SAUCE

A very fancy entrée but nonetheless a very easy dish to make and one that's great for entertaining.

> **PREPARATION TIME: 7 minutes
> COOKING TIME: 12 minutes
> STANDING TIME: 3 minutes**

1 tablespoon unsalted butter
2 ³/₄-inch-thick salmon steaks (about 6 ounces each)
¹/₂ cup heavy cream
1 shallot, minced
12 threads saffron, crumbled
2 ounces bay scallops (¹/₄ cup), cut in half crosswise
Pinch salt, or to taste
Dash hot red pepper sauce, or to taste
Pinch grated lemon zest

1. Melt the butter in a microwave-safe 10-inch glass pie plate on high power for 30 seconds. Place the salmon in the pie plate; turn to coat with butter. Cover with microwave-safe plastic wrap, and vent on one side.

2. Microwave on medium power (50%) until a milky substance comes to the surface and the fish is slightly firm to the touch, 3 to 5 minutes. Turn the steaks over. Microwave, covered and vented, on medium power (50%) just until cooked through, about 3 minutes.

3. Meanwhile, combine the cream, shallot, and saffron in a microwave-safe 2-cup glass measure. Cover with microwave-safe plastic wrap and vent one side. Microwave on high power until the cream is thick, about 4 minutes. Immediately stir in the remaining ingredients. Cover and let stand 3 minutes to cook the scallops. Taste and adjust seasonings. Serve the sauce hot, spooned over the salmon steaks.

SERVES 2

SALMON STEAKS WITH LIME, GARLIC, AND CILANTRO*

This recipe can easily be increased. For three salmon steaks, add a total of 1 to 2 minutes cooking time; for four salmon steaks, add a total of 2 to 3 minutes.

BETTER BY MICROWAVE

▶ PREPARATION TIME: 5
minutes
MARINATING TIME: 20
minutes
COOKING TIME: 6 minutes
STANDING TIME: 1 to 2
minutes

2 ½-inch-thick salmon steaks
   (about 6 ounces each)
2 tablespoons fresh lime juice
1 tablespoon minced cilantro,
   including tender stems
1 tablespoon olive oil
1 clove garlic, crushed
Freshly ground pepper
Fresh lime wedges, for garnish
Sprigs of cilantro, for garnish

1. Arrange the salmon steaks in a microwave-safe 10-inch glass pie plate. Whisk the lime juice, cilantro, olive oil, garlic, and a grinding of pepper in a small bowl. Spoon over the salmon; cover with microwave-safe plastic wrap and marinate at room temperature about 20 minutes.

2. Vent one side of the plastic wrap and microwave on high power 3 minutes. Turn plate a half-turn and microwave until salmon is almost cooked through, 2 to 3 minutes more. Let stand, covered, 1 to 2 minutes.

3. Carefully remove the skin and serve the salmon with the juices spooned over each portion. Garnish with lime wedges and cilantro sprigs.

SERVES 2

SWORDFISH STEAKS

BENGALI SWORDFISH*

This mildly spiced swordfish has subtle Indian seasonings and is low in fat and long on flavor. Buy the freshest swordfish you can find, and be very careful not to overcook it. To make this dish even lower in fat try the new nonfat yogurt on the market. Served with rice, a chutney, and a green vegetable, this makes a first-rate meal.

▶ **PREPARATION TIME:** 15
  minutes
COOKING TIME: 4 minutes

2 tablespoons plain nonfat or
  lowfat yogurt
1 scallion, trimmed and minced
1 small clove garlic, minced
1 tablespoon minced cilantro
¼ teaspoon grated lime zest
¼ teaspoon minced fresh
  ginger
⅛ teaspoon **each** salt and
  freshly ground pepper
Pinch **each** ground cumin seed
  and crushed hot red pepper
  flakes
2 1-inch-thick swordfish steaks
  (about 8 ounces each)
Lime slices or wedges and cilantro sprigs, for garnish

1. Place all the ingredients except the swordfish steaks, lime slices, and cilantro sprigs in a small bowl and combine thoroughly.

2. Place the swordfish in a 9-inch microwave-safe glass pie plate. Spread the sauce over the top of the steaks. Cover with microwave-safe plastic wrap and vent one side. Microwave on high power until the fish is just cooked through, 3 to 4 minutes, rotating the plate a half-turn after each minute.

3. Transfer the swordfish to serving plates, garnish with lime and cilantro sprigs, and serve at once.

SERVES 2

SWORDFISH MARINATED IN OLIVE OIL, LEMON, AND OREGANO*

The rich flavor of swordfish works well with the fresh, assertive flavors of the olive oil, lemon, and oregano in this recipe. It reminds us of lunch on a terrace overlooking the bright blue Aegean Sea. Any firm-fleshed, richly flavored fish—shark comes instantly to mind—can be used instead.

▶ **PREPARATION TIME:** 5 minutes
MARINATING TIME: 30 minutes
COOKING TIME: 4 minutes

2 tablespoons olive oil, preferably extra-virgin
2 tablespoons fresh lemon juice
2 strips lemon zest, 2 inch × ½ inch, cut into julienne
1 teaspoon chopped fresh oregano leaves, or ¼ teaspoon dried oregano
1 clove garlic, crushed
2 1-inch-thick swordfish steaks (about 8 ounces each)
Freshly ground pepper
Fresh oregano sprigs, if available, for garnish
Lemon wedges, for garnish

1. Combine the olive oil, lemon juice, lemon zest, oregano, and garlic in a microwave-safe 10-inch glass pie plate. Add the swordfish steaks and turn to coat with the marinade. Marinate at room temperature 30 minutes (or refrigerate and marinate up to 1 hour).

2. Cover with microwave-safe plastic wrap and vent on one side. Microwave on high power for 3 to 4 minutes, or until just cooked through, turning the plate a half-turn every minute. Spoon the marinade over the steaks; sprinkle generously with the pepper and garnish with the sprigs of fresh oregano, if available, and lemon wedges.

SERVES 2

SWORDFISH WITH RED PEPPER SAUCE*

> **PREPARATION TIME:** 8 minutes
> **COOKING TIME:** 5 minutes

1 tablespoon olive oil
1 shallot, minced
1 clove garlic, minced
1 6-ounce jar roasted red peppers, drained and chopped
4 sun-dried tomatoes (packed in oil), diced
Pinch **each** dried thyme and grated orange zest
Salt and freshly ground pepper to taste
2 1-inch-thick swordfish steaks (about 8 ounces each)

1. Stir together the oil, shallot, and garlic in a microwave-safe 9-inch glass pie plate. Cover the dish with microwave-safe plastic wrap and vent one side. Microwave on high power for 1 minute.

2. Place the shallot mixture with the remaining ingredients except the fish steaks in a food processor or blender and process until very smooth.

3. Place the fish steaks in the same pie plate. Microwave, covered and vented, on high power for 2 minutes, turning the fish over after 1 minute. Spread the steaks with most of the pepper sauce. Microwave covered and vented for 2 minutes longer, turning the fish after 1 minute.

4. Spoon the remaining sauce onto serving plates and place fish steaks on top. Serve hot.

SERVES 2

TROPICAL FISH*

F resh tropical mango makes a simple room-temperature salsa for this delicious and colorful dish. Serve with a vegetable such as tiny fresh green beans or summer squash, and a frosty glass of lemonade. You can enjoy this refreshing and nutritious dish even more knowing it's very low in fat and calories. Other fish like flounder or red snapper could be substituted—just be careful not to overcook them.

▶ *PREPARATION TIME: 15 minutes*
COOKING TIME: *4 minutes*

---

1 ripe mango (12 ounces)
    seeded, pared, and diced
2 tablespoons minced sweet red
    onion
1 tablespoon fresh lime juice
1 tablespoon minced cilantro
1/2 teaspoon minced fresh
    ginger
1/4 teaspoon minced garlic
1/8 teaspoon grated lime zest
Pinch **each** salt and crushed hot
    red pepper flakes
2 1-inch-thick swordfish steaks
    (about 8 ounces each)
Lime wedges, for garnish

---

1. Stir together the mango, red onion, lime juice, cilantro, ginger, garlic, lime zest, salt, and red pepper flakes in a small bowl until well mixed. Taste and adjust seasoning.

2. Place the swordfish in a microwave-safe 9-inch glass pie plate. Cover with microwave-safe plastic wrap and vent one side. Microwave on high power until the fish is just cooked through, 3 to 4 minutes, rotating the plate a half-turn after each minute.

3. Transfer the swordfish to serving plates and garnish with mango salsa and lime wedges.

SERVES 2

SEAFOOD MEDITERRANEAN STYLE

MOROCCAN SNAPPER IN PARCHMENT*

Moroccan Snapper, cooked and served in parchment paper and fragrant with herbs and spices, is a stunning presentation.

▸ **PREPARATION TIME:** 20 minutes
COOKING TIME: 3 minutes

½ **each** red and yellow bell pepper, stemmed, seeded, cut into very thin strips
4–6 Niçoise olives, halved and pitted
1 scallion, trimmed and sliced on diagonal
1 teaspoon olive oil, preferably extra-virgin
1 small garlic clove, minced
2 teaspoons minced fresh parsley
Pinch **each** ground cumin seed, ground coriander seed, crushed hot red pepper flakes, grated lemon zest, salt, and freshly ground pepper
2 red snapper fillets (about 6 ounces each)
2–4 lemon slices

1. Place all the ingredients except the snapper and lemon slices in a mixing bowl and combine thoroughly.

2. Cut two pieces of parchment paper into sections 12 × 8 inches each. Fold the parchment paper in half lengthwise. Place a snapper fillet on one side of the fold on each piece of paper. Spoon the bell pepper mixture over the fish and top with one or two lemon slices. Fold the other side of each paper over the fish, then double-fold all edges to seal the packages securely.

3. Place the packets on a large microwave-safe plate. Microwave on high power 3 minutes, rotating the plate a half-turn after each minute.

4. Transfer the packages to serving plates and cut open with scissors at the table. Serve immediately.

SERVES 2

FLOUNDER WITH THYME AND RED BELL PEPPER STRIPS*

▸ **PREPARATION TIME:** 10
  minutes
COOKING TIME: 12 minutes
STANDING TIME: 1 minute

1 sweet white or yellow onion
  (about 8 ounces), halved
  and cut into thin lengthwise
  strips
1 red bell pepper, stem and
  seeds removed, halved, and
  cut into thin 1/8-inch lengthwise slices
2 tablespoons olive oil, preferably extra-virgin
1/4 teaspoon fresh or dried
  thyme leaves
1–1 1/4 pounds flounder fillets,
  cut into 4 even portions
1 tablespoon fresh lemon juice
1 tablespoon pitted and slivered
  brine-cured black olives
Salt and freshly ground pepper

1. Combine the onion, red peppers, oil, and thyme in a microwave-
safe 10-inch glass pie plate; stir to
blend. Microwave uncovered on high
power for 5 minutes. Stir well. Cover
with microwave-safe plastic wrap
and vent one side; microwave on high
power for 2 minutes.

2. Push the cooked vegetables
aside to make room for the fish fillets;
arrange the fish with the narrow tails
tucked under so that the portions
cook evenly. Spoon some of the
cooked vegetables over the fish and
sprinkle with the lemon juice. Cover
with microwave-safe plastic wrap
vented on one side; microwave 4 to
5 minutes, or until the fish turns
opaque, turning dish a quarter-turn
halfway through the cooking. Let
stand, covered, 1 minute.

3. Sprinkle with the olives and
season with salt and pepper to taste
before serving.

SERVES 4

FLOUNDER ROULADES WITH SPINACH, TOMATOES, AND FRESH BASIL*

> ▶ **PREPARATION TIME:** 15 minutes
> **COOKING TIME:** 18 minutes

2 tablespoons finely chopped
   sweet red onion
1 tablespoon olive oil
1 clove garlic, minced
1 15-ounce can whole tomatoes,
   drained, coarsely cut up
1 tablespoon plus 1 teaspoon
   chopped fresh basil
1/2 teaspoon grated orange zest
2 teaspoons fresh lemon juice
Salt and freshly ground pepper
1 pound flounder or sole fillets,
   cut into 8 serving pieces
1 10-ounce bag fresh spinach
   leaves, rinsed but not dried,
   stems discarded, large
   leaves torn in two
1/2 medium sweet red onion, cut
   into very thin vertical slivers
   (about 1/2 cup)
Fresh basil leaves, roughly torn

1. Combine the onion, oil, and garlic in a microwave-safe 10-inch glass pie plate; microwave uncovered on high power for 4 minutes, stirring once. Add the tomatoes; microwave for 8 minutes, or until boiling and slightly thickened, stirring once. Add 1 tablespoon of the basil and the orange zest; season to taste with salt and pepper. Set aside until ready to use.

2. Sprinkle a scant 1/2 teaspoon of the lemon juice and a pinch of the chopped fresh basil on each fillet; roll up, starting with the thin end of the fillet. Arrange like the spokes of a wheel in a microwave-safe 10-inch glass pie plate; cover with microwave-safe plastic wrap and vent one side. Microwave 2 to 2 1/2 minutes, turning the plate a half-turn after each minute, until the fish is opaque. Let stand, covered, while cooking the spinach.

3. Combine the spinach and the red onion in a microwave-safe 3-quart glass casserole with a lid; microwave covered 2 minutes. Let stand while reheating the tomato sauce in microwave, uncovered, 1 minute or until warm.

4. To serve, lift a serving of cooked spinach with two forks or a slotted spoon to drain off the excess liquid; arrange a bed of spinach in the center of four dinner plates, dividing evenly. Lifting with a spatula (to drain off the juice), place two flounder roll-ups on each plate, centered on the spinach. Top with a spoonful of the warm tomato sauce and garnish with torn basil leaves.

SERVES 4

FISH STEAKS PROVENÇAL*

To sop up the flavorful juices in this delicious dish, serve rice or orzo, a rice-shaped pasta, on the side.

▸ **PREPARATION TIME:** 10 minutes
COOKING TIME: 18 minutes
STANDING TIME: 1 minute

½ cup finely chopped onion
1 tablespoon olive oil
1 clove garlic, crushed
1 strip orange zest, ½ inch × 2 inches
1 14½-ounce can Italian plum tomatoes, drained
2 small zucchini (about 6 ounces total), trimmed, cut into ¼-inch slices, and then halved crosswise
1 tablespoon coarsely chopped fresh parsley
1 teaspoon capers, rinsed and drained
6 brine-cured black olives, pitted and coarsely chopped
½ teaspoon fresh or dried rosemary (see Note)
4 ½-inch-thick halibut, cod, or salmon steaks (about 6 ounces each)
2 tablespoons orange juice
½ teaspoon salt, or to taste
Freshly ground pepper
1 tablespoon julienne strips fresh basil

1. Combine the onion, oil, garlic, and orange zest in a microwave-safe 3-quart glass casserole with a lid. Cover and cook on high power for 2 minutes. Stir in the tomatoes, zucchini, parsley, capers, black olives, and rosemary. Cover and cook on high power for 6 minutes; stir well. Let stand, uncovered, while cooking the fish.

2. Place the fish in a microwave-safe 10-inch glass pie plate and sprinkle with the orange juice. Cover with microwave-safe plastic wrap and vent one side; microwave 4 to 6 minutes, or until the fish is opaque, turning the dish a quarter-turn halfway through the cooking. Let stand, covered, 1 minute.

3. To serve, drain the liquid from the fish; remove and discard the skin and center bones. Place on a serving platter. Remove the orange zest from the vegetables; season the mixture with salt and pepper to taste. Microwave 30 seconds to reheat, if necessary. Spoon the sauce evenly over the fish and garnish with the julienne strips of basil.

SERVES 4

NOTE: If using the dried rosemary, chop it with the fresh parsley to rehydrate before adding to the casserole.

RED SNAPPER WITH ORANGE, ROSEMARY, AND OLIVE OIL*

▸ *PREPARATION TIME: 10 minutes*
COOKING TIME: 6 minutes
STANDING TIME: 1 minute

2 tablespoons olive oil, preferably extra-virgin
3 strips orange zest, 3 inches ×
   ½ inch, cut into very thin
   julienne
1 clove garlic, halved and
   bruised
½ teaspoon dried rosemary or
   fresh rosemary stripped
   from stem
1 pound red snapper fillets, cut
   into 4 even portions
1 tablespoon fresh lemon juice
Freshly ground pepper
Sprigs of fresh rosemary, if
   available, for garnish

1. Combine the oil, orange zest, garlic, and rosemary in a microwave-safe 10-inch glass pie plate. Microwave uncovered on high power for 2 minutes. Stir well.

2. Dip the red snapper fillets in the hot oil, turning to coat evenly. Arrange the fish in the pie plate, placing the thin ends toward the center of the dish and sprinkle with lemon juice. Cover with microwave-safe plastic wrap and vent one side. Microwave on high power for 2 minutes. Turn the dish a quarter-turn and microwave 1 to 2 minutes longer, or until the fish is opaque. Let stand, covered, 1 minute before serving.

3. Transfer to serving dishes, arranging the strips of orange zest on top of the fillets, dividing evenly. Add a grinding of black pepper. Garnish with sprigs of fresh rosemary, if available.

SERVES 4

SHELLFISH

MUSSELS WITH RED ONION AND PARSLEY*

The glossy black shells of the mussels and the purple rings of onion make a very dramatic presentation. This dish makes a nice appetizer for four or dinner for two people. Serve with crusty French bread to sop up the juices. Good warm or at room temperature.

▶ **SOAKING TIME:** 10 minutes
PREPARATION TIME: 10 minutes
COOKING TIME: 7 minutes

24 mussels, scrubbed, soaked, bearded
½ cup dry white wine
1 strip orange zest, 1 inch × ½ inch
1 clove garlic, bruised with side of knife
¼ teaspoon fennel seeds
1 small sprig fresh basil
½ cup thinly sliced red onion rings
2 tablespoons olive oil
2 tablespoons chopped fresh parsley

1. Prepare the mussels.
2. Combine the wine, orange zest, garlic, and fennel seeds in a microwave-safe 3-quart glass baking dish with a lid. Microwave covered on high power for 2 minutes
3. Add the mussels and basil. Microwave covered for 4 to 5 minutes, or until all the mussels are opened, stirring thoroughly every 1½ minutes and turning the dish a half-turn. Remove any mussels that are wide open when you stir, and reserve, covered, while the remaining mussels continue cooking.
4. To serve, sprinkle with the onion rings, oil, and parsley and stir to blend. Strain the mussel juices and pour on top.
SERVES 2

* Usually sold by the pound, there are approximately 20 mussels to a pound.

SCALLOPS WITH BACON AND APPLE

With this classic combination of scallops, bacon, and apple juice we like the flavor of apple slices, sautéed in butter in a hot skillet, and served on the side.

> **PREPARATION TIME:** *5 minutes*
> **COOKING TIME:** *9 minutes*

2 slices bacon
8 ounces (about 8 pieces) small sea scallops, rinsed, patted dry
¼ cup apple juice
1 teaspoon unsalted butter, cut into ¼-inch pieces
1 teaspoon fresh lemon juice
Minced fresh chives, for garnish

1. Arrange the bacon in a microwave-safe 10-inch glass pie plate; microwave on high power for 2 minutes, turning dish a half-turn after 1 minute. Transfer to a paper towel; drain. Cut each strip into 4 equal lengths; reserve. Pour off the excess bacon drippings, leaving a thin film still coating the plate.

2. Arrange the scallops around the edges of the pie plate; cover with a piece of microwave-safe plastic wrap and vent on one side. Microwave on high power for 1 minute; turn the plate a half-turn; microwave 1 minute. Transfer the partially cooked scallops to a microwave-safe serving plate; place a piece of bacon on top of each scallop.

3. Add the apple juice to the scallop juices in the pie plate. Microwave uncovered for 4 minutes, or until boiling and slightly reduced. Stir in the butter until melted; add the lemon juice. Spoon the juices over the scallops and bacon. Microwave the completed dish uncovered for 1 minute, to reheat. Sprinkle with chives and serve with sautéed apple slices (see headnote).

SERVES 2

SEA SCALLOPS WITH WHITE WINE AND SAFFRON BUTTER

This rather elegant combination of scallops, rice, and julienned vegetables is perfect for a quiet dinner for two. Cook the rice on top of the stove while the vegetables and scallops are cooking in the microwave.

▶ *PREPARATION TIME: 15 minutes*
COOKING TIME: 13 minutes
STANDING TIME: 7 minutes

---

1 small carrot, pared and trimmed
1 small yellow summer squash (about 3 ounces), trimmed
1 small zucchini (about 3 ounces), trimmed
2 scallions, trimmed
1/2 cup water
1 tablespoon unsalted butter
1/2 teaspoon grated lemon zest
1/4 cup dry white wine
Pinch saffron threads
12 ounces (6 to 9 pieces) uniformly sized sea scallops, rinsed, patted dry
Hot cooked rice, tossed with sliced green tops of scallion
1 tablespoon unsalted butter
Salt
Fresh sprigs lemon thyme, if available, for garnish

---

1. Cut the carrots, yellow summer squash, zucchini, and scallions in thin julienne strips, each about 2½ inches long. Place the carrots in a microwave-safe 10-inch glass pie plate; add the water. Cover with microwave-safe plastic wrap and vent on one side; microwave on high power for 3 minutes.

2. Uncover; drain off the liquid and add the squashes, scallions, but-ter, and lemon zest; stir to blend. Microwave covered for 2 minutes. Let stand, covered, until ready to serve.

3. Place the wine and saffron in a microwave-safe 10-inch glass pie plate; microwave covered on high power for 3 minutes. Add the scallops and turn to coat with the wine. Cover with microwave-safe plastic wrap and vent on one side; microwave for 2 minutes.

4. Immediately strain the wine and scallop juices into a microwave-safe 2-cup glass measure. Cover the scallops and let stand 2 minutes to continue cooking. Meanwhile, microwave the wine and scallop juices uncovered for 2½ minutes, or until boiling and slightly reduced.

5. To serve, arrange the rice in three small mounds around the edges of two dinner plates. Place small bundles of the vegetables between the mounds of rice, dividing evenly. Place the scallops in the center of each plate, dividing evenly. Whisk the butter and a pinch of salt into the wine and saffron mixture and spoon over the scallops and vegetables. Garnish with the lemon thyme, if available.

SERVES 2

CLAMS WITH BLACK BEAN SAUCE*

Buy the smallest littleneck clams you can find, or the tiny—not much larger than your thumb—West Coast clam called Manilla Bay.

▸ **SOAKING TIME:** 10 minutes
PREPARATION TIME: 10 minutes
COOKING TIME: 10 minutes

24 littleneck clams, or 36 Manilla Bay clams (about 1¾ pounds total weight)

Black Bean Sauce:
2 tablespoons peanut oil
1 tablespoon thin slivers fresh ginger
1 clove garlic, cut into thin slices
2 tablespoons Chinese rice wine or dry sherry
1 tablespoon fermented black beans, finely chopped
1 tablespoon soy sauce, preferably low-sodium
1 teaspoon Oriental sesame oil
¼ teaspoon crushed hot red pepper flakes
1 tablespoon torn cilantro leaves

1. Scrub and soak clams.

2. Make the sauce. Combine the peanut oil, ginger, and garlic in a microwave-safe 3-quart glass casserole with a lid. Microwave covered on high power for 2 minutes, or until the oil is hot and the ginger and garlic are fragrant. Add the wine, black beans, soy sauce, sesame oil, and red pepper flakes; microwave covered for 1 minute.

3. Stir in the clams. Microwave covered for 6 minutes, or until all of the clams have opened, turning the dish a half-turn and shaking the dish to redistribute clams halfway through the cooking.

4. Arrange the clams on a deep platter, spoon the juices on top, and sprinkle with the cilantro. Return any unopened clams to the casserole; microwave covered for 30 to 45 seconds, or until opened. Discard any still unopened.

SERVES 2

CLAMS WITH SAUSAGE AND SAFFRON RICE

This combination of flavors—saffron, sausage, and clams—was borrowed from a Spanish paella.

> ▸ **SOAKING TIME:** 10 minutes
> **PREPARATION TIME:** 5
> minutes
> **COOKING TIME:** 27 minutes
> **STANDING TIME:** 8 minutes

18 littleneck clams
8 ounces sweet Italian sausage,
    casings removed, meat
    crumbled
½ cup chopped onion
1 clove garlic, minced
1½ cups homemade or canned
    chicken broth
⅔ cup long-grain white rice
½ cup diced fresh or drained
    canned tomato
6 threads saffron, or a pinch of
    powdered saffron
½ cup frozen tiny peas

1. Scrub and soak clams.

2. Combine the sausage, onion, and garlic in a microwave-safe 3-quart glass casserole with a lid. Microwave uncovered on high power until the sausage is cooked and the onion is tender, 6 minutes, stirring once halfway through the cooking.

3. Stir in the broth, rice, tomato, and saffron. Cover and cook 15 minutes, turning the dish a half-turn once. Let stand covered for 5 minutes.

4. Arrange the clams on top of the rice; spoon the frozen peas around the clams. Microwave covered until the clams begin to steam open, about 6 minutes. Let stand 3 minutes before serving.

SERVES 2

SHRIMP

BASIC COOKED SHRIMP*

This is a quick technique for cooking shrimp to perfection for use in salads or shrimp cocktail.

▶ **PREPARATION TIME: 5 minutes**
COOKING TIME: 2 minutes
STANDING TIME: 1 minute

1 pound large (about 20) shrimp, peeled and deveined

Spread the shrimp in a single layer in a microwave-safe 10-inch glass pie plate. Cover with microwave-safe plastic wrap and vent one side. Microwave on high power for 1 minute. Rearrange the shrimp so that the uncooked pieces are around the edges of the plate and the more-cooked pieces are toward the center. Re-cover and microwave 1 minute. Let stand, covered, 1 minute. Rinse with cold water to cool down and prevent overcooking.

SERVES 4

SHRIMP-STUFFED POTATOES

This recipe, inspired by a recipe from Claude Guigon, the executive chef at Sun Valley resort, Idaho, is the sort of rib-sticking, nourishing fare one yearns for after a rigorous day on the slopes.

▸ **PREPARATION TIME:** 10 minutes
COOKING TIME: 14 minutes

---

2 large baking potatoes (about 6 ounces each)
8 ounces shelled and deveined shrimp, coarsely chopped
1 tablespoon olive oil
½ clove garlic, crushed
Pinch dried thyme
¼ cup milk, half-and-half, or heavy cream
½ cup coarsely shredded Cheddar cheese (about 2 ounces)
2 tablespoons minced chives or green part of scallion
Salt and freshly ground pepper

---

1. Scrub the potatoes and pierce at least twice on each side with a fork. Microwave on high power for 7 to 9 minutes, or until the potatoes feel almost tender when pierced with a skewer; wrap in a kitchen towel and let stand until ready to use.

2. Combine the shrimp, olive oil, garlic, and thyme in a microwave-safe 9-inch glass pie plate; stir to blend. Cover with microwave-safe plastic wrap and vent one side; microwave 2 minutes. Uncover; stir well; cover and let stand 1 minute. Drain off the excess liquid before using.

3. Meanwhile, cut a thin slice from one side of each cooked potato. Using a teaspoon, scoop out the cooked potato, leaving a firm shell. Reserve the shells. In a large bowl, mash the cooked potato, the drained cooked shrimp, the milk or cream, half of the cheese, and half of the chives until blended; add salt and pepper to taste.

4. Spoon back into the reserved potato shells and sprinkle with the remaining ¼ cup cheese, dividing evenly. Place on a microwave-safe plate and microwave 1 minute, or until the cheese is melted. Sprinkle with the remaining 1 tablespoon chives, and serve hot.

SERVES 4

SHRIMP IN SPICY TOMATO SAUCE*

Serve this delicious sauce over flat spinach fettuccine. If you like a spicier sauce, increase the red pepper flakes to taste.

▶ **PREPARATION TIME:** 15 minutes
COOKING TIME: 14 minutes
STANDING TIME: 1 minute

½ cup chopped onion
¼ cup olive oil, preferably extra-virgin
2 tablespoons slivered prosciutto or smoked ham
1 clove garlic, minced
1 cup canned crushed tomatoes
¼ teaspoon crushed hot red pepper flakes, or more to taste
1 pound (about 24) medium shrimp, shelled and deveined
1 tablespoon chopped Italian parsley
Salt and freshly ground pepper

1. Combine the onion, oil, prosciutto, and garlic in a microwave-safe 10-inch glass pie plate. Microwave uncovered on high power for 4 minutes, stirring once. Add the tomatoes and red pepper flakes. Microwave for 8 minutes, or until boiling and slightly thickened, stirring once during the cooking.

2. Stir in the shrimp. Cover with microwave-safe plastic wrap and vent one side; microwave 1 minute. Stir the shrimp in the center of the dish to the edges and the cooked shrimp on the edges to the center. Recover and microwave 1 minute, or until the shrimp are almost cooked through. Let stand, covered, 1 minute to finish cooking. Stir in the parsley, add salt and pepper to taste, and serve hot.

SERVES 4

SHRIMP WITH GARLIC AND WINE SAUCE*

Good served with hot rice, or for a change of pace try orzo, a tiny, rice-shaped pasta.

▶ **PREPARATION TIME:** 15 minutes
COOKING TIME: 12 minutes
STANDING TIME: 1 minute

3 tablespoons unsalted butter, cut into ¼-inch pieces
2 cloves garlic, crushed
½ cup dry white wine
1 pound large (about 20) shrimp, shelled and deveined
2 teaspoons finely chopped fresh parsley
1 teaspoon fresh lemon juice
Salt and freshly ground black pepper

1. Melt the butter in a microwave-safe 10-inch glass pie plate on high power for 2 minutes. Stir in the garlic; microwave uncovered for 3 minutes, stirring once. Add the wine; microwave 5 minutes.

2. Stir in the shrimp and sprinkle with the parsley. Cover with microwave-safe plastic wrap and vent one side; microwave for 1 minute. Stir the shrimp and carefully move the partially cooked shrimp toward the center and the uncooked shrimp toward the outside edges of the plate. Microwave, covered and vented, 1 minute longer. Let stand, covered, 1 minute. Drizzle with the lemon juice, add salt and pepper to taste, and serve hot.

SERVES 4

FISH STEWS

FRESH TOMATO AND SEAFOOD STEW WITH ORANGE AND BASIL*

Save this recipe for the height of summer when fresh tomatoes are irresistibly juicy and garden fresh basil is packed with flavor. For a true Mediterranean-style feast, rub thick slices of Italian bread with the cut side of a garlic clove, drizzle with olive oil, and toast on both sides on a hot grill or under the broiler—in Italy these are called crostini. Place a crostino in the bottom of each soup bowl and ladle the soup on top.

▶ **PREPARATION TIME:** 5 minutes
COOKING TIME: 13 minutes
STANDING TIME: 7 minutes

¼ cup very hot tap water
5 or 6 saffron threads, or a generous pinch of ground saffron
1 pound ripe tomatoes, cored and cut into ½-inch chunks
2 tablespoons julienne strips of fresh basil leaves

2 strips orange zest, 3 inches × ½ inch
1 clove garlic, crushed
¼ cup dry white wine
1 pound cod or halibut, skinned and boned, cut into 4 large chunks
12 large shrimp, peeled and deveined
Salt and freshly ground pepper
4 pieces crostini (see headnote)

1. Combine the hot water and saffron threads in a microwave-safe 3-quart glass casserole with a lid; microwave covered on high power for 1 minute. Let stand, covered, 5 minutes.

2. Stir the tomatoes and 1 tablespoon of the basil into the saffron. Twist the orange zest to release the oils; add the orange zest and the garlic to the tomatoes. Microwave covered for 5 minutes. Stir in the wine; microwave *uncovered* until the liquid boils, 2 to 3 minutes. Add the fish and shrimp; microwave covered for 4 minutes, turning the dish once. Carefully rearrange the pieces of fish and shrimp and spoon the liquid over the seafood. Let stand, covered, 2 minutes.

3. Before serving, taste the broth and add salt and pepper to taste.

Place a piece of crostino in the bottom of each soup bowl; divide the seafood and broth evenly among the soup plates. Garnish each with a few pieces of the remaining basil.

SERVES 4

GULF SHORE SEAFOOD STEW*

This seafood dish contains flavors popular in the cuisine of the Southwest: cilantro, jalapeno, lime, and avocado.

▶ **PREPARATION TIME:** 20 minutes
COOKING TIME: 12 minutes

½ ripe California avocado, peeled, pitted, and diced
2 small tomatoes, seeded and diced

1 tablespoon minced cilantro
2 medium red onions, cut into ¼-inch dice
2 cloves garlic, minced
1 tablespoon olive oil, preferably extra-virgin
2 cups diced seeded peeled tomatoes

1 cup dry white wine
1 tablespoon tequila
1 fresh jalapeno pepper, seeded
    and minced
1 bay leaf
1/2 teaspoon chili powder
1/4 teaspoon **each** ground
    cumin seed, grated lime
    zest, and salt
Pinch dried oregano
12 ounces red snapper fillets,
    cut into 2½ × 1-inch strips
6 large mussels, scrubbed,
    soaked, and bearded
6 large shrimp (in shells)
Lime wedges, for serving

1. Combine the avocado, tomato, and cilantro in a small bowl and set aside at room temperature for garnish.

2. Coat the onions and garlic with the oil in a microwave-safe 11 × 9-inch glass baking dish. Cover with microwave-safe plastic wrap and vent one side. Microwave on high power for 2 minutes.

3. Stir in the tomatoes, wine, tequila, jalapeno, bay leaf, chili powder, cumin seed, lime zest, salt, and oregano. Microwave, covered and vented, for 6 minutes, stirring every 2 minutes. Gently stir in the snapper. Continue to microwave, covered and vented, until the fish is opaque in the center, about 2 minutes. Let stand.

4. Microwave the mussels in a microwave-safe 9-inch glass pie plate, covered and vented, until opened, about 1 minute. Strain the juices and add with the mussels to the stew. Discard any unopened mussels.

5. Microwave the shrimp in the same dish, covered and vented, until pink and just firm to the touch, about 1 minute. Shell and devein the shrimp, then stir into the stew. Serve hot, topped with the avocado and tomato garnish and lime wedges.

SERVES 2

SEAFOOD IN SAFFRON-TOMATO BROTH WITH RED ONION GREMOLATA*

Saffron, the stamen of the crocus, harvested in Spain, lends a distinctively pervasive flavor to the tomato broth.

▶ **SOAKING TIME:** 20 minutes
PREPARATION TIME: 15 minutes
COOKING TIME: 14 minutes

6 mussels, scrubbed, soaked, and bearded
6 clams, scrubbed and soaked
4 extra-large shrimp, shelled and deveined
6 ounces fresh swordfish, halibut, or cod, skin and bones removed, cut into 4 serving pieces
1/4 cup very hot tap water
Generous pinch saffron threads, or 1/8 teaspoon ground saffron
1/4 cup olive oil, preferably extra-virgin
1 clove garlic, slivered
1 14 1/2-ounce can Italian-style plum tomatoes with juices, pureed in food processor or pressed through food mill or sieve
Salt and freshly ground pepper
2 pieces crostini (see page 173)

Red Onion Gremolata:
1 tablespoon chopped Italian parsley
1 tablespoon chopped sweet red onion
1 strip lemon zest, about 2 inches × 1/2 inch, cut into very thin strips

1. Prepare all the seafood and refrigerate until ready to cook.

2. Combine the hot water and saffron threads in a microwave-safe 1-cup glass measure; microwave 1 minute; set aside, covered, until ready to use.

3. Make the Red Onion Gremolata: Finely chop the parsley, red onion, and lemon zest together until well blended; set aside.

4. Combine the olive oil and garlic in a microwave-safe 3-quart glass casserole with a lid. Microwave uncovered on high power for 1 minute. Stir in the tomatoes and the saffron and water mixture; microwave uncovered for 5 minutes.

5. Add the seafood; spoon the hot tomato broth over the fish; sprinkle with half of the gremolata mixture. Cover and microwave for 8 minutes, stirring gently but thoroughly halfway through the cooking time. Using tongs, transfer all the

opened clams and mussels to a side dish; cover with foil to keep warm. Microwave the remaining seafood covered for 1 to 2 minutes, or until all the shellfish is opened and the shrimp and fish steak are opaque in the center. Return the reserved shellfish to the casserole and spoon the hot tomato broth over all. Season to taste with salt and freshly ground pepper.

6. Place the crostini in shallow serving bowls and top with the seafood and tomato broth, dividing evenly. Sprinkle with the remaining gremolata before serving.

SERVES 2

CHAPTER 7

MAIN DISH SALADS

The microwave's efficiency, convenience, super-quick cooking powers, easy clean-up, and ability to keep the kitchen cool make it our favorite cooking method when we need cooked chicken breast, scallops, salmon fillet, or vegetables for a salad.

These recipes give us the wonderfully fresh flavors that we care about. The fact that the scallops in the Warm Scallop Salad with Cilantro and Lime Dressing, the salmon in the Thai Salmon Salad, or the chicken in the Provençal Chicken Salad were all cooked in the microwave in merely a twinkle of the cook's unharried and unhassled eye is another plus. (Less substantial salads appear in the Side Dish chapter.)

RECIPES

Red Peppers Stuffed with Warm Rice Salad
Poached Chicken Breasts for Chicken Salads*
Pecos River Chicken Salad*
Provençal Chicken Salad
Warm Chicken Salad with Peanut Sauce
Sesame-Cilantro Chicken Salad*
Chicken, Mango, and Orange Salad*
Fresh Figs, Chicken, and Arugula
Shrimp and Spinach Salad*
Shrimp and Feta Potato Salad
Thai Salmon Salad*
Poached Fish Salad with Spinach and New Potatoes*
Warm Scallop Salad with Cilantro and Lime Dressing*

* Especially good for you.

RED PEPPERS FILLED
WITH WARM RICE SALAD

▶ **PREPARATION TIME:** 10
  minutes
COOKING TIME: 20 minutes
STANDING TIME: 5 minutes

½ cup long-grain rice
1½ cups water
¾ teaspoon salt
3 tablespoons olive oil
1 tablespoon red wine vinegar
1 small clove garlic, crushed
Freshly ground pepper
1 large or 2 small red bell pep-
    pers, halved, seeds and
    stems discarded
¼ cup **each** chopped green bell
    pepper, carrot, and celery
1 scallion, trimmed and
    chopped
½ cup shredded Monterey Jack
    cheese (2 ounces)

1. Combine the rice, water, and
½ teaspoon of the salt in a microwave-safe 2-quart glass casserole
with a lid; microwave covered on
high power for 15 minutes. Let stand,
covered, 5 minutes.

2. Meanwhile, whisk the oil,
vinegar, garlic, the remaining ¼ teaspoon salt, and a grinding of pepper
in a small microwave-safe glass bowl.
Lightly brush the inside and outside
of the pepper halves with the vinaigrette, reserving some to toss with the
rice. Place the peppers, cut-side
down, in a microwave-safe 2-quart
glass casserole with a lid. Microwave
2 minutes. Let stand, covered, until
ready to fill.

3. Combine the hot cooked rice
with the chopped green pepper, carrot, and celery, the scallion, and ¼
cup of the cheese. Microwave the remaining vinaigrette 30 seconds, or
until warmed through; add to the rice
mixture and toss. Spoon into the pepper halves. Sprinkle with the remaining cheese; microwave, uncovered,
until heated through, about 2 minutes.

SERVES 2

POACHED CHICKEN BREASTS FOR CHICKEN SALADS*

Poached chicken breasts are delicious "as is," but they are also the starting point for a variety of wonderful salads.

This recipe serves two but is easily halved or doubled. To microwave half a skinned, boned chicken breast, follow the procedure below and microwave on high power for 2 to 3 minutes. Microwave two whole skinned, boned, and split chicken breasts on high power for 6 to 8 minutes. Always turn the chicken halfway through, and use the same proportion of liquid. You'll know it's done when no pinkness remains and the juices run clear.

▸ **PREPARATION TIME:** 3
  minutes
COOKING TIME: 4 minutes

1 whole chicken breast, skinned,
  boned, split, and trimmed
  of fat
1 tablespoon homemade or
  canned chicken broth, white
  wine, citrus juice, or water

Arrange the chicken in a microwave-safe 9-inch glass pie plate with the thicker portions toward the outside of the dish. Drizzle with the chicken broth. Cover with microwave-safe plastic wrap and vent one side. Microwave on high power for 3 to 4 minutes, turning chicken over after 2 minutes.

SERVES 2

PECOS RIVER CHICKEN SALAD*

▸ **PREPARATION TIME:** 25
  minutes
COOKING TIME: 4 minutes
CHILLING TIME: 1 hour

1 Poached Chicken Breast (recipe above), cooled and torn
into ½-inch strips 2–3
inches long

¼ cup minced cilantro
¼ cup minced sweet red onion
1 plum tomato, seeded and
    diced
½ California avocado, peeled,
    pitted, and diced
2 tablespoons olive oil
2 tablespoons fresh lime juice
Pinch **each** ground cumin seed
    and chili powder, or to taste
1 cup **each** finely shredded red
    and green cabbage
2 tablespoons coarsely chopped
    dry-roasted peanuts

1. Place all the ingredients ex-cept the cabbage and peanuts in mix-ing bowl and toss to combine. Refrigerate at least 1 hour to allow flavors to blend.

2. Arrange the shredded cabbage on serving plates and spoon the salad over the top. Sprinkle with roasted peanuts and serve at once.

SERVES 2

PROVENÇAL CHICKEN SALAD

D eep, wonderful earthy flavors make this a welcome light entrée during any season.

▶ **PREPARATION TIME:** 30
    minutes
COOKING TIME: 9 minutes

1 Poached Chicken Breast (rec-
    ipe page 182), cooled and
    torn into ½-inch strips 2–3
    inches long
⅓ cup minced fresh parsley
¼ cup balsamic vinegar
3 tablespoons olive oil, prefera-
    bly extra-virgin
2 shallots, minced
2 cloves garlic, minced

1 anchovy fillet, drained,
    mashed with a fork
Salt and freshly ground pepper
2 skinned and seeded roasted
    red bell peppers, cut into
    ½-inch strips
8 ounces haricots verts or very
    thin green beans, trimmed
⅓ cup water
10 Niçoise olives
1 tablespoon capers, drained

1. Place the chicken in a shallow bowl. Stir together the parsley, vinegar, olive oil, shallots, garlic, anchovy, salt, and pepper to taste in a mixing bowl. Toss the chicken with half the dressing.

2. Place the roasted peppers in a second shallow bowl. Pour half of the remaining dressing over the peppers and toss to coat.

3. Place the haricots verts and water in a microwave-safe 2-quart glass casserole with a lid. Microwave covered on high power for 3 to 5 minutes, until crisp tender, stirring twice. Drain and toss with the remaining dressing.

4. Arrange the chicken, peppers, and beans on four serving plates. Add the olives and sprinkle with capers. Serve at room temperature.

SERVES 4

WARM CHICKEN SALAD WITH PEANUT SAUCE

For best flavor make this salad just before serving using the still warm, just poached chicken (and allow 7 minutes more for preparation/cooking time).

▶ **PREPARATION TIME:** 10 minutes
COOKING TIME: 3 minutes

2 whole chicken breasts (about 6 ounces each), boned, skinned, and trimmed of fat
5 cups trimmed, rinsed, and shredded romaine leaves
1 small red bell pepper, seeded and cut into thin strips
1/4 cup thinly sliced scallions, cut on the diagonal
1/3 cup lightly packed cilantro sprigs
1/2 cup thin slices seedless cucumber

Peanut Sauce:
1/2 cup smooth peanut butter
1 1/2 tablespoons low-sodium soy sauce
1 tablespoon fresh lemon juice
1 teaspoon chopped garlic
1 teaspoon chopped fresh ginger
1 teaspoon Oriental sesame oil
1/2 teaspoon hot chili-flavored sesame oil, or 1/4 teaspoon crushed hot red pepper flakes
1/2 cup reserved poaching liquid
Salt

1. Split the chicken breasts in two and place smooth-side down on the work surface. Separate the fillets from the breasts and arrange in a single layer in a microwave-safe 10-inch glass pie plate. Cover with microwave-safe plastic wrap and vent one side. Microwave on high power for 2 minutes. Let stand, covered, 1 minute. Pour off and reserve the broth.

2. Make the Peanut Sauce: Blend the peanut butter, soy sauce, lemon juice, garlic, ginger, sesame oil, and chili oil in a food processor until smooth. Transfer to a large bowl. Gradually stir in up to ½ cup of the reserved poaching liquid, 1 tablespoon at a time, until the sauce is of pouring consistency. Add salt to taste.

3. Spread a bed of romaine on a large serving platter. Cut the warm chicken breasts diagonally into ¼-inch slices and toss with the red bell pepper strips. Arrange in the center of the romaine. Sprinkle with half the scallions; drizzle with half the warm peanut sauce. Garnish with the remaining scallions and the cilantro sprigs. Arrange the cucumber slices around the edges of the platter. Serve warm, passing the remaining warm peanut sauce on the side.

SERVES 4

SESAME-CILANTRO CHICKEN SALAD*

S erve this for a leisurely weekend lunch or a quick weekday supper, or pack it to take on a picnic—it's perfect for all three.

▶ **PREPARATION TIME:** 20
  minutes
COOKING TIME: 8 minutes
CHILLING TIME: 1 hour

2 Poached Chicken Breasts (recipe page 182), cooled and torn into ½-inch strips 2–3 inches long
1 medium cucumber, pared, seeded, and thinly sliced
6 small scallions, trimmed and minced
6 tablespoons fresh lime juice

¼ cup minced cilantro
2 tablespoons minced fresh ginger, or to taste
2 tablespoons Oriental sesame oil
2 jalapeno peppers or other fresh chili, seeds and ribs removed, minced
2 bunches watercress, tough stems trimmed, rinsed, and dried
1 tablespoon toasted sesame seeds

1. Place all the ingredients except the watercress and sesame seeds in a mixing bowl and toss to combine. Refrigerate at least 1 hour to allow flavors to blend.

2. Arrange the watercress on serving plates and spoon the chicken salad over the top. Sprinkle with toasted sesame seeds and serve at once.

SERVES 4

CHICKEN, MANGO, AND ORANGE SALAD*

Great textures and flavors make this wonderful, refreshing salad an irresistible treat.

▶ **PREPARATION TIME:** 25 minutes
COOKING TIME: 4 minutes

1 Poached Chicken Breast (recipe page 182), cooled and torn into 1/2-inch strips 2–3 inches long
1 ripe mango (about 12 ounces), seeded, pared, and cut into medium dice
2 navel oranges
1 bunch watercress, tough stems trimmed
1 bunch arugula, tough stems trimmed
1 small head romaine, leaves separated
2 teaspoons coarsely chopped fresh rosemary leaves
1/2 teaspoon salt, or to taste
1/4 teaspoon freshly ground pepper, or to taste

3 tablespoons olive oil, preferably extra-virgin
2 tablespoons balsamic vinegar
Orange slices, for garnish

1. Place the mango in a large salad bowl. Cut the peel and white pith from oranges. Working over the same bowl to catch the juices, cut the orange segments from membranes and place the segments in the bowl.

2. Rinse and dry the greens; tear into bite-sized pieces and add with the rosemary and the chicken to the salad. Season with salt and pepper.

3. Drizzle the oil over the salad and toss to coat. Add the vinegar and toss again. Garnish with the orange slices and serve at once.

SERVES 4

FRESH FIGS, CHICKEN, AND ARUGULA

These luscious flavors and textures are great together. Feast on the salad when you have some time to relax and enjoy it—it's easy to make.

> **PREPARATION TIME: 20 minutes**
> **COOKING TIME: 4 minutes**

1 bunch arugula, tough stems trimmed
1 bunch watercress, tough stems trimmed
1 cup shredded radicchio
5 tablespoons olive oil, preferably extra-virgin
1½ tablespoons balsamic vinegar, or to taste
2 teaspoons honey
2 teaspoons Dijon mustard
⅛ teaspoon each salt and freshly ground pepper, or to taste
1 Poached Chicken Breast (recipe page 182), cooled and torn into ½-inch strips 2–3 inches long
⅓ cup toasted pine nuts
6 dried apricots, cut into thin strips
3 slices prosciutto, cut into thin strips
3 large black figs, stemmed, thinly sliced crosswise

1. Rinse and dry the arugula, watercress, and radicchio; combine in a large salad bowl and refrigerate covered.

2. Whisk the oil, vinegar, honey, mustard, salt, and pepper together in a small bowl. Let stand at room temperature.

3. Just before serving, add the chicken, pine nuts, apricots, and prosciutto to the salad greens and toss to combine. Add all but 1 tablespoon of the vinaigrette and toss well to coat. Divide the salad between two serving plates. Top with sliced figs and drizzle the figs with remaining dressing. Serve at once.

SERVES 2

SHRIMP AND SPINACH SALAD*

H ere's a healthful dish especially great for spring or summer—and very versatile. Arugula or watercress can be used instead of spinach, or a combination of all three. Tarragon, parsley, or chervil can take the place of the basil, and bay scallops can be used instead of shrimp.

▶ **PREPARATION TIME:** 15 minutes
COOKING TIME: 7 minutes

1/4 cup olive oil
1 tablespoon fresh lemon juice
1 shallot, minced
1 teaspoon Dijon mustard
1/8 teaspoon **each** salt and freshly ground pepper, or to taste
10 ounces spinach (smallest leaves possible), stemmed, rinsed, dried, and torn into bite-sized pieces (about 4 cups)
1 small red onion, sliced into thin rings
1/3 cup shredded fresh basil leaves
1 pound (about 24) medium shrimp, shelled and deveined

1. Whisk together the oil, lemon juice, shallot, mustard, salt, and pepper in a microwave-safe 1-cup glass measure.

2. Place the spinach in a large salad bowl and toss with the onion and basil.

3. Place the shrimp in a deep microwave-safe 12-inch oval glass baking dish, leaving the center of the dish open. Cover with microwave-safe plastic wrap and vent one side. Microwave on high power for 1 to 3 minutes, until the flesh becomes barely opaque but not tough, stirring twice. Add to the spinach.

4. Add the shrimp-cooking liquid to the dressing. Microwave uncovered for 1 to 1½ minutes, until very hot. Whisk, and pour over the salad, tossing completely. Serve immediately.

SERVES 4

SHRIMP AND FETA POTATO SALAD

This main course potato salad, great for a picnic, offers a terrific combination of Mediterranean flavors.

▸ **PREPARATION TIME:** 20
  minutes
COOKING TIME: 20 minutes
STANDING TIME: 2 minutes
CHILLING TIME: 1 hour

---

2 pounds all-purpose potatoes
  (about 6 medium), pared
  and cut in 3/4-inch dice
1/4 cup water
1 pound small shrimp
2 tablespoons lemon juice
3 ounces feta cheese, coarsely
  crumbled
1 medium red bell pepper,
  seeded and diced
1/2 medium cucumber, pared,
  cut in half lengthwise,
  seeded, and diced
1/3 cup diced sweet red onion
5 tablespoons white wine
  vinegar
1/4 cup chopped pitted black
  Mediterranean olives
2 tablespoons olive oil, preferably extra-virgin
1/4 teaspoon dried oregano
1/4 teaspoon freshly ground
  pepper
2 tablespoons minced fresh
  mint

---

1. Place the potatoes in a micro-wave-safe 3-quart glass casserole with a lid and sprinkle with the water. Microwave covered on high power for 11 to 14 minutes, stirring three times, until done. Drain well and let cool to room temperature.

2. Arrange the shrimp in a circle around the outer edge of a micro-wave-safe 12-inch oval glass baking dish, leaving the center of the dish open, and sprinkle with the lemon juice. Cover with microwave-safe plastic wrap and vent one side. Microwave for 3 to 6 minutes, stirring once and checking often so as not to overcook. Let stand, covered, for 2 minutes. Shell and devein the shrimp.

3. Place the potatoes and shrimp in a medium mixing bowl. Stir in all the remaining ingredients except the mint and stir to combine. Refrigerate until cold, at least 1 hour. Stir in the mint just before serving.

SERVES 4

THAI SALMON SALAD*

This is a delightful salad, with lots of interesting flavors that work really well together. The nam pla sauce can be found in Oriental markets or specialty shops.

▸ **PREPARATION TIME:** 20 minutes
COOKING TIME: 4 minutes

6 tablespoons fresh lime juice (about 3 limes)
3 tablespoons safflower oil
2 tablespoons nam pla (Oriental fish sauce)
1 tablespoon minced fresh lemon grass
1 small clove garlic, minced
1 teaspoon soy sauce, preferably low-sodium
1 teaspoon sugar
1/2 teaspoon minced fresh ginger
Pinch **each** grated lime zest and crushed hot red pepper flakes
2 1/2-inch-thick salmon steaks (about 6 ounces each)
4 cups rinsed, dried, shredded romaine leaves
1 bunch radishes, trimmed and thinly sliced
1 cup fresh mint leaves
1/2 cup cilantro leaves
2 small red onions, sliced and separated into rings

1. Combine the lime juice, safflower oil, nam pla, lemon grass, garlic, soy sauce, sugar, ginger, lime zest, and pepper flakes in a small bowl.

2. Place the salmon in a microwave-safe 9-inch glass pie plate. Cover with microwave-safe plastic wrap and vent one side. Microwave on high power until just cooked through, 2 to 4 minutes, rotating a half-turn after each minute. Let cool. Pour off the liquid, then flake the salmon, removing skin and bones.

3. Combine the remaining ingredients in a large salad bowl. Add about half the dressing to the salmon and toss to combine. Add the remaining dressing to the greens and toss to coat. Add the salmon to the salad and serve at once.

SERVES 4

POACHED FISH SALAD WITH SPINACH AND NEW POTATOES*

This flavorful salad makes a delicious luncheon or light supper entrée. Serve with sour dough rolls from the bakery and a crisp Sancerre or California Fume Blanc.

▸ **PREPARATION TIME:** 15 minutes
COOKING TIME: 10 minutes

5 tablespoons olive oil
2 tablespoons fresh lemon juice
1 teaspoon whole-grain mustard
¼ teaspoon salt
Freshly ground pepper
12 ounces flounder or sole fillets, cut into portions
6 small new potatoes (about 12 ounces), scrubbed and cut into ⅛-inch-thick slices
6 ounces slender fresh green beans, stem ends trimmed
1 tablespoon water
4 ounces trimmed, rinsed, and dried fresh spinach (about 2 cups packed)
2 scallions, trimmed and cut in thin diagonal slices
2 radishes, trimmed and thinly sliced
1 small carrot, trimmed, pared, and cut into julienne
½ small cucumber, pared and thinly sliced

1. Whisk the oil, lemon juice, mustard, salt, and a grinding of black pepper until blended. Set aside.

2. Arrange the fish fillets in a single layer, thin portions pointing toward the center in a microwave-safe 9-inch glass pie plate; lightly brush the fillets with 1 tablespoon of the dressing. Cover with microwave-safe plastic wrap and vent one side. Microwave on high power until the fish is opaque, 2 to 3 minutes, turning the dish a half-turn after each minute. Uncover and let stand until ready to serve. (The fish will continue to cook while it is standing.)

3. Spread the potato slices in the bottom of a 2-quart microwave-safe glass casserole with a lid. Place the beans in an even layer on the top of the potatoes; sprinkle with the water. Cover and microwave for 6 to 7 minutes, or until the potatoes are tender when pierced with a fork, stirring once or twice. Let stand, covered, until ready to serve.

4. In a large bowl, combine the spinach leaves with 2 tablespoons of the dressing; toss to coat. Arrange the spinach leaves on a large serving dish. Arrange the potato slices and green beans over the spinach and top with the pieces of fish fillet; drizzle with the remaining dressing. Garnish the platter with the scallion, radish, carrot, and cucumber slices.

SERVES 2

WARM SCALLOP SALAD WITH CILANTRO AND LIME DRESSING*

This simple scallop salad makes a delicious luncheon or light summer supper dish for two. Serve with crusty French bread, a chilled dry white wine, and fresh fruit for dessert.

▶ *PREPARATION TIME: 15 minutes*
COOKING TIME: 2 minutes

4 tablespoons olive oil
2 tablespoons fresh lime juice
1 teaspoon Oriental sesame oil
1/4 teaspoon salt
8 ounces bay scallops (about 1/2-inch diameter), rinsed and patted dry
1/8 teaspoon crushed hot red pepper flakes
1/4 cup plain lowfat yogurt
1 small head red-leaf or other tender garden lettuce, rinsed, dried, and torn into pieces (about 4 cups)
1/4 cup thinly sliced red onion
1/4 cup cilantro leaves
1 small cucumber, peeled and thinly sliced
1/4 medium red bell pepper, seeded and cut into thin slivers
1 small ripe avocado, peeled and pitted, cut into 1/2-inch-thick wedges
1 tablespoon thinly sliced green scallion tops

1. Whisk the olive oil, lime juice, sesame oil, and salt in a small bowl. Arrange the scallops in a single layer on a microwave-safe 9-inch glass pie plate; sprinkle with 1 tablespoon of the dressing and the red pepper flakes. Toss to coat. Set aside.

2. Whisk the yogurt into the remaining dressing and set aside. Combine the lettuce, onion, and cilantro leaves in a large bowl. Place the cucumber and red bell pepper in a second smaller bowl.

3. Cover the scallops with microwave-safe plastic wrap and vent one side. Microwave on high power for 2 minutes, turning the dish a half-turn halfway through cooking. Immediately uncover and strain off the excess liquid. Add the scallops to the cucumber and red pepper mixture; add 2 tablespoons of the dressing, and toss.

4. Add 2 tablespoons of the remaining dressing to the lettuce mixture, and toss. Divide the lettuce between two large plates. Mound the scallop mixture in the center. Drizzle with any remaining dressing. Garnish the plates with the avocado slices and scallions, and serve at once.

SERVES 2

VEGETABLES

This is a big chapter, but it should be. Vegetables are microwave-friendly. They microwave fast—the cooking time is often reduced by almost half. The freshest vegetables retain their just-picked flavor and—researchers tell us—more of the heat-sensitive nutrients often lost when cooked conventionally.

By using the microwave as a convenient kitchen accessory, vegetables can be cooked in the microwave just minutes before the entrée has finished cooking conventionally. Or, if you plan the menu to include a microwaved entrée with a standing time, the vegetable can be cooking in the microwave while the entrée completes its standing time.

You no longer have to plan ahead when baking potatoes or cooking beets, artichokes, or winter squash. The microwave cuts the cooking times of these traditionally slow-cooking vegetables anywhere from 25 to 30 percent.

We had a great time creating wonderful flavor combinations—Broccoli with Garlic and Hot Pepper

Oil, Green Beans with Lemon and Mint, Zucchini Papparadelle, and Braised Leeks with Pear, to name just a few.

Before you begin, be sure to read the tips for microwaving vegetables, below.

MICROWAVE TIPS FOR VEGETABLES

▶ Always microwave vegetables on high power.
▶ Always cover vegetables with a microwave-safe lid or microwave-safe plastic wrap vented on one side.
▶ Vegetables with skins (e.g., acorn squash and baking potatoes) should be pierced several times with a fork or they might explode while cooking.
▶ If a recipe gives a range of cooking time, always check after the minimum time suggested. If you need to cook a vegetable longer than the suggested time, check for doneness at frequent intervals.
▶ Finally—and most important—always select the freshest, best-looking vegetables you can buy. Microwaving vegetables is great, but it won't hide flaws!

R E C I P E S

SPRING AND SUMMER

Artichokes, with Dipping Sauces
Asparagus with Three-Citrus Butter
Ratatouille*
Swiss Chard with Sour Cherries and Pine Nuts*
Green Beans with Lemon and Mint*
Fresh Corn with Peppered Olive Oil*
Sesame Snow Peas*
Shredded Carrots with Chervil Butter
Radishes with Scallions and Parsley*

Summer Squash with Gremolata*
Zucchini Papparadelle*
Zucchini with Balsamic Vinegar and Mint*
Spaghetti Squash with Fresh Tomato Sauce*
Primavera Vegetables with Lemon-Mustard Dressing
Sweet Peas with Lemon Butter

FALL AND WINTER

New England Acorn Squash
Quick Beets with Parsley
Brussels Sprouts with Caraway
Broccoli with Garlic and Hot Pepper Oil*
Cauliflower with Lemon and Parsley
Sweet and Sour Cabbage
Sweet Red Onions with Sage Butter
Braised Leeks with Pear
Leeks with Lemon Thyme
Shiitake with Garlic and Herb Butter
Braised Fennel with Parmigiano-Reggiano Cheese

COMFORTING POTATOES

Potatoes and Mushrooms in Lemon Cream
Potatoes with Three Bubbly Cheeses
Tiny New Potatoes with Red Pepper- and Garlic-Infused Oil*
Potatoes with Greens and Pancetta
Little Red Potatoes with Butter and Chives
Potatoes with Olive Oil, Capers, and Olives*
Ginger-Mashed Sweet Potatoes
Sweet Potatoes with Curried Onion and Yogurt Topping

VEGETABLE PUREES

Pureed Acorn Squash with Maple Syrup
Orange-Rutabaga Puree
Celery Root and Potato Puree
Turnip-Potato Puree

* Especially good for you.

SPRING AND SUMMER

ARTICHOKES, WITH DIPPING SAUCES

Now you can decide to serve artichokes at the last minute! Cooked conventionally, artichokes can take nearly an hour to prepare, but using the microwave you can have two artichokes on the table in 15 minutes. They're great plain (and without sauces are very low in calories), but they're even better served with one of the following dipping sauces. The "bagna cauda" sauce is delicious, but if you're not an anchovy fan try a squeeze of lemon instead of the anchovy.

▶ **PREPARATION TIME:** 5
   minutes
COOKING TIME: 10 minutes
STANDING TIME: 5 minutes

2 medium artichokes
1 lemon, halved
2 tablespoons water

   1. Cut off the artichoke stems flush with the bottom leaves and pull off small, dark outer leaves. Cut off the top inch of the cone with a knife, then trim the points from all the leaves with scissors. Rub the cuts with lemon halves as soon as they are made.
   2. Place the artichokes in a microwave-safe 2-quart glass casserole with a lid. Add the water. Microwave

covered on high power for 10 minutes. Let stand covered for 5 minutes longer. Serve hot with one of the following dipping sauces.

SERVES 2

HERB BUTTER

2 tablespoons unsalted butter
1 teaspoon minced fresh
   parsley
1 teaspoon snipped fresh chives
Pinch freshly ground pepper

   Melt the butter in a small microwave-safe bowl on high power for about 1 minute. Stir in the herbs and pepper. Serve hot.

"BAGNA CAUDA"

1 tablespoon unsalted butter
1 tablespoon olive oil, prefera-
    bly extra-virgin
1/8 teaspoon minced fresh garlic
1/4 teaspoon anchovy paste

Pinch freshly ground pepper

Heat the butter, olive oil, and garlic in a microwave-safe small bowl on high power for about 1 minute. Stir in the remaining ingredients and serve hot.

ASPARAGUS WITH THREE-CITRUS BUTTER

Asparagus is the most seasonal of vegetables and one of the oldest vegetables known to man—a favorite of the ancient Romans. It is a cousin of the lily, and just as lovely. It is the aristocrat of vegetables, and since it is so special and so good, it should be cooked with extra care: The microwave is the perfect tool for the job. The cooking time depends on the size and condition of the asparagus. If the stalks are large and require longer cooking, peeling them is recommended. Asparagus should be cooked until tender only, never until soft and mushy. Snap or cut off the woody end of the stalk end and cut all the stalks to the same length. Since asparagus has two textures, arrange it in a starburst pattern with the tender tips at the center, if possible. One pound of trimmed asparagus will be cooked in 2 to 6 minutes—depending on the degree of doneness desired, the size and age, the cooking medium, and whether or not you cover it, among other variables. Try checking and stirring it around after a couple of minutes or so to get it cooked just as you'd like. Remember, it will continue to cook a bit after it's removed from the microwave.

▶ **PREPARATION TIME:** 10
    minutes
COOKING TIME: 7 minutes

2 tablespoons unsalted butter
1 tablespoon orange juice

1/4 teaspoon **each** grated or-
    ange, lemon, and lime zest
1 pound very thin stalks aspar-
    agus, ends trimmed
Salt and freshly ground pepper
    to taste

1. Place the butter, orange juice, and all three citrus zests in a microwave-safe 12-inch glass baking dish. Microwave uncovered on high power for 30 to 60 seconds, to melt the butter. Stir well to blend.

2. Toss the asparagus in the flavored butter and arrange in a single layer in a starburst pattern with the tender tips in the center of the dish, if possible. Cover with microwave-safe plastic wrap and vent one side; microwave until the asparagus is crisp-tender, 2 to 6 minutes depending on the thickness of the stalks. Season with salt and pepper. Serve hot.

SERVES 4

RATATOUILLE*

Ratatouille is a Provençal vegetable stew that originated in Nice, a classic slow-cooking dish that adapts itself very well to the microwave. Rather than an hour or so of cooking, in the microwave it takes only 20 minutes. Ratatouille is a very versatile dish that can be served hot, warm, room temperature, or cool—as the center of a meal, an hors d'oeuvre, or an accompaniment. It is good served in any season; hot as a hearty vegetable dish in winter with roast lamb or duck, or cool in summer flavored with lemon juice and served with grilled chicken. Or use ratatouille as a filling for omelets or savory tarts, as a stuffing for vegetables such as eggplant and peppers, cool as a salad with ground coriander, or prepare a hot gratin with bread crumbs and freshly grated Parmigiano-Reggiano cheese.

▶ **PREPARATION TIME:** 20 minutes
COOKING TIME: 20 minutes
STANDING TIME: 10 minutes

---

1 medium eggplant (about 1 pound), cut into 1-inch dice
1/2 cup olive oil, preferably extra-virgin
2 medium zucchini (about 6 ounces each), scrubbed and cut into 1-inch dice

1 16-ounce can Italian plum tomatoes, drained and coarsely chopped
1 **each** red and yellow bell pepper, cut into 1-inch dice
1 small bulb fennel, diced
1 medium onion, diced
3 tablespoons tomato paste
2 teaspoons minced fresh basil
1 clove garlic, minced
1/2 teaspoon **each** salt and freshly ground pepper
1/4 cup chopped fresh parsley

¹⁄₄ cup grated Parmigiano-Reggiano cheese

---

1. Place the eggplant and 6 tablespoons of the olive oil in a microwave-safe 12-inch oval baking dish. Toss to coat the eggplant well and spread evenly in the dish. Cover the dish with microwave-safe plastic wrap and vent one side. Microwave on high power until softened, about 5 minutes.

2. Add the remaining olive oil and the zucchini, tomatoes, bell peppers, fennel, onion, tomato paste, basil, garlic, and salt. Toss well to coat and spread evenly in the dish. Microwave, covered and vented, about 15 minutes, until the vegetables are tender, stirring three times.

3. Stir in the pepper and parsley and let stand 10 minutes. Sprinkle with cheese. Taste and adjust seasoning. Serve warm.

SERVES 6

VARIATIONS

▸ Add a bay leaf—making certain to remove it before serving.
▸ Right before serving, top the ratatouille with some pitted Niçoise olives.
▸ Add fresh artichoke hearts.
▸ *If the ratatouille is to be served chilled*, chop the vegetables a little smaller, and add a pinch of ground coriander and a dash of fresh lemon juice.
▸ Oregano and thyme are sometimes used with the basil and parsley.

SWISS CHARD WITH SOUR CHERRIES AND PINE NUTS*

Doneness is a personal preference; some (especially those from the South) like greens cooked to death, others prefer them firm to the bite. Test for the doneness that suits you. You may substitute spinach, beet, or dandelion greens for the Swiss chard—all are rich in iron and are excellent sources of Vitamins A and C and fiber. You may also use collard, mustard greens, or kale, but they require longer cooking. Serve this dish with grilled meats, fish, or poultry; it's the perfect accompaniment to any simple entrée.

> **PREPARATION TIME:** 10 minutes
> **COOKING TIME:** 4 minutes

---

1 bunch Swiss chard (about 1 pound)
1 tablespoon olive oil, preferably extra-virgin
1 clove garlic, minced
1 tablespoon chopped dried sour cherries or golden raisins
1–2 teaspoons balsamic vinegar
Salt and freshly ground pepper to taste
1 tablespoon toasted pine nuts (optional)

1. Trim the thick stems from the chard and cut the leaves into 2-inch lengths. You should have about 8 cups. Wash and dry the leaves. Place in a microwave-safe 2-quart glass casserole with a lid.

2. Stir together the olive oil and garlic and drizzle over the Swiss chard. Toss to blend completely. Stir in the dried cherries.

3. Cover and microwave on high power for 2 to 4 minutes, to desired doneness. Toss with the vinegar and salt and pepper to taste. Serve hot, garnished with toasted pine nuts, if desired.

SERVES 2

GREEN BEANS WITH LEMON AND MINT*

This dish has a really nice clean, sparkling flavor. It's one of our favorites for summertime—or any time we want to feel like it's summer.

> **PREPARATION TIME:** 5 minutes
> **COOKING TIME:** 11 minutes

---

2 tablespoons unsalted butter
1 teaspoon fresh lemon juice
1/2 teaspoon grated lemon zest
1/8 teaspoon **each** salt and freshly ground pepper, or to taste

10 ounces fresh green beans, trimmed
1/3 cup water
2 teaspoons minced fresh mint

---

1. Microwave the butter in a small microwave-safe bowl on high power until melted. Add the lemon juice, zest, salt, and pepper.

2. Place the green beans and water in a microwave-safe 2-quart glass casserole with a lid. Microwave covered on high power for 6 to 8 minutes, depending on desired doneness, stirring twice.

3. Drain the beans and put back into the dry casserole. Pour the butter mixture over the beans and toss to blend completely. Reheat until heated through, about 1 to 2 minutes. Top with minced fresh mint, and serve hot or room temperature.

SERVES 4

FRESH CORN WITH PEPPERED OLIVE OIL*

E ver since tasting an unusual salad from the south of France made with fresh corn kernels and coarsely crushed black peppercorns, we have been intrigued by the combination. Here is the result. Double the amount of olive oil if you like to really slather your corn with it.

▶ *PREPARATION TIME: 10 minutes*
COOKING TIME: 2 minutes per ear
STANDING TIME: 5 minutes

2 to 4 ears of corn, husked

Black Pepper Oil:
2 tablespoons flavorful olive oil, preferably extra-virgin
1 small clove garlic, bruised with side of knife
1/2 teaspoon whole peppercorns, crushed with mortar and pestle, or 1/4 teaspoon freshly ground pepper
Salt

1. Place the ears of corn in a single layer in a microwave-safe 10-inch glass square or round baking dish. Cover with microwave-safe plastic wrap and vent one side. Microwave on high power for 2 minutes per ear, turning the dish a quarter-turn after every 2 minutes. Let stand, covered, 5 minutes.

2. Meanwhile, place the oil in a microwave-safe 1-cup glass measure. Add the garlic; microwave uncovered for 2 minutes, or until the oil is heated and the garlic is sizzling, but not browned. Carefully remove the garlic and discard. Add the black pepper to the hot oil. Brush the corn with the oil and sprinkle lightly with salt.

SERVES 2

SESAME SNOW PEAS*

Here's a great vegetable side dish that takes only 6 minutes to prepare and cook, and is very low in calories. It's quicker than many frozen vegetables, and it's a great example of how the microwave can prepare vegetables that are really quick, tasty, and very good for you.

▸ **PREPARATION TIME:** 5
   minutes
COOKING TIME: 1 minute

*6 ounces snow peas, strings
   removed
1 teaspoon safflower oil
1 teaspoon sesame seeds
¼ teaspoon Oriental sesame oil
Salt and freshly ground pepper
   to taste*

Place the snow peas, safflower oil, sesame seeds, and sesame oil in a microwave-safe glass 9-inch pie plate; toss to coat the peas with the oil and spread evenly in the dish. Cover with microwave-safe plastic wrap and vent one side. Microwave on high power until the snow peas are crisp-tender, about 1 minute. Season to taste with salt and pepper and serve hot.

SERVES 2

SHREDDED CARROTS WITH CHERVIL BUTTER

Any of the very aromatic herbs like chervil, tarragon, or lemon thyme are especially good in this dish. Look for the small packages of assorted fresh herbs now conveniently available fresh in the produce section of many supermarkets.

▸ **PREPARATION TIME:** 5
   minutes
COOKING TIME: 7 minutes
STANDING TIME: 2 minutes

*2 tablespoons unsalted butter
1 tablespoon grated onion
5 or 6 medium carrots, pared
   and coarsely shredded
   (about 2½ cups)*

2 teaspoons finely chopped
   fresh chervil or 1 teaspoon
   finely chopped fresh tarragon or lemon thyme
Salt and freshly ground pepper
Leaves of fresh chervil, tarragon, or lemon thyme, for
   garnish

1. Melt the butter in a microwave-safe 2-quart glass casserole

with a lid, uncovered, on high power
for 1 to 2 minutes. Stir in the onion;
microwave uncovered for 2 minutes,
or until tender.

2. Stir in the carrots until
blended. Cover and microwave for 3
minutes; stir in chervil. Let stand,
covered, 2 minutes. Season to taste
with salt and pepper. Garnish with a
few leaves of fresh herb.

SERVES 4

RADISHES WITH SCALLIONS AND PARSLEY*

Radishes should be served as a vegetable more often—their terrific pep-
pery flavor compliments so many entrées. This recipe will make you
a convert.

▶ **PREPARATION TIME:** 10
   minutes
COOKING TIME: 6 minutes

3 bunches radishes (about 40
   small)
2 tablespoons unsalted butter
2 scallions, trimmed and
   minced
1 tablespoon minced fresh
   parsley
1/4 teaspoon salt, or to taste
1/8 teaspoon freshly ground
   pepper

1. Trim the radishes and grate
them coarsely in a food processor or
with a hand grater.

2. Place the butter, scallions,
and parsley in a microwave-safe 2-
quart glass casserole with a lid. Microwave covered on high power for
about 2 minutes, until the butter is
melted and the scallions are softened.
Stir in the radishes and salt, and microwave for 3 to 4 minutes, to desired
doneness. Remove from oven and stir
in the pepper. Taste and adjust the
seasoning, and serve hot.

SERVES 4

SUMMER SQUASH WITH GREMOLATA*

This fresh, clean-tasting vegetable dish is good served hot, at room temperature, or cool, so you can make it at the last minute or early in the day.

PREPARATION TIME: 10 minutes
COOKING TIME: 8 minutes

2 tablespoons minced fresh parsley
1 teaspoon grated lemon zest
1 small clove garlic, minced
2 **each** medium zucchini and yellow squash (5 ounces each), scrubbed and trimmed
2 tablespoons homemade or canned chicken broth or water
¼ teaspoon salt, or to taste
⅛ teaspoon freshly ground pepper, or to taste

1. Make the gremolata: Stir together the parsley, lemon zest, and minced garlic in a small bowl.

2. Slice each squash into thin diagonal slices. Stack them in manageable piles and cut into thin strips. Place the squash in a microwave-safe glass 8-inch cake dish. Add the chicken broth or water and salt and stir to mix. Cover with microwave-safe plastic wrap and vent one side. Microwave on high power for 6 to 8 minutes, stirring every 2 minutes, until crisp-tender or desired doneness. Stir in the pepper, taste and adjust seasonings, and sprinkle with the gremolata.

SERVES 4

ZUCCHINI PAPPARADELLE*

This simple vegetable side dish was named after the broad fettuccine-like noodle it resembles.

PREPARATION TIME: 10 minutes
COOKING TIME: 3 minutes
STANDING TIME: 1 minute

3 or 4 small zucchini (about 12 ounces total), scrubbed and trimmed

1 tablespoon unsalted butter,
cut into small pieces
1 teaspoon fresh lemon juice
Salt and freshly ground pepper

---

1. Using a vegetable parer, cut long broad lengthwise ribbons from the zucchini; discard the first and last strip.

2. Place the zucchini in a microwave-safe 2-quart glass casserole with a lid. Microwave covered on high power for 3 minutes, stirring once. Let stand, covered, 1 minute. Stir in the butter and lemon juice, add salt and pepper to taste, and toss to blend.

SERVES 4

ZUCCHINI WITH BALSAMIC VINEGAR AND MINT*

Vegetables have become culinary stars—no longer hated by most kids and some adults. What a relief. This Italian-inspired dish is very low in calories—and should be a favorite with everyone. If there's time, let it sit a little while before serving to allow the flavors to blend and deepen.

▸ **PREPARATION TIME:** 10
minutes
COOKING TIME: 3 minutes
STANDING TIME: 2 minutes

---

1 medium zucchini (about 9
ounces), scrubbed and cut
into 1½-inch × ½-inch
strips
1 shallot, minced
1 teaspoon olive oil, preferably
extra-virgin
1 tablespoon balsamic vinegar
1 tablespoon minced fresh mint
Salt and freshly ground pepper
to taste

Fresh mint sprigs, for garnish

---

1. Place the zucchini and shallot in a microwave-safe 9-inch glass pie plate; add the oil, toss to coat, and spread evenly in the dish.

2. Cover the dish with microwave-safe plastic wrap and vent one side. Microwave on high power until the zucchini is crisp-tender, about 3 to 4 minutes. Let stand 2 minutes, then stir in the remaining ingredients. Serve warm or at room temperature, garnished with additional fresh mint sprigs, if desired.

SERVES 2

SPAGHETTI SQUASH WITH FRESH TOMATO SAUCE*

Spaghetti squash cooks very fast in the microwave. Serve it hot with melted butter, salt and pepper, and grated cheese, or top it with the following fresh tomato sauce.

▸ **PREPARATION TIME:** 10 minutes
COOKING TIME: 29 minutes

1 spaghetti squash (3–3½ pounds)

Fresh Tomato Sauce:
⅓ cup finely chopped onion
3 tablespoons olive oil, preferably extra-virgin
3 cups cored diced fresh tomatoes
2 tablespoons chopped fresh basil
1 small clove garlic, crushed
Salt and freshly ground pepper
Grated Parmigiano-Reggiano cheese

1. Pierce the squash completely through the hard flesh with a large fork or tip of a paring knife at least six times at evenly spaced intervals.

Place on a piece of paper towel and microwave on high power for 7 minutes. Turn the squash over and microwave 7 minutes more. Protecting your hands with mitts, remove the squash from the oven. Wrap in a clean kitchen towel and let stand while making the sauce.

2. Combine the onion and oil in a microwave-safe 10-inch glass pie plate; microwave uncovered for 5 minutes. Stir in the tomatoes; microwave for 10 minutes, or until the sauce is slightly thickened, stirring once. Add the basil, garlic, salt, and pepper; let stand while preparing the squash.

3. To serve, cut the squash in half lengthwise; discard seeds. Using a fork, pull out the pulp in long spaghetti-like strands. Place in a shallow serving bowl, top with sauce and serve with grated cheese.

SERVES 4

PRIMAVERA VEGETABLES WITH LEMON-MUSTARD DRESSING

Preceded by Hearty Lentil and Mushroom Soup (recipe page 60), this combination of vegetables is a good choice as an entrée for a vegetarian menu. The Lemon-Mustard Sauce is excellent when used as a multipurpose sauce over plain cooked broccoli spears, boiled potatoes, or beets.

▸ **PREPARATION TIME:** 10 minutes
COOKING TIME: 7 minutes

4 medium carrots, pared and cut into ¼-inch-thick sticks
2 cups broccoli flowerets with 1-inch stems attached
1 medium zucchini (about 4 ounces), scrubbed and trimmed and cut into 3 × ½-inch lengths
1 tablespoon water

Lemon-Mustard Sauce:
3 tablespoons fresh lemon juice
2 teaspoons Dijon-style mustard
1 teaspoon granulated sugar
¼ teaspoon salt
Freshly ground pepper
½ cup olive oil
1 scallion, trimmed, white part finely chopped, green part thinly sliced

1. Arrange the vegetables in a microwave-safe 10-inch glass pie plate, with the broccoli stems facing outward and the sticks of carrot and zucchini spread on top; sprinkle with water. Cover with a double layer of dampened paper towel and a piece of microwave-safe plastic wrap; vent one side. Microwave on high power for 6 minutes, or until the vegetables are crisp-tender, turning the dish a quarter-turn twice.

2. Meanwhile, make the sauce: Combine the lemon juice, mustard, sugar, salt, and a grinding of pepper in a small bowl or a food processor. Gradually add the oil and whisk or process until the mixture is emulsified. Stir the scallion into the sauce.

3. Serve the vegetables hot, drizzled with the sauce.

SERVES 4

SWEET PEAS WITH LEMON BUTTER

This is best prepared with fresh-shelled peas, but in a pinch tiny sweet frozen peas can be used. Try using a variety of fresh herbs.

▶ **PREPARATION TIME:** 10 minutes
COOKING TIME: 2 minutes

1 tablespoon unsalted butter, at room temperature
1/2 teaspoon grated lemon zest
1 pound fresh whole peas, shelled (about 1–1 1/2 cups)
1 tablespoon water
1/2 teaspoon minced fresh chives, tarragon, or mint (optional)

Mash the butter and lemon zest together on a saucer; set aside. Combine the peas and water in a microwave-safe 1½-quart glass casserole with a lid. Microwave covered for 2 minutes, or until tender, stirring once. Stir in the lemon butter and the fresh herb of your choice, if using, and serve at once.

SERVES 2

FALL AND WINTER

NEW ENGLAND ACORN SQUASH

With a microwave, you can decide to serve acorn squash at the last minute. It only takes about 15 minutes—rather than 1 hour when cooked conventionally. It's available all year, but the peak season is October to December. Select heavy, firm, unblemished squash and store them in a well-ventilated spot at room temperature—do not refrigerate.

▸ **PREPARATION TIME:** 5 minutes
COOKING TIME: 11 minutes
STANDING TIME: 5 minutes

---

2 medium acorn squash (1 pound each)
2 tablespoons unsalted butter
1 tablespoon maple syrup
Pinch **each** salt and ground cinnamon
Dash hot red pepper sauce
4 cinnamon sticks for garnish (optional)

---

1. Cut the acorn squash in half crosswise and scrape out the seeds and strings. Slice off a thin piece from the bottom of each squash so it will stand up straight.

2. Combine the butter, maple syrup, salt, ground cinnamon, and hot red pepper sauce in a microwave-safe 1-cup glass measure and microwave uncovered on high power until the butter is melted, about 1 minute.

3. Place squash in a microwave-safe 2-quart glass casserole with a lid. Evenly divide the butter mixture between the cavities of the squash halves. Cover and microwave for 10 minutes, turning the casserole twice. Let stand covered 5 minutes. Serve, garnished with cinnamon sticks if desired.

SERVES 4

QUICK BEETS WITH PARSLEY

Try substituting safflower oil for the unsalted butter, especially if you are going to serve these delicious beets chilled as a salad.

▸ **PREPARATION TIME:** 8 minutes
COOKING TIME: 20 minutes
STANDING TIME: 3 minutes

---

1 pound 2-inch diameter un-peeled whole beets with 1-inch stems (about 10 beets), well scrubbed
½ cup water
2 tablespoons unsalted butter
2 scallions, trimmed and minced
1 teaspoon Dijon mustard
1 teaspoon tarragon white wine vinegar, or to taste
⅛ teaspoon **each** grated lemon zest, salt, and freshly ground pepper
2 teaspoons minced fresh parsley

1. Place the beets and water in a microwave-safe 2-quart glass casserole with a lid. Cover and microwave on high power for 12 to 15 minutes, stirring three times, until tender when pierced with a fork. Let stand, covered, 3 minutes. Drain. Peel when cool enough to handle, and slice into thin slices.

2. Place the butter in the same clean casserole. Microwave uncovered until melted, about 1 minute. Stir in the scallions and microwave covered 2 minutes, until the scallions are softened. Stir in the mustard, vinegar, lemon zest, and salt, then stir in the sliced beets. Microwave covered for about 2 minutes, until heated through. Stir in the pepper, taste and adjust seasoning, and serve hot, garnished with parsley.

SERVES 4

BRUSSELS SPROUTS WITH CARAWAY

Even people who think they don't like Brussels sprouts will like these. Shredding Brussels sprouts before cooking means they'll cook evenly and won't get waterlogged, so they'll taste better. Select firm compact heads with tight leaves, and avoid those with wilted or yellow leaves.

▶ **PREPARATION TIME:** 15
minutes
COOKING TIME: 6 minutes

2 10-ounce packages fresh
Brussels sprouts
2 tablespoons unsalted butter
¼ teaspoon caraway seeds
¼ teaspoon salt
1 teaspoon balsamic or red
wine vinegar
⅛ teaspoon freshly ground
pepper

1. Trim the Brussels sprouts and remove any tough outer leaves. Shred the leaves by slicing each one into three pieces crosswise. Separate into "rings" (about 8 cups worth).

2. Microwave the butter, caraway seeds, and salt in a microwave-safe 2-quart glass casserole with a lid, uncovered, on high power until melted, about 1 minute.

3. Add the Brussels sprouts and toss to coat well. Microwave covered for 3 to 5 minutes, stirring twice, until the Brussels sprouts are the desired doneness and bright green. Stir in the vinegar and freshly ground pepper, taste and adjust seasoning, and serve hot.

SERVES 4

BROCCOLI WITH GARLIC AND HOT PEPPER OIL*

The pungency of the garlic is greater when it is crushed in a garlic press than when it is sliced thin. We prefer the more subtle flavor and aroma of sliced garlic in this classic dish of broccoli, olive oil, and lemon.

▶ **PREPARATION TIME:** 5
minutes
COOKING TIME: 7 minutes

1 bunch broccoli, stems
trimmed, cut into flowerets
2 tablespoons water
2 tablespoons olive oil, preferably extra-virgin
1 clove garlic, cut into thin slices
¼ teaspoon crushed hot red
pepper flakes
Lemon wedges

1. Place the broccoli in a microwave-safe 3-quart glass casserole with a lid, add the water, and microwave covered on high power for 3 minutes. Turn the dish and microwave until the broccoli is tender, 1 to 2 minutes longer. Uncover and let stand.

2. Combine the oil, garlic, and red pepper flakes in a microwave-safe 1-cup glass measure. Microwave uncovered for 2 minutes, or until the garlic sizzles; stir once.

3. Transfer the broccoli to a serving dish and drizzle with the hot oil mixture. Garnish with lemon wedges.

SERVES 4

CAULIFLOWER WITH LEMON AND PARSLEY

Cauliflower is on lots of the "good for you" lists, and is especially high in Vitamin C and calcium. It's available all year, but the peak season is October and November. Choose heavy, compact heads with clean white buds; avoid the ones with brown spots, which are a sign of age.

▶ **PREPARATION TIME:** 10 minutes
COOKING TIME: 7 minutes
STANDING TIME: 3 minutes

2 tablespoons unsalted butter
1 small head cauliflower (1 pound trimmed), cut into flowerets 2 inches long × 1½ inches wide
⅛ teaspoon salt, or to taste
2 teaspoons minced fresh parsley
1 teaspoon fresh lemon juice
¼ teaspoon grated lemon zest
Dash hot red pepper sauce

1. Microwave the butter uncovered in a microwave-safe deep 10-inch glass pie plate on high power until melted, about 1 minute. Add the cauliflower and salt and toss to coat with butter. Arrange the cauliflower in concentric circles with the buds toward the outside of the dish. Cover with microwave-safe plastic wrap and vent one side. Microwave for 5 to 6 minutes, turning the dish twice, until crisp-tender and easily pierced with a fork. Let stand, covered, for 3 minutes. Drain in a colander.

2. Meanwhile, mix the remaining ingredients in a small bowl. Toss with the cauliflower to blend completely. Taste and adjust seasonings, and serve at once.

SERVES 4

SWEET AND SOUR CABBAGE

This dish is perfect served with roast pork or poultry—its zingy flavor is a great complement to a simple entrée.

▸ **PREPARATION TIME:** 10 minutes
COOKING TIME: 11 minutes
STANDING TIME: 2 minutes

2 tablespoons unsalted butter
3 cups thinly shredded (1/4-inch) red cabbage (about 1/4 medium cabbage)
1 Granny Smith apple, peeled, cored, and finely diced
1 medium onion, thinly sliced
2 tablespoons red wine vinegar
2 tablespoons dark brown sugar
1 tablespoon golden raisins
1/2 teaspoon salt
1/8 teaspoon ground allspice

1/4 teaspoon freshly ground pepper

1. Melt the butter in a microwave-safe 2-quart glass casserole with a lid, about 1 minute. Stir in the cabbage, apple, onion, vinegar, brown sugar, golden raisins, salt, and allspice. Cover and microwave on high power for 8 to 10 minutes, stirring four times, until the cabbage is very soft. Let stand, covered, for 2 minutes.

2. Add freshly ground pepper and taste and adjust seasonings. Serve hot or warm.

SERVES 4

SWEET RED ONIONS WITH SAGE BUTTER

▸ **PREPARATION TIME:** 5 minutes
COOKING TIME: 7 minutes
STANDING TIME: 5 minutes

1 1/2 pounds small sweet red onions (about 6 to 8), peeled, trimmed, and quartered

2 tablespoons unsalted butter
1/2 teaspoon minced fresh sage leaves, or 1/4 teaspoon crumbled dried sage
Salt and freshly ground pepper

1. Arrange the onions, cut-side down, in a single layer in a microwave-safe 10-inch glass pie plate. Cut 1 tablespoon of the butter into small pieces and place on top of the onions. Cover with microwave-safe plastic wrap and vent on one side; microwave on high power for 5 minutes.

2. Meanwhile, work the sage into the remaining tablespoon of butter with a fork. Uncover the onions and carefully turn cut-side up. Cut the sage butter into small bits and place on top of the onions. Microwave covered for 2 minutes. Let stand, covered, 5 minutes. Season with salt and pepper, and serve hot.

SERVES 4

BRAISED LEEKS WITH PEAR

Pear is a perfect addition to braised leeks; the very subtle fruit flavor lightens the dish and makes it sparkle. As with almost all microwave cooking, smaller pieces of food cook better than larger ones, so we sliced these leeks.

▸ **PREPARATION TIME: 8 minutes**
COOKING TIME: 16 minutes
STANDING TIME: 2 minutes

8 leeks (1-inch diameter), dark green tips and roots trimmed
½ cup heavy cream
¼ cup homemade or canned chicken broth
1 ripe pear, peeled, cored, and finely chopped
½ bay leaf
⅛ teaspoon salt, or to taste
Pinch freshly ground pepper, or to taste
2 teaspoons snipped fresh chives

1. Slice the leeks crosswise on the diagonal ¼ inch thick. Place the leeks in a colander and wash well under cold running water. Dry on paper towels.

2. Stir together the leeks, cream, chicken broth, pear, bay leaf, and salt in a microwave-safe 8-inch glass cake dish. Microwave uncovered on high power for 14 to 16 minutes, until the leeks are softened and the liquid is absorbed, stirring four times. Let stand 2 minutes.

3. Remove the bay leaf and stir in freshly ground pepper. Taste and adjust seasoning. Top with chives and serve hot.

SERVES 4

LEEKS WITH LEMON THYME

Lemon thyme is especially delicious with leeks, but if it's unavailable, use plain fresh thyme instead and mash ¼ teaspoon grated lemon zest into the butter to approximate the aromatic level of the fresh herb. Leeks can be sandy, so be sure to follow the rinsing directions carefully. To ensure even cooking—and to enable you to rinse more thoroughly—cut the leeks in half lengthwise.

▶ **PREPARATION TIME:** *5 minutes; plus 10 minutes soaking*
COOKING TIME: *10 minutes*
STANDING TIME: *2 minutes*

---

4 leeks (1-inch diameter), dark green tops and roots trimmed, split lengthwise
2 tablespoons water
1 tablespoon butter, cut into 4 pieces
Sprigs of fresh lemon thyme (see headnote)
Salt and freshly ground white pepper

---

1. Rinse the leeks well in warm water to remove any sand; soak in clean warm water 10 minutes; then carefully rinse in cold water to crisp.

2. Place the leeks in a microwave-safe 10-inch glass pie plate in a single layer and add the water. Cover with microwave-safe plastic wrap and vent one side; microwave on high power for 8 to 10 minutes, or until leeks are tender, turning plate once.

3. Uncover, carefully drain off all of the liquid, and place a piece of butter on each leek. Spread the sprigs of lemon thyme on the leeks, cover with the plastic wrap, and let stand 2 minutes before serving. Season with salt and pepper.

SERVES 2

SHIITAKE WITH GARLIC AND HERB BUTTER

S hiitake are cultivated "exotic" mushrooms also known as Golden Oak and Black Forest mushrooms. Once available only dried and imported exclusively from Japan, they are now raised on mushroom farms in this country and are available in many supermarkets. The caps are thick and meaty, but the stems are tough and fibrous and should be discarded.

▸ **PREPARATION TIME: 5 minutes**
COOKING TIME: 7 minutes

1 tablespoon unsalted butter
2 teaspoons minced fresh
    parsley
1 small clove garlic, crushed
½ teaspoon fresh thyme leaves,
    or a pinch dried thyme
1 3½-ounce package shiitake
    mushrooms, wiped clean,
    stems removed
Salt and freshly ground pepper

1. Melt the butter in a microwave-safe 10-inch glass pie plate uncovered on high power for 1 minute. Stir in the parsley, garlic, and thyme; microwave on high for 2 minutes, stirring once.

2. Add the shiitake, turning to coat with the butter, and arrange smooth-side down. Cover with microwave-safe plastic wrap and vent one side. Microwave for 4 minutes, or until tender, turning the shiitake smooth-side up halfway through the cooking. Uncover and microwave 1 to 2 minutes longer. Serve hot, with the garlic and herb butter spooned over the top.

SERVES 2

BRAISED FENNEL WITH PARMIGIANO-REGGIANO CHEESE

Once again, the microwave and the conventional broiler are used in combination to create a delicious vegetable side dish.

PREPARATION TIME: *5 minutes*
COOKING TIME: *5 minutes*
STANDING TIME: *5 minutes*
BROILING TIME: *2 minutes*

1 bulb fennel (12–16 ounces)
1 tablespoon water
1 tablespoon unsalted butter, cut into 4 pieces, at room temperature
10–12 large curls of Parmigiano-Reggiano cheese

1. Trim a thin slice from the bottom of the fennel bulb. Cut off the leafy green tops and most of the darker green portion on the ribs of the fennel. Pull off any loose outside ribs, or if the bulb is tight, simply trim away any bruised portions. Cut the bulb into lengthwise quarters.

2. Arrange the fennel in a small flame-resistant and microwave-safe baking dish (Corning Ware or bake-proof pottery is good) just large enough to hold the fennel snugly. Add the water and spread each wedge with a softened piece of butter. Cover with microwave-safe plastic wrap and vent one side. Microwave on high power for 5 minutes until tender. Let stand, covered, 5 minutes.

3. Meanwhile, preheat the broiler. Using a vegetable parer, shave 3 large curls of cheese onto each portion of fennel. Broil about 3 inches from the heat source until browned and bubbly, about 2 minutes. Serve warm or at room temperature.

SERVES 4

COMFORTING POTATOES

POTATOES AND MUSHROOMS IN LEMON CREAM

This rich and delicious dish is great for entertaining—it's so special you can serve a very simple (and easy) main dish and the meal will still seem festive. For an even fancier dish, try shiitake mushrooms.

PREPARATION TIME: 10 minutes
COOKING TIME: 18 minutes
STANDING TIME: 3 minutes

3 medium-small all-purpose potatoes (about 1 pound), pared and sliced 1/4-inch thick
1 cup heavy cream
2 strips lemon zest (2 1/2 inches × 1/2 inch)
1 clove garlic, peeled and left whole
1/4 pound mushroom caps (about 4 large), sliced thin
1/4 teaspoon salt
1 tablespoon minced fresh parsley leaves
1/8 teaspoon freshly ground pepper

1. Soak the potato slices in cold water while preparing the remaining ingredients.

2. Place the cream, lemon zest, and garlic in a microwave-safe 2-quart glass measure. Microwave uncovered on high power for about 7 minutes, until thickened and reduced by half. Remove and discard the lemon zest and garlic.

3. Blot the potato slices dry with paper towels. Combine the potatoes, mushroom slices, cream mixture, and salt in a microwave-safe 8-inch square glass baking dish. Microwave uncovered for 9 to 11 minutes, stirring four times, just until done. Stir in the parsley and pepper, cover, and let stand for 3 minutes. Taste and adjust seasoning. Serve hot.

SERVES 4

POTATOES WITH THREE BUBBLY CHEESES

A perfect example of how to use your microwave intelligently: The bacon and potatoes are cooked in the microwave and the cheeses are melted and browned under the broiler. Since the broiler is going to be on, plan your menu so that you can use it to cook juicy lamb or veal chops before melting the cheese-smothered potatoes. Serve this tempting menu with a palate-cleansing salad of bitter and sweet salad greens.

▶ *PREPARATION TIME: 15 minutes*
COOKING TIME: 11 minutes
STANDING TIME: 2 minutes
BROILING TIME: 2 minutes

1½ pounds baking potatoes, peeled and cut into ¼-inch-thick julienne strips (like French fries)
1 slice bacon, cut into ¼-inch dice
Freshly ground pepper
2 ounces shredded mozzarella cheese (about ½ cup loosely packed)
2 ounces shredded Gruyère or Jarlsberg cheese (about ½ cup loosely packed)
2 ounces shredded sharp white Cheddar cheese (about ½ cup loosely packed)

1. Soak the potato slices in cold water while preparing the remaining ingredients.

2. Place the diced bacon in an approximately 10-inch round or oval flame-proof and microwave-safe shallow baking dish or platter (bake-proof pottery or Corning Ware is a good choice). Microwave on high power until the bacon is partially cooked, 1 to 2 minutes.

3. Drain the potatoes and blot dry with paper towels. Add to the bacon; stir to coat. Cover with microwave-safe plastic wrap and vent one side; microwave for 8 or 9 minutes, or until the potatoes are evenly cooked, stirring once halfway through the cooking time.

4. Uncover; add a generous grinding of pepper and sprinkle evenly with the three cheeses. Broil about 4 inches from heat source until the cheeses are browned and bubbly, about 2 minutes. Serve at once.

SERVES 4

TINY NEW POTATOES WITH RED PEPPER-AND GARLIC-INFUSED OIL

Try some of the fascinating new varieties of potatoes now available. Among our favorites are the Ruby Gold and Yellow Finnish.

▶ **PREPARATION TIME: 5 minutes**
COOKING TIME: 12 minutes

2 tablespoons olive oil, preferably extra-virgin
½ teaspoon crushed hot red pepper flakes
1¼ pounds tiny new potatoes, scrubbed and halved
2 tablespoons water
1 clove garlic, crushed
Salt

1. Combine the oil and red pepper flakes in a microwave-safe 1-cup glass measure. Microwave uncovered on high power for 2 minutes. Remove from the microwave and set aside.

2. Combine the potatoes and water in a microwave-safe 10-inch glass pie plate; cover with microwave-safe plastic wrap and vent one side. Microwave for 10 minutes, or until the potatoes are evenly tender when pierced with the tip of a small knife; turn the dish a half-turn twice during the cooking time. Let stand, covered, until ready to serve.

3. Stir the garlic into the red pepper-infused oil; microwave uncovered until the garlic sizzles slightly, about 1 minute; do not brown.

4. Drain the water from the potatoes; place in a serving bowl and season with salt to taste. Drizzle with the hot oil; toss, and serve.

SERVES 4

POTATOES WITH GREENS AND PANCETTA

For this dish, use escarole, broccoli rabe, kale, or the large, dark green outside leaves of romaine lettuce. The kale and broccoli rabe will require a slightly longer cooking time than the escarole or romaine, so test for tenderness as the cooking time progresses in Step 1. Pancetta is an un-smoked bacon salt-cured and rolled up like a giant sausage; it is sold by the slice in Italian markets. If unavailable, substitute prosciutto—or in a pinch, even mildly cured baked ham can be used.

▶ **PREPARATION TIME:** 10
  minutes
COOKING TIME: Up to 22
  minutes
STANDING TIME: 5 minutes

---

1 1/2 pounds rinsed and trimmed
  broccoli rabe or torn (1-inch
  pieces) escarole, kale, or
  dark green outside leaves of
  romaine (about 4 cups)
1/3 cup very hot water
2 cups pared and sliced baking
  potatoes
2 tablespoons olive oil
1 slice pancetta, trimmed and
  slivered (about 2
  tablespoons)
1 clove garlic, crushed
Salt and freshly ground pepper

---

1. Combine the greens and water in a microwave-safe 3-quart glass casserole with a lid. Microwave covered on high power for 5 minutes. Stir well; microwave covered 5 to 8 minutes longer for broccoli rabe or kale or 3 to 5 minutes for escarole or romaine.

2. Stir in the potatoes and microwave covered until the potatoes are evenly cooked, 5 to 8 minutes. Let stand, covered.

3. Place the oil in a microwave-safe 9-inch glass pie plate and add the pancetta. Microwave uncovered until the meat is sizzling, 2 to 2½ minutes. Stir in the crushed garlic.

4. Season greens and potato mixture with salt and freshly ground black pepper to taste, and stir in the hot oil mixture. Serve hot or at room temperature.

SERVES 4

LITTLE RED POTATOES
WITH
BUTTER AND CHIVES

Try using minced fresh mint or parsley—or your favorite herb or combination of herbs—instead of the chives.

▶ **PREPARATION TIME:** 5
   minutes
COOKING TIME: 12 minutes
STANDING TIME: 3 minutes

1½ pounds little red potatoes
   (about 12, 2½ inches ×
   1½ inches), well scrubbed
2 tablespoons unsalted butter
¼ teaspoon salt
2 scallions, trimmed and finely
   minced
⅛ teaspoon freshly ground
   pepper
1 tablespoon snipped fresh
   chives

1. Remove a strip of peel about ½ inch thick around each potato with a vegetable peeler or a paring knife. Blot the potatoes dry with paper towels.

2. Melt the butter in a microwave-safe 2-quart glass casserole with a lid on high power, about 1 to 2 minutes. Stir in the potatoes and salt, coating the potatoes with butter. Place the largest potatoes around the outside of the dish and the smaller ones in the center. Cover and microwave for 8 to 10 minutes, stirring twice, until just tender. Stir in the pepper and let stand covered for 3 minutes. Taste and adjust seasonings. Sprinkle with chives. Serve hot.

SERVES 4

POTATOES WITH OLIVE OIL, CAPERS, AND OLIVES*

This dish is delicious without the capers and olives, but extra-special with them, and they give it a great look.

▶ **PREPARATION TIME:** 15
   minutes
COOKING TIME: 12 minutes
STANDING TIME: 3 minutes

---

4 medium all-purpose potatoes
   (about 1½ pounds), pared
   and sliced ¼ inch thick
1 medium red onion, sliced thin
   (about 1 cup)

1 large shallot, cut into rings
1 tablespoon olive oil, preferably extra-virgin
1 clove garlic, minced
¼ teaspoon salt
2 teaspoons balsamic or red
   wine vinegar, or to taste
Large pinch crushed hot red
   pepper flakes, or to taste

¼ cup pitted and chopped
    black Mediterranean olives
2 teaspoons drained capers

___

1. Soak the potato slices in cold water while preparing the remaining ingredients.

2. Combine the red onion, shallot, oil, and garlic in a 2-quart microwave-safe casserole with a lid. Microwave covered on high power just until softened, about 2 minutes.

3. Drain the potatoes and blot dry with paper towels. Stir the potatoes and salt into the onion mixture. Cover and microwave for 8 to 10 minutes, until the potatoes are just done.

4. Stir in the vinegar and pepper flakes. Stir in the olives and capers or sprinkle them on top of the potatoes. Cover with a lid and let stand 3 minutes. Taste and adjust seasonings. Serve hot.

SERVES 4

GINGER-MASHED SWEET POTATOES

S weet potatoes, an excellent source of Vitamin A and low in calories, are available all year, but their best season is August to November. Select firm, dry sweet potatoes and avoid those with damp spots or mold.

▶ **PREPARATION TIME:** 10
    minutes
COOKING TIME: 13 minutes
STANDING TIME: 2 minutes

___

3 medium sweet potatoes
    (about 8 ounces each),
    pared and cut in 1-inch dice
2 tablespoons homemade or
    canned chicken broth or
    water
½ cup heavy cream
2 scallions (white part only),
    trimmed and minced
1 teaspoon minced fresh ginger
¼ cup Major Grey's Mango
    Chutney, minced

¼ teaspoon **each** salt and
    freshly ground pepper

___

1. Place the sweet potatoes in a microwave-safe deep 9-inch glass pie plate and toss with the chicken broth. Cover with microwave-safe plastic wrap and vent one side. Microwave on high power until completely cooked, about 10 minutes, stirring three times. Let stand 2 minutes. Drain in a colander.

2. Meanwhile, place the cream, scallions, and ginger in a microwave-safe 2-cup glass measure. Microwave uncovered for 3 minutes, stirring once, until slightly thickened.

3. Mash the potatoes with a ricer, a potato masher, or an electric mixer until smooth. Add the cream mixture and blend well. Add the re- maining ingredients and incorporate. Taste and adjust seasoning. Serve immediately, or make ahead and refrigerate, and reheat right before serving.

SERVES 4

SWEET POTATOES WITH CURRIED ONION AND YOGURT TOPPING

Serve this unusual sweet potato dish with grilled or pan-cooked ground lamb burgers.

> **PREPARATION TIME:** 5 minutes
> **COOKING TIME:** 23 minutes

2 large sweet potatoes (about 8–10 ounces each), peeled and halved lengthwise
2 cups coarsely chopped onion
2 tablespoons unsalted butter, cut into small pieces
1 1/2 teaspoons curry powder
1/2 teaspoon ground cumin seed
1 tablespoon dried currants or raisins
Salt and freshly ground pepper
1/2 cup plain nonfat yogurt
1 tablespoon minced cilantro (optional)

1. Arrange the potatoes, cut-side down, in a microwave-safe 10-inch glass pie plate. Cover with microwave-safe plastic wrap and vent one side; microwave on high power for 7 to 8 minutes, or until the potatoes are evenly tender, turning the dish a half-turn once. Let stand, covered, while cooking the onions.

2. Spread the onions in a microwave-safe 3-quart glass casserole with a lid; dot with the butter. Microwave covered for 5 minutes; stir in the curry powder and cumin until blended. Cover and microwave 5 minutes. Stir in the currants and microwave until the onions are tender, about 2 to 3 minutes longer.

3. Place the cooked sweet potatoes in the casserole with the onions; spoon the onions on top. Microwave covered just to heat up the potatoes, about 2 minutes. Sprinkle with salt and pepper. Serve the yogurt, sprinkled with the cilantro if desired, in a small bowl. Place a spoonful of yogurt on each hot sweet potato half.

SERVES 4

VEGETABLE PUREES

PUREED ACORN SQUASH WITH MAPLE SYRUP

O ne of the advantages of the microwave is its ability to cook slow-cooking vegetables in just a fraction of the time, turning a traditionally lengthy preparation for a simple dish like this pureed acorn squash into an almost spontaneous thought.

▶ **PREPARATION TIME:** *5 minutes*
COOKING TIME: *12 minutes*
STANDING TIME: *5 minutes*

1 large acorn squash (about 2
    pounds), rinsed
2 tablespoons water
2 tablespoons unsalted butter,
    cut into pieces
2 tablespoons maple syrup
Salt and freshly ground pepper

1. Carefully cut the acorn squash in half lengthwise. Scrape out the seeds. Place cut-side down in a microwave-safe 10-inch glass pie plate. Add the water. Cover with microwave-safe plastic wrap and vent one side. Microwave on high power for 12 minutes, turning the dish a quarter-turn twice, until the squash is tender when pierced with a fork. Let stand, covered, 5 minutes.

2. Protecting your hand with a double thickness of paper toweling, spoon out the softened squash flesh and transfer to a food processor. Add the butter and maple syrup and process until the mixture is pureed. Season to taste with salt and pepper, and serve at once.

SERVES 4

ORANGE-RUTABAGA PUREE

This is a very nice fall or winter vegetable dish, and one that can be made ahead and reheated at the last minute if desired. To save time, grate the vegetables in the food processor.

▶ **PREPARATION TIME:** 10
   minutes
COOKING TIME: 23 minutes

8 ounces rutabaga, pared and
   coarsely grated
2 small carrots, pared and
   coarsely grated
1 medium potato (4 ounces),
   pared and coarsely grated
1 cup water
1 tablespoon heavy cream
1 tablespoon unsalted butter, at
   room temperature
Pinch grated orange zest
⅛ teaspoon salt, or to taste

Hot red pepper sauce to taste

Place the rutabaga, carrots, potato, and water in a microwave-safe 3-quart glass casserole with a lid. Microwave covered on high power for 18 to 20 minutes, until very soft. Drain completely. Puree the rutabaga mixture in a food processor or food mill. Stir in the cream, butter, orange zest, salt, and hot pepper sauce. Taste and adjust seasonings. Reheat for 2 to 3 minutes if necessary.

SERVES 2

CELERY ROOT AND POTATO PUREE

Celeriac, or celery root as it is popularly known, is a large bulbous root with a pronounced celery flavor. It makes delicious soups and vegetable purees, and is a natural paired with potatoes and cream, as it is here. It is often served with venison, pheasant, squab, or other game dishes.

▶ **PREPARATION TIME:** 10
   minutes
COOKING TIME: 20 minutes
STANDING TIME: 5 minutes

1 bulb celery root (1¼ pounds)
   trimmed, pared, and cut
   into ¼-inch dice (2½ to 3
   cups)

½ cup very hot tap water
2 cups diced, pared baking po-
tatoes (about 2 small
potatoes)
2 tablespoons unsalted butter
2 tablespoons heavy cream
Salt and freshly ground white
pepper, to taste

1. Combine the celery root and water in a microwave-safe 3-quart glass casserole with a lid. Microwave covered on high power for 10 min- utes, stirring once. Stir in the pota- toes; microwave covered until the potatoes and celery root are evenly tender, 8 to 10 minutes. Let stand, covered, 5 minutes.

2. Press the cooked celery root, potatoes, and liquid through a food mill or a large sieve placed over a bowl. (Or puree the mixture in the food processor and then press through a sieve to make a smoother puree.) Stir in the butter and heavy cream, and salt and pepper to taste.

SERVES 4

TURNIP-POTATO PUREE

Turnips are wonderful and sadly underused. Try this simple dish and get reacquainted with this delicious vegetable. For a really quick way to grate the turnips and the potato, use the steel blade of the food processor.

▶ **PREPARATION TIME:** 10
    minutes
COOKING TIME: 24 minutes

12 ounces turnips (2 medium
large), pared and coarsely
grated
4 ounces all-purpose potato (1
medium), pared and
coarsely grated
1 small leek, green tops and
roots trimmed, sliced thin,
washed well, and drained
1 cup water
1 tablespoon unsalted butter
¼ teaspoon salt, or to taste

⅛ teaspoon freshly ground
white pepper, or to taste

Place the turnips, potato, leek, and water in a microwave-safe 3- quart glass casserole with a lid. Mi- crowave covered on high power for 18 to 22 minutes, until very soft. Drain completely. Puree the turnip mixture in a food processor with but- ter, salt, and pepper until smooth. Re- heat for 1 to 2 minutes on high power if necessary.

SERVES 4

CHAPTER 9

SIDE DISHES: POLENTA, STUFFINGS, AND SALADS

Like Custard Sauce and Béchamel Sauce, polenta is one of those slow-cooking, constantly stirred dishes requiring lots of patience and a fair amount of muscle to prepare. The microwave has revolutionized these techniques, and, at the same time, managed to leave the taste intact. In fact, we will probably never again find ourselves—hands protected by mitts—laboriously stirring for 20 minutes, trying to duck splattering, boiling polenta. No, we'll cook our favorite polenta recipes in the microwave for about 10 minutes, stirring thoroughly at least twice during the cooking time, and we won't feel a moment of guilt—except maybe later when we help ourselves to seconds.

Stuffings in the microwave? Sounds odd at first, but it really makes perfect sense. Especially if you use the combined efforts of the oven (as in toasting the bread cubes in the Bread and Fruit Stuffing) or the stovetop (as in cooking the brown rice—which is not at all time-saving or very successful in the microwave—in the Brown Rice Stuffing). Once again, your old-fashioned range and your new-fangled microwave make a terrific team.

The potato and other vegetable salads are all interesting variations on a standard theme—with the added bonus of being simpler to prepare when one or more of the components is neatly cooked in the microwave. Whether cooking green beans for the Green Bean and Fennel Salad or simply cooking bacon for the Wilted Watercress Salad, the microwave proves over and over again that it is, indeed, a useful kitchen appliance.

R E C I P E S

POLENTA EXPRESS

Polenta with Heavy Cream
Cheese Polenta with Provençal Sauce
Polenta with Ricotta and Dried Cherries
Southwestern Polenta
Sweet Potato Polenta*

STUFFINGS

Bread and Fruit Stuffing
Cornbread Stuffing
Microwave Cornbread
Brown Rice Stuffing*

POTATO SALADS

Potato and Turnip Salad*
Warm Potato Salad Vinaigrette
Sweet Potato Salad*
Vegetable Potato Salad

OTHER VEGETABLE SALADS

Green Bean and Fennel Salad*
Warm Green Bean, Red Onion, and Basil Salad*
Marinated Artichokes*
Sweet and Sour Cauliflower*
Warm Beet Salad with Orange and Basil*
Wilted Watercress Salad

* Especially good for you.

POLENTA EXPRESS

POLENTA WITH HEAVY CREAM

Just before serving, brown the bubbly cheese and thickened cream swimming on top of this heavenly polenta dish under the broiler. This could be served as a main course with roasted sweet red peppers and grilled sausage on the side.

▶ **PREPARATION TIME:** 5 minutes
COOKING TIME: 19 minutes
STANDING TIME: 10 minutes
BROILING TIME: 5 minutes

2 cups unsalted homemade or canned chicken broth
1 cup water
1 cup yellow cornmeal
½ teaspoon salt
4 ounces mozzarella cheese, shredded or cut in thin slices
1 cup heavy cream
1 tablespoon grated Parmigiano-Reggiano cheese

1. Microwave the chicken broth in a microwave-safe 3-quart glass casserole with a lid, covered, on high power until very hot, 3 minutes. In a separate bowl, stir the water and cornmeal together until smooth. Gradually stir the cornmeal and water mixture into the hot chicken broth until smooth; add the salt. Microwave uncovered 3 minutes. Stir thoroughly with a spoon or whisk until there are absolutely no lumps. Microwave 3 minutes longer.

2. Generously butter a microwave-safe and flame-resistant 10-inch pie plate or baking dish (Corning Ware or flame-proof pottery are good choices). Spread half the polenta in a smooth layer on the bottom, sprinkle with half the mozzarella, and drizzle with half the heavy cream. Spoon the remaining polenta on top and spread as evenly as possible. Top with the remaining mozzarella and heavy cream; sprinkle with the grated cheese.

3. Microwave uncovered for 5 minutes. Turn the dish a half-turn and lift the edges of the polenta so some of the cream will run to the bottom of the plate. Microwave 5 minutes. Remove from the oven and let stand 10 minutes.

4. Meanwhile, preheat the broiler. Broil the polenta 3 inches from the heat until the top is browned and bubbly, 3 to 5 minutes.

SERVES 4

CHEESE POLENTA WITH PROVENÇAL SAUCE

This is a very satisfying and very tasty side dish, and it can be prepared in the same amount of time it would take for the polenta alone if made conventionally. Serve it with a very simple entrée, like roast chicken or pork.

▶ **PREPARATION TIME:** 20 minutes
COOKING TIME: 18 minutes
STANDING TIME: 30 minutes

2 cups water
²/₃ cup yellow cornmeal
2 tablespoons olive oil
Salt and freshly ground pepper
½ cup shredded mozzarella cheese, preferably fresh
1 small onion, diced
2 cloves garlic, minced
½ cup canned Italian crushed tomatoes
⅓ cup minced red bell pepper
1 bay leaf
1 teaspoon fresh thyme leaves

Pinch **each** grated orange zest and fennel seeds
20 Niçoise olives, pitted and chopped
2 sun-dried tomatoes (packed in oil), diced
2 teaspoons drained capers
1 tablespoon minced fresh basil

1. Whisk together the water, cornmeal, 1 tablespoon of the oil, and ½ teaspoon salt in a microwave-safe 3-quart casserole with a lid. Cover and microwave on high power for 6 minutes, whisking completely three times. Stir in the mozzarella and a grinding of pepper and turn out into a lightly oiled 8-inch-square baking pan. Let stand 30 minutes, or until firm.

2. Meanwhile, stir the remaining 1 tablespoon oil and the onion together in a microwave-safe 9-inch glass pie plate. Cover with microwave-safe plastic wrap and vent one side. Microwave for 1 minute. Stir in the garlic and microwave, covered and vented, 2 minutes longer.

3. Stir in the crushed tomatoes, red bell pepper, bay leaf, thyme, orange zest, and fennel seeds. Microwave, covered and vented, 2 minutes. Remove from the oven and stir in the olives, sun-dried tomatoes, capers, and salt and pepper to taste. Taste and adjust seasonings.

4. Cut the polenta into four squares and then diagonally into eight triangles, and microwave uncovered on a microwave-safe platter for 2 to 3 minutes, until heated through. Place on serving plates. Heat sauce for 1 to 3 minutes, until very hot. Spoon the sauce over the polenta and serve immediately, topped with minced basil.

SERVES 4

POLENTA WITH RICOTTA AND DRIED CHERRIES

This is a great dish to serve with grilled or roasted meat or poultry.

▸ **PREPARATION TIME:** 5 minutes
COOKING TIME: 15 minutes
STANDING TIME: 2 minutes

2 cups water
1 1/2 cups homemade or canned chicken broth
1 cup yellow cornmeal
1/4 teaspoon salt, or to taste
1/2 cup dried cherries
1 1/2 teaspoons grated lemon zest
1 cup part skim or whole ricotta cheese, at room temperature
2 tablespoons unsalted butter, at room temperature
3 dashes hot red pepper sauce, or to taste

1. Place the water and chicken broth in a microwave-safe 3-quart glass casserole with a lid. Whisk in the cornmeal and salt. Cover and cook on high power for 10 to 12 minutes, until the liquid is almost completely absorbed, whisking three times, and adding the cherries for the last 3 minutes of cooking. Remove from the oven, add the lemon zest, and let stand, covered, 2 minutes.

2. Whisk in the ricotta, butter, and hot pepper sauce. If necessary, reheat in the microwave for 1 to 3 minutes, just until heated through. Serve hot.

SERVES 6

SOUTHWESTERN POLENTA

This polenta may be cut into any shape you desire, and you can pan-fry it on top of the stove for a crunchy exterior instead of reheating it in the microwave. It goes well with grilled steak or chicken. Brown the polenta triangles right on the grill.

▶ **PREPARATION TIME: 8 minutes**
COOKING TIME: 9 minutes
STANDING TIME: 30 minutes

2 cups water
2/3 cup yellow cornmeal
1/2 teaspoon salt, or to taste
1/2 cup shredded Monterey Jack cheese (about 2 ounces)
1/4 cup minced cilantro
1 teaspoon ground cumin seed
Hot red pepper sauce to taste

1. Whisk together the water, cornmeal, and salt in a microwave-safe 3-quart glass casserole with a lid. Cover and microwave on high power for 6 minutes, whisking completely twice.

2. Remove from the oven and stir in the cheese, cilantro, cumin, and red pepper sauce. Spread in a lightly oiled 8-inch-square baking pan. Let stand 30 minutes or until firm.

3. Cut the polenta into four squares and then diagonally into eight triangles. Heat uncovered on a microwave-safe platter for 2 to 3 minutes, until heated through.

SERVES 4

SWEET POTATO POLENTA*

The sweet potato transforms this dish into a vibrant orange. The texture is smoother than other potatoes.

▶ **PREPARATION TIME:** 10 minutes
COOKING TIME: 19 minutes
STANDING TIME: 3 minutes

---

1 pound sweet potatoes (2 medium), pared and cut into medium dice
⅓ cup water
3 cups whole or lowfat milk
¾ cup yellow cornmeal
2 tablespoons unsalted butter
1½ teaspoons salt, or to taste
¼ teaspoon dried sage
½ teaspoon freshly ground pepper, or to taste

---

1. Place the diced sweet potatoes and water in a microwave-safe 3-quart glass casserole with a lid. Microwave covered on high power for 8 to 10 minutes, until cooked through and soft. Let stand covered for 3 minutes. Drain the sweet potatoes and puree until completely smooth in a food processor or food mill, scraping the sides, about 2 minutes.

2. In the same clean casserole, whisk together the milk, cornmeal, butter, salt, and sage. Cover and microwave for 7 to 9 minutes, until almost all the liquid is absorbed, whisking completely three times. Remove from the oven and whisk until smooth.

3. Whisk together the pureed sweet potatoes, polenta, and fresh ground pepper. Taste and adjust seasoning. Serve hot.

SERVES 4

STUFFINGS

For many people, stuffing is the main reason for cooking turkey or chicken. Here is some advice for stuffings:

▶ These stuffings can go from microwave to table or can be put into the bird right before it is cooked. Roast birds only in conventional ovens.

▶ Microwave stuffings can be cooked while the bird is being carved.

▶ The stuffings may be prepared a day in advance and refrigerated, but don't stuff the bird until just before cooking.

▶ Always remove the stuffing from a leftover bird and refrigerate it separately, to reduce the risk of food infection.

▶ The microwave is ideal for reheating leftover stuffing, because it remains moist and fresh. Reheat a stuffing on high power uncovered until heated through.

▶ Stuffing expands as it cooks, so mix it with a light hand and pack it lightly to allow plenty of room for expansion.

▶ Don't add too much liquid or the stuffing will become soggy.

BREAD AND FRUIT STUFFING

Dried cherries are fantastic in this dish, but if they're difficult for you to find, use golden raisins or diced dried apples. Or try the dried fruit of your choice—currants, peaches, apricots, or pears would all be wonderful. This is an excellent stuffing for duck or goose.

▶ **PREPARATION TIME:** 20 minutes
COOKING TIME: 12 minutes

12 slices white bread, cut in ¾-inch dice (about 6 cups)
¼ cup unsalted butter (½ stick)
1 small Granny Smith apple, peeled, cored, and diced (about 1 cup)
1 rib celery, trimmed and minced (about 1 cup)
½ cup dried cherries
4 large scallions, trimmed and minced (about 1 cup)
2 tablespoons minced fresh parsley
¼ teaspoon **each** dried thyme, salt, and freshly ground pepper
1–3 tablespoons homemade or canned chicken broth

1. Place the bread cubes on a baking sheet in a slow (250°) conventional oven to dry out.

2. Meanwhile, microwave the butter in a microwave-safe 2-quart glass measure on high power until melted, about 1 minute. Stir in the apple, celery, and dried cherries and mix well. Cover with microwave-safe plastic wrap and vent one side. Microwave on high power for 6 minutes, stirring twice.

3. Add the dried bread cubes, scallions, parsley, thyme, salt, and pepper, and stir to blend well. Add just enough broth to moisten. Taste and adjust seasoning. (If desired, stuff into the bird at this point and cook conventionally.) Cover with plastic wrap and vent one side. Or microwave on high power for about 5 minutes, or until heated through.

MAKES 7 CUPS (Enough stuffing for an 8-pound bird or 4 Cornish hens)

CORNBREAD STUFFING

This is great with turkey. Or, for a sensational combination, try it with ham. The cornbread can be made in advance.

▶ **PREPARATION TIME:** 30 minutes (plus 45 minutes to make and cool the cornbread)
COOKING TIME: 12 minutes

1 recipe Microwave Cornbread (see page 241)
¼ cup unsalted butter (½ stick)
5 ounces Canadian-style bacon, diced small

3 stalks celery, trimmed and
   minced
1 red bell pepper, seeded and
   diced
1 medium onion, sliced thin
2 scallions, trimmed and
   minced
1 tablespoon fresh sage or
   1 1/2 teaspoons dried sage
1/2 teaspoon **each** salt and
   freshly ground pepper, or to
   taste

1. Make the cornbread according to the recipe below, and cool completely. Cut the cornbread into 3/4-inch cubes, and place on a baking sheet in a slow (250°) oven to dry.

2. Meanwhile, melt the butter in a microwave-safe 2-quart glass casserole with a lid on high power about 1 minute. Stir in the Canadian bacon, celery, bell pepper, and onion. Cover with microwave-safe plastic wrap and vent one side. Microwave on high power for 6 minutes, stirring twice.

3. Add the cornbread cubes, scallions, sage, salt, and pepper and stir to blend completely. Taste and adjust seasonings. (If desired, stuff into bird at this point and cook conventionally.) Cover with plastic wrap, and vent one side. Or microwave on high power for 5 minutes, or until heated through.

MAKES 7 CUPS (Enough stuffing for an 8-pound bird)

MICROWAVE CORNBREAD

This cornbread recipe was adapted from the recipe on the cornmeal box—and it works remarkably well in the microwave.

▶ **PREPARATION TIME:** 5
   minutes
COOKING TIME: 6 minutes
STANDING TIME: 5 minutes
COOLING TIME: 30 minutes

2 teaspoons baking powder
1/2 teaspoon salt
1 cup milk
1/4 cup safflower oil
1 large egg

1 1/4 cups all-purpose flour
3/4 cup cornmeal
2 tablespoons sugar

1. Combine the dry ingredients. Mix together the milk, oil, and egg and stir into the dry ingredients with

a fork just until moistened.

2. Pour the batter into an ungreased microwave-safe 8-inch glass cake dish. Microwave on high power for 5 to 6 minutes, or until the surface appears dry, rotating the dish after 2 minutes. Let stand 5 minutes, then cool completely on a rack.

BROWN RICE STUFFING*

Healthful, delicious nutty-flavored brown rice stuffing is a pleasant alternative to more standard bread stuffings. This one, wonderfully jazzed up with Italian vegetables and herbs, is a real treat, and a perfect stuffing for poultry and fish.

▶ **PREPARATION TIME:** 20 minutes
COOKING TIME: 13 minutes

1 medium onion (4 ounces), sliced thin
1/4 cup olive oil
1 clove garlic, minced
8 medium mushrooms (4 ounces), stemmed, sliced
1 **each** red and yellow bell pepper, seeded, diced
1 small bulb fennel (about 6 ounces), trimmed and diced small (about 1 cup)
4 cups cooked brown rice
1 teaspoon dried basil
1 teaspoon **each** dried rosemary and salt
1/4 teaspoon freshly ground pepper
1/4 cup toasted pine nuts
1–3 tablespoons homemade or canned chicken broth

1. Stir together the onion, olive oil, and garlic in a microwave-safe 2-quart glass casserole with a lid. Microwave covered on high power for 4 minutes, until the onions are softened, stirring once.

2. Stir in the mushrooms, peppers, and fennel. Microwave covered for 4 minutes, stirring once. Stir in the cooked brown rice, basil, rosemary, salt, pepper, pine nuts, and just enough chicken stock to moisten. (If desired, stuff into the bird at this point and cook conventionally.) Microwave, covered and vented, on high power for about 5 minutes, or until heated through.

MAKES 7 CUPS (Enough stuffing for an 8-pound bird)

POTATO SALADS

POTATO AND TURNIP SALAD*

Here's an unusual twist to potato salad. Potatoes and turnips are a wonderful combination. Try fresh thyme or parsley instead of the dill for a variation; all are delicious.

▶ **PREPARATION TIME: 20 minutes**
COOKING TIME: 20 minutes
STANDING TIME: 6 minutes

1 pound all-purpose potatoes (4 medium), pared and cut in ½-inch dice
1 cup water
¼ cup olive oil
3 scallions, trimmed and minced
2 teaspoons fresh lemon juice
2 teaspoons minced fresh dill
1 teaspoon balsamic vinegar
1 teaspoon Dijon mustard
½ teaspoon salt, or to taste
¼ teaspoon freshly ground pepper, or to taste
½ pound turnips (3 medium), pared and cut in ½-inch dice

1. Place the potatoes in a microwave-safe 3-quart glass casserole with a lid. Pour ¾ cup of the water over the potatoes. Microwave covered on high power for 7 to 10 minutes, or until done. Let stand, covered, 3 minutes. Drain the potatoes and place in a medium bowl. Stir in the olive oil, scallions, lemon juice, dill, vinegar, mustard, salt, and pepper and blend completely.

2. Place the turnips and the remaining ¼ cup water in the same clean 3-quart casserole. Cover and microwave for 8 to 10 minutes, until done. Let stand, covered, for 3 minutes. Drain completely and stir into the potato mixture. Taste and adjust seasoning. Serve warm, at room temperature, or chilled.

SERVES 4

WARM POTATO SALAD VINAIGRETTE

A microwave version of a classic potato salad, this is great for a simple supper accompanied by roasted or barbecued chicken.

▶ **PREPARATION TIME:** 15 minutes
COOKING TIME: 17 minutes
STANDING TIME: 2 minutes

6 slices bacon
2 pounds all-purpose potatoes (about 6 medium), pared and cut into ½-inch dice
¼ cup water
1 shallot, minced
3 tablespoons apple cider vinegar
2 tablespoons safflower oil
¼ teaspoon dried thyme
¼ teaspoon each salt and freshly ground pepper, or to taste
¼ cup minced fresh parsley

1. Place the bacon in a single layer on three layers of folded paper towels in a microwave-safe glass 8-inch square baking dish. Cover with a paper towel. Microwave on high power for 5 minutes. Remove the plastic wrap and let stand for 2 minutes.

2. Place the potatoes in a microwave-safe 3-quart glass casserole with a lid. Sprinkle with the water and shallot. Cover and microwave for 12 minutes, stirring three times.

3. Cut the bacon into ½-inch pieces and add to the potatoes. Add the vinegar, oil, thyme, salt, and pepper; stir to combine. Transfer to a serving dish and sprinkle with the parsley. Serve warm.

SERVES 6

SWEET POTATO SALAD*

An unusual and tasty version of potato salad, this might even become your favorite.

▶ **PREPARATION TIME:** 15
  minutes
COOKING TIME: 10 minutes
CHILLING TIME: 1 hour

---

2 pounds sweet potatoes (4
    medium), pared and cut
    into ½-inch dice
¼ cup water
¾ cup plain lowfat or nonfat
    yogurt
¼ cup minced cilantro
3 scallions, trimmed and
    minced
1 tablespoon minced fresh
    ginger
1 tablespoon fresh lime juice
¼ teaspoon grated lime zest
Salt to taste

¼ tablespoon freshly ground
    pepper

---

1. Place the potatoes in a microwave-safe 3-quart glass casserole with a lid and sprinkle with the water. Cover and microwave on high power for 8 to 10 minutes, stirring three times. Drain. Let cool slightly for about 5 minutes.

2. Stir in the remaining ingredients. Refrigerate at least 1 hour until cold before serving.

SERVES 6

VEGETABLE POTATO SALAD

▶ **PREPARATION TIME:** 20
  minutes
COOKING TIME: 9 minutes
STANDING TIME: 2 minutes
CHILLING TIME: 1 hour

---

2 pounds small red new potatoes (12–16), scrubbed and
  quartered
1/4 cup water
4 ounces fresh green beans,
  trimmed and cut into 1-inch
  pieces
1/2 cup sour cream
10 radishes, trimmed and thinly
  sliced
3 scallions, trimmed and
  minced
2 small carrots, pared and
  thinly sliced
1/4 cup minced fresh parsley
1/2 teaspoon salt
1/4 teaspoon freshly ground
  pepper

1. Place the potatoes in a micro-wave-safe 3-quart glass casserole with a lid and sprinkle with the water. Cover and microwave on high power for 9 minutes, stirring twice. Remove from the oven and stir in the beans. Let stand, covered, 2 minutes. Remove the cover and let the vegetables cool to room temperature.

2. Stir in the remaining ingredients and refrigerate at least 1 hour until cold before serving.

SERVES 6

OTHER VEGETABLE SALADS

GREEN BEAN
AND FENNEL SALAD*

S elect crisp, tender, and very fresh green beans for this sophisticated yet classically simple salad.

▶ **PREPARATION TIME: 10 minutes**
COOKING TIME: 6 minutes

1/3 cup coarsely chopped walnuts
1 bulb fennel (about 8 ounces), outer stalks and tops trimmed, rinsed
8 ounces fresh green beans, stem ends trimmed, cut into 1/2-inch lengths
2 tablespoons water
3 tablespoons olive oil, preferably extra-virgin
2 tablespoons red wine vinegar
1/2 clove garlic, crushed
1/4 teaspoon salt
Freshly ground pepper

---

1. Spread the walnuts on a paper plate or a piece of microwave-safe pa- per towel and heat on high power for 1 minute. Set aside.

2. Finely chop enough of the tender feathery tops of the fennel to measure 1 tablespoon. Cut the fennel bulb lengthwise into quarters and slice into thin crosswise slices; set aside.

3. Place the green beans in a mi- crowave-safe 2-quart glass casserole with a lid and sprinkle with the water. Microwave covered on high power for 4 minutes, or until tender, stirring once. Immediately transfer to a colander, rinse with cool water, and drain.

4. Whisk the oil, vinegar, garlic, salt, and pepper together in a salad bowl. Add the walnuts, sliced fennel, chopped fennel tops, and green beans; toss to blend. Serve at room temperature.

SERVES 4

WARM GREEN BEAN, RED ONION, AND BASIL SALAD*

▶ **PREPARATION TIME:** 5 minutes
COOKING TIME: 6 minutes
STANDING TIME: 5 minutes

8 ounces fresh green beans, stem ends trimmed, left whole
½ cup hot tap water
1 tablespoon extra-virgin olive oil
¼ cup thin lengthwise slices sweet red onion
2 large leaves fresh basil, cut into julienne

Salt and freshly ground pepper

Combine the beans and water in a microwave-safe 3-quart glass casserole with a lid. Microwave covered on high power for 6 to 7 minutes, stirring once. Let stand, covered, 5 minutes; drain. Add the oil, onion, basil, salt, and pepper; toss and serve warm or at room temperature.

SERVES 2

MARINATED ARTICHOKES*

▶ **PREPARATION TIME:** 15 minutes
COOKING TIME: 10 minutes
STANDING TIME: 5 minutes

2 large artichokes (about 5 ounces each)
3 tablespoons fresh lemon juice
2 tablespoons water
3 tablespoons olive oil, preferably extra-virgin
1 clove garlic, crushed

1 bay leaf
1 teaspoon minced fresh oregano leaves, or a pinch dried oregano
Salt and freshly ground pepper

1. Snap off the bottom leaves of the artichokes; peel the tough outer skin from the stems. Using a large, heavy knife, cut the artichokes in half lengthwise. Drizzle the cut sides of the artichokes generously with 2 tablespoons of the fresh lemon juice. Place cut-side down in a broad microwave-safe 3-quart glass casserole with a lid. Add the water, 1 tablespoon of the olive oil, the garlic clove, and the bay leaf to the casserole. Microwave covered on high power for 6 minutes, turning the casserole a half-turn once.

2. Uncover and turn artichokes cut-side up; baste with the juices, cover, and microwave on high power for 3 to 4 minutes, or until almost tender. Let stand, covered, 5 minutes.

3. To serve, drain off the liquid and discard the garlic and bay leaf. Using a teaspoon, carefully remove the choke from the center of each artichoke half. Sprinkle the artichokes with the remaining 2 tablespoons olive oil and 1 tablespoon lemon juice; add the oregano, a pinch of salt, and a grinding of black pepper. Serve two halves per person. Spoon the juices over the artichokes.

SERVES 2

SWEET AND SOUR CAULIFLOWER*

Serve this simple Oriental-style pickle with the Salmon Steaks with Lime, Garlic, and Cilantro (recipe page 153).

▶ **PREPARATION TIME:** *10 minutes*
COOKING TIME: *7 minutes*
STANDING TIME: *2 minutes*
CHILLING TIME: *1 hour*

2 cups cauliflower flowerets (about ½ a small head)
2 medium carrots, trimmed, pared, and cut into ¼-inch diagonal slices
2 tablespoons water
2 tablespoons white vinegar
1½ teaspoons granulated sugar
¼ teaspoon salt
1 teaspoon minced seeded fresh green chili pepper
1 scallion, trimmed and cut into thin diagonal slices

1. Combine the cauliflower and carrot in a microwave-safe 2-quart glass casserole with a lid and sprinkle with the water. Microwave covered on high power until the vegetables are crisp-tender, about 6 minutes, stirring once halfway through the cooking. Let stand, covered, 2 minutes.

2. Meanwhile, combine the vinegar, sugar, and salt in a 1-cup glass measure. Drain the liquid from the vegetables into the vinegar mixture. Microwave uncovered for 1 minute, or until very hot. Stir to dissolve the sugar.

3. Add the hot vinegar, chili pepper, and scallions to the vegetables; toss to blend. Refrigerate at least 1 hour until well chilled before serving.

SERVES 4

WARM BEET SALAD WITH ORANGE AND BASIL*

Because of their smooth nonfibrous texture, beets cook quickly in the microwave. We guarantee, if you are a beet lover, you will never boil another beet once you have tried this method. Serve this salad warm or slightly chilled.

▶ **PREPARATION TIME:** 10 minutes
COOKING TIME: 15 minutes
STANDING TIME: 10 minutes

8 medium beets (each about 2 inches in diameter), tops trimmed to 1 inch, washed and scrubbed
½ cup very hot tap water
2 tablespoons olive oil, preferably extra-virgin
1 tablespoon fresh lemon juice
1 teaspoon finely shredded orange zest
½ clove garlic, crushed
½ teaspoon salt
Freshly ground pepper
2 tablespoons julienne fresh basil

½ cup thin lengthwise slices sweet red or white onion
Whole basil leaves, for garnish
4 thin orange slices, for garnish (optional)

1. Combine the beets and water in a microwave-safe 3-quart glass casserole with a lid. Microwave covered on high power for 15 minutes, or until the beets are evenly tender when pierced with a fork, stirring once halfway through the cooking. Let stand, covered, for 10 minutes, or until cool enough to handle.

2. Remove the tops and peel the beets. Cut into ¼-inch-thick slices.

3. In a mixing bowl whisk together the oil, lemon juice, orange zest, garlic, salt, and pepper. Add the beets and basil; toss to blend. Serve warm, on individual salad plates topped with the onion slivers; gar-nish each serving with a whole basil leaf and a twisted orange slice, if desired.

SERVES 4

WILTED WATERCRESS SALAD

▶ *PREPARATION TIME: 10 minutes*
COOKING TIME: 3 minutes

2 cups watercress sprigs, rinsed, tough stems trimmed
¼ cup thinly sliced red onion
2 fresh mushroom caps, sliced
¼ cup grated Gruyère cheese
2 slices bacon, diced
1 tablespoon homemade or canned chicken broth
2 teaspoons olive oil
2 teaspoons minced shallots
1 teaspoon balsamic vinegar
½ teaspoon Dijon mustard
Pinch freshly ground pepper

1. Combine the watercress, on-ion, mushrooms, and cheese in a serving bowl.

2. Place the bacon in a micro-wave-safe 9-inch glass pie plate. Cover lightly with a sheet of waxed paper. Microwave on high power un-til crisp, 1 to 2 minutes. Transfer the bacon to paper towels to drain, then sprinkle over the salad.

3. Measure 1 teaspoon of the ba-con fat into a small microwave-safe bowl. Add the remaining ingredients and mix. Microwave until very hot, 30 to 60 seconds. Immediately pour over the watercress mixture, toss well, and serve.

SERVES 1

CHAPTER 10

DESSERTS

Our appetite for dessert borders on the shameful—consequently, this chapter is sizable. But you will hear no apologies from us. We include dozens of wonderful recipes from simple and stylish poached fruits to sublime and sophisticated "made from scratch" ice creams like the knockout Bittersweet Chocolate Ice Cream that will make chocolate lovers swoon.

The best microwaved desserts are often the most healthful. As with other foods that are successfully cooked in the microwave, fruits retain their flavor, color, texture, and shape beautifully, and because they are high in sugar content, their cooking time is short. So microwaved fruit desserts have a twofold virtue: they are in line with today's emphasis on healthful eating, and they take very little time to prepare.

We have included a few very good fruit crisps, but generally the microwave does not do very well with baked goods so you will not find any cakes or cookies. However, we know you will enjoy the fantastic dessert sauces, the extensive choice of recipes for chocoholics, the delicious candies, and the hasty puddings.

Be sure to read the tips for microwaving chocolate on page 282 before making any of the chocolate recipes.

R E C I P E S

POACHED FRUIT

Apricot-Strawberry Compote*
Blueberry-Peach Compote*
Figs with Lemon, Honey, and Thyme*
Grapes with Tarragon*
Oranges in Bay Leaf Syrup*
Pears Poached in Earl Grey Tea*
Poached Seckel Pears*
Pears Poached in Red Wine with Orange and Ouzo*
Poached Pears with Lemon and Honey
Prunes in Cognac and Jasmine Tea*
Honey-Pear Compote*
Rhubarb in Ginger Syrup*

BAKED FRUIT

Baked Apples
Pears in Cassis Cream
Brown-Sugar-Glazed Banana Slices
Baked Honey, Butter, and Cinnamon Pears

FRUIT CRISPS

Cranberry-Apple Crisp
Lemony Pear and Currant Crisp
Strawberry-Rhubarb Crisp
Apple-Almond Crisp

APPLESAUCES

Chunky Applesauce with Pears*
Warm Baked Applesauce
Rosy Applesauce*
Plum Applesauce*

HOMEMADE ICE CREAM

Bittersweet Chocolate Ice Cream
Caramel Ice Cream
Cappuccino Ice Cream

FOR CHOCOLATE LOVERS ONLY

Hot Fudge Sauce
Mocha Sauce
Chocolate-Lemon Tart
Heavenly Hazelnut Fudge
Chocolate Custard
Frozen Chocolate and Coffee Pie
Old-fashioned Chocolate Pudding

FRUIT AND CHOCOLATE

Orange Segments with Chocolate Sauce*
Chocolate-Dipped Strawberries
Frozen Chocolate-Dipped Bananas

HASTY PUDDINGS

Fruity Indian Pudding
Cherry-Lemon Rice Pudding
Orange Bread Pudding with Chocolate Sauce

DESSERT SAUCES

Red Plum Sauce*
Blueberry Syrup*
Blueberry-Lemon Sauce*
Brown Sugar and Banana Sauce
Ginger Custard Sauce*
Custard Sauce
Butterscotch Sauce
Caramel Sauce
Peanut Butter-Fudge Sauce

CANDIES

Mexican Coffee Truffles
Chocolate-Dipped Ginger and Cashews
Chocolate Hazelnut Clusters
Candied Orange Peel*
Hazelnut Brittle
Chocolate-Almond Caramels

PIES

Pear-Apple Pie
Lemon-Strawberry Pie

* Especially good for you.

POACHED FRUIT

Poached fruits—both fresh and dried—are classic and popular desserts, and the microwave does them to perfection. Its moist heat creates the ideal environment for poaching.

Early success with a recipe for a classic poached pear with lemon and honey encouraged us to continue working on the subject. Before we knew it, our kitchens were fragrant with oranges poaching in a simple syrup spiked with pungent bay leaves, pears in Earl Grey tea, and rhubarb swimming in a rosy pink ginger-scented syrup. And as an added bonus, they were poaching in as little as half the conventional cooking time.

APRICOT-STRAWBERRY COMPOTE*

Give yourself a treat and spend less than 10 minutes to prepare it. This flavorful fruit dessert has got a lot of flavor and a great color.

▶ **PREPARATION TIME: 5 minutes**
COOKING TIME: 3 minutes
COOLING TIME: 10 minutes
CHILLING TIME: 1 hour

1/4 cup dry white wine
1/4 cup cranberry juice
1 strip lemon zest, 2 inches ×
    1/2 inch
1 teaspoon minced crystallized
    ginger

6 dried apricots, cut into thin
    strips
1/8 teaspoon vanilla extract
2 fresh strawberries, hulled and
    quartered
Julienne lemon zest, for garnish

1. Combine the wine, cranberry juice, strip of zest, and ginger in a microwave-safe small bowl. Microwave uncovered on high power for 2

minutes. Add the apricots; microwave 1 minute. Stir in the vanilla. Let cool to room temperature, then refrigerate until cold, at least 1 hour.

2. Just before serving, remove the lemon zest and stir in the strawberries. Serve cold garnished with julienne lemon zest.

SERVES 1

BLUEBERRY-PEACH COMPOTE*

A great dessert for the middle of winter, when you'd like to pretend it's summer.

▶ **PREPARATION TIME:** 5 minutes
COOKING TIME: 2 minutes
STANDING TIME: 2 minutes

1 16-ounce bag frozen unsweetened sliced peaches, thawed
1/2 cup water
Juice of 1 orange (about 6 tablespoons)
2 tablespoons sugar
1 teaspoon orange-flavored liqueur such as Grand Marnier or Cointreau

1/2 cup fresh or thawed frozen blueberries
1 tablespoon julienne orange zest

Combine the peaches, water, orange juice, sugar, and liqueur in a microwave-safe 2-quart glass casserole with a lid. Cover and microwave on high power for 2 minutes. Stir in the blueberries and orange zest and let stand, covered, 2 minutes. Serve warm.

SERVES 4

FIGS WITH LEMON, HONEY, AND THYME*

A lovely winter dessert either on its own, topped with crème fraîche or sour cream, or as a topping for ice cream or pound cake. It has great Mediterranean flavor.

▶ **PREPARATION TIME:** 5
  minutes
COOKING TIME: 10 minutes
STANDING TIME: 5 minutes

1 cup fruity white wine
½ cup apple juice
2 tablespoons honey
1 teaspoon fresh thyme leaves
1 pound dried Calmyrna figs
    (18–20), stems trimmed,
    halved, each half cut into 5
    thin strips
4 strips lemon zest, 3 inches ×
    ¾ inch

Whisk together the wine, apple juice, honey, and thyme leaves in a microwave-safe 2-quart glass casserole with a lid. Stir in the figs and lemon zest. Cover and microwave on high power for 8 to 10 minutes, until the figs are softened. Let stand, covered, for 5 minutes. Serve warm.

SERVES 4

GRAPES WITH TARRAGON*

▶ **PREPARATION TIME:** 2
  minutes
COOKING TIME: 7 minutes
COOLING TIME: 10 minutes
CHILLING TIME: 1 hour

1 cup water
¼ cup sugar
1 tablespoon Pernod or other
    anise-flavored liqueur
3 sprigs fresh tarragon, plus ad-
    ditional sprigs for garnish
2 8-ounce bunches seedless red
    grapes, rinsed and drained

1. Stir the water, sugar, Pernod, and 3 tarragon sprigs together in a microwave-safe 2-quart glass casserole with a lid. Microwave uncovered on high power until the sugar dissolves, about 3 minutes.

2. Stir well, add the grapes, and cover. Microwave 3 to 4 minutes, turning the grapes after 2 minutes. Let cool to room temperature, then refrigerate until cold, 1 hour.

3. Remove and discard the tarragon sprigs, Serve the grapes in the poaching liquid, garnished with fresh tarragon sprigs.

SERVES 2

ORANGES IN BAY LEAF SYRUP*

This delicious fruit dessert has a complex, spicy flavor. It's best when served icy cold in clear glass bowls.

▸ **PREPARATION TIME:** 10 minutes
COOKING TIME: 12 minutes
COOLING TIME: 10 minutes
CHILLING TIME: 1 hour

1 cup water
½ cup sugar
2 strips orange zest, 4 inches × 1 inch
2 strips lemon zest, 2 inches × ½ inch
2 large bay leaves
1 cinnamon stick
6 whole cloves
8 whole allspice berries
8 whole black peppercorns
4 large naval oranges
Julienne zest of ½ orange, for garnish

1. Combine the water, sugar, orange and lemon zest, bay leaves, cinnamon stick, whole cloves, allspice, and black peppercorns in a microwave-safe 2-quart glass measure. Microwave uncovered on high power for 12 minutes, until slightly reduced, thickened, and strongly flavored.

2. Strain the liquid and cool to room temperature, then chill until very cold. (If you are in a hurry, place the syrup in a bowl set inside a larger bowl of ice water and whisk until very cold.)

3. When ready to serve, pare and section the oranges over a serving bowl, saving the juices. Add the orange sections and juices to the strained syrup and serve in chilled glass bowls; garnish with orange zest.

SERVES 4

PEARS POACHED IN EARL GREY TEA*

This is a versatile recipe—try using other types of tea such as jasmine, Darjeeling, black currant, or herb. These pears may be served warm or chilled. Cool the pears in the poaching liquid if there is time; they will absorb more of the flavor from the tea.

▶ **PREPARATION TIME:** 5
    minutes
COOKING TIME: 4 minutes
COOLING TIME: 10 minutes
CHILLING TIME: 2 hours

1 cup boiling water
2 Earl Grey tea bags
1 strip lemon zest, 2 inches ×
    ½ inch
2 tablespoons honey
2 teaspoons fresh lemon juice
1 large firm ripe pear
2 lemon slices, for garnish
Fresh mint leaves, for garnish

1. Combine the boiling water, tea bags, lemon zest, honey, and lemon juice in a microwave-safe 2-cup glass measure. Cover with a saucer and let steep for several minutes. Remove the tea bags and stir.

2. Meanwhile, peel, halve, and core the pear. Place the pear halves, cut-side down, in a microwave-safe 8-inch glass cake dish. Pour the tea mixture over and around the pears. Cover with microwave-safe plastic wrap and vent one side. Microwave on high power for 1 minute. Turn the pears over and microwave, covered and vented, until the pears are tender when pierced with a fork, 2 to 4 minutes longer.

3. Remove the pears from the oven and let cool to room temperature. Refrigerate until cold, 1 to 2 hours. Serve cold with lemon slices and mint.

SERVES 2

POACHED SECKEL PEARS*

Seckel pears are the very tasty, very spicy, very small pears that are available in fall and early winter. Try to find twelve that are all about the same size (see below) so the pears will all cook at the same rate.

▶ **PREPARATION TIME:** 20
    minutes
COOKING TIME: 20 minutes

12 firm, ripe Seckel pears (2
    inches long × 1½ inches
    wide)
4 cups water
Juice of 1 lemon
2 cups dry red wine
½ cup sugar
2 sprigs fresh rosemary
½ bay leaf
Zest of 1 orange, cut in thick
    strips

1. Peel the pears with a swivel-blade vegetable peeler, leaving the stem on. Carefully, with the tip of the peeler, core the pears. Cut a small piece off the bottom of each of the pears so they will stand straight. Place the pears in a bowl with the water and the lemon juice.

2. Whisk together the wine, sugar, rosemary, bay leaf, and orange zest in a microwave-safe 2-quart glass casserole with a lid. Drain the pears and add them to the wine mixture. Cover and microwave on high power for 10 to 12 minutes, stirring twice, until the pears are tender when pierced with a fork.

3. Remove the pears with a slotted spoon and set aside. Remove and discard the rosemary, bay leaf, and orange zest. Microwave the wine mixture uncovered for 8 minutes. Let the wine cool slightly and put the pears back into the wine mixture. Serve warm, at room temperature, or chilled.

SERVES 4

PEARS POACHED IN RED WINE WITH ORANGE AND OUZO*

Ouzo is an unsweetened anise aperitif; if it's not available, use any anise-flavored liqueur (anisette, Sambucca). This is an unusual combination of flavors and very delicious.

▶ **PREPARATION TIME:** 10 minutes
COOKING TIME: 15 minutes
COOLING TIME: 20 minutes
CHILLING TIME: 2 hours

2 cups dry red wine
1/3 cup sugar
3 strips orange zest, 4 inches × 1 inch
1 tablespoon ouzo
1 teaspoon balsamic or red wine vinegar

3 firm ripe pears, peeled, halved, and cored

1. Stir together the red wine, sugar, orange zest, ouzo, and balsamic vinegar in a microwave-safe 8-inch glass cake dish. Add the pears, cut-side down, cover with a microwave-safe dinner plate, and microwave on high power for 8 to 10 minutes, turning halfway through, until the pears are tender when pierced with a fork.

2. Remove the pears to a plate with a slotted spoon. Return the poaching liquid to the microwave and microwave uncovered for 3 to 5 minutes, until slightly reduced. Let the liquid cool slightly and pour over the pears. Cool to room temperature and chill for at least 2 hours, and up to 36.

3. Remove the orange zest and serve the chilled pears cut-side up in glass bowls with the poaching liquid.

SERVES 6

POACHED PEARS WITH LEMON AND HONEY

S erve these delicately flavored pears at room temperature or chilled, topped with a spoonful of sweetened sour cream.

▶ **PREPARATION TIME:** 10 minutes
COOKING TIME: 5 minutes
STANDING TIME: 5 minutes
COOLING TIME: 20 minutes

4 firm-ripe small pears (about 1½ pounds)
2 tablespoons honey
1 tablespoon fresh lemon juice
Ground nutmeg
½ cup sour cream or crème fraîche (optional)
1 tablespoon granulated sugar (optional)

1. Using a small sharp knife or a vegetable parer, remove the skins from the pears leaving the stem intact. Cut a thin slice from the bottom of each pear so that they will stand up.

2. Stand the pears, evenly spaced and not touching each other, in a microwave-safe 2-quart glass casserole with a lid. In a separate bowl, stir the honey and lemon together until blended. Spoon over the pears. Microwave covered on high power for 5 minutes. Remove from oven; let stand, covered, 5 minutes.

3. Uncover; sprinkle with ground nutmeg. Cool at room temperature, basting frequently with the juices. Stir the sour cream and sugar together, if using; refrigerate until ready to serve.

SERVES 4

PRUNES IN COGNAC AND JASMINE TEA*

These prunes are a terrific dessert—good warm, at room temperature, or chilled; they will keep several weeks in the refrigerator.

▶ **PREPARATION TIME:** 5 minutes
COOKING TIME: 6 minutes
STANDING TIME: 2 minutes

12 ounces pitted prunes
1 cup strong hot brewed jasmine tea
¼ cup sugar
3 tablespoons Cognac or brandy
2 pieces lemon zest, 2 inches × ½ inch
1 cinnamon stick
½ teaspoon vanilla extract

Place all the ingredients in a microwave-safe 2-quart glass casserole with a lid. Cover and microwave on high power for 6 minutes, until the prunes are very soft. Let stand, covered, 2 minutes.
SERVES 4

HONEY-PEAR COMPOTE*

This very simple dish, which uses pears in season, makes a great winter dessert.

▶ **PREPARATION TIME:** 10 minutes
COOKING TIME: 3 minutes

1 cup water
2 tablespoons honey
2 teaspoons fresh lemon juice
3 ripe medium pears, peeled, cored, and sliced
2 dried pear halves, cut lengthwise into strips
1 cinnamon stick
3 whole cloves

Mix the water, honey, and lemon juice in a microwave-safe 2-quart glass casserole with a lid. Add the remaining ingredients and stir thoroughly. Cover and microwave on high power for 3 minutes—the dried pears should be soft. Remove the cinnamon stick and cloves, if desired, and serve warm.

SERVES 4

Honey-Pear Compote with Raspberries*: Add ½ cup fresh or thawed frozen raspberries to the cooked compote and microwave, covered, for 2 minutes longer before serving.

RHUBARB IN GINGER SYRUP*

We have adapted this recipe from a favorite technique for cooking rhubarb in a shallow baking dish in the oven. The natural—and plentiful—rhubarb juices, flavored with thin slices of fresh ginger, melt the sugar into a pretty pink syrup. Stirring with a vigorous hand is taboo when it comes to rhubarb. Stir very gently, with a skewer or a chopstick, and the rhubarb will remain fairly chunky. Good served warm or chilled, on ice cream or yogurt or by itself.

▶ *PREPARATION TIME: 5 minutes*
COOKING TIME: 10 minutes
STANDING TIME: 5 minutes

1½ pounds rhubarb, rinsed, trimmed, and cut into ½-inch pieces
½ cup water
½ cup sugar, or more if a sweeter syrup is desired
4 paper-thin slices fresh ginger

Combine the rhubarb, water, sugar, and ginger in a microwave-safe 3-quart glass casserole with a lid. Microwave covered on high power for 8 to 10 minutes, stirring very gently twice. Let stand, covered, 5 minutes before serving.

SERVES 4

V A R I A T I O N

Strawberry and Rhubarb in Ginger Syrup:* After the rhubarb is cooked, add 1 cup of thin-sliced strawberries to the casserole; poke down into the rhubarb with a skewer (do not stir). Cover and let stand 5 minutes, as directed above.

BAKED FRUIT

Calling these fruits "baked" might be a misnomer, since we both agree that baking is what a microwave probably does not do—at least in the truest sense of the word. To us, baking means a golden brown crust and the heady aroma of flour and butter toasting away in a cave of dry heat. But these "baked" fruit recipes were adapted very successfully, from favorite conventionally baked fruit recipes, and are well worth sharing with you. Although microwave baking has cut the conventional baking time in half, the flavor is still very much intact.

BAKED APPLES

Baked apples are definitely comfort food, and these will make you feel well taken care of. Try using crystallized ginger instead of the walnuts, or a mixture of walnuts and ginger.

▸ **PREPARATION TIME:** 7 minutes
COOKING TIME: 5 minutes

¼ cup unsweetened apple juice
1 tablespoon unsalted butter
1 teaspoon honey
1 teaspoon fresh lemon juice
Pinch ground cinnamon
2 McIntosh apples, cored from stem end leaving bottom intact and apple whole
2 cinnamon sticks
¼ cup walnuts, coarsely chopped
Vanilla ice cream (optional)

1. Place the apple juice, butter, honey, lemon juice, and cinnamon in a microwave-safe 1-cup glass measure. Microwave uncovered on high power until the butter is melted, about 1 minute. Stir well.

2. Place the apples in a microwave-safe 9-inch glass pie plate and

pour the apple juice mixture into each cavity, dividing evenly. Place the cinnamon sticks and walnuts inside the apples and pour the remaining juice mixture over the nuts.

3. Microwave uncovered on high power for 2 minutes. Tilt the plate and spoon the liquid in the plate over the apples. Microwave 2 minutes longer. Serve warm, with vanilla ice cream if desired.

SERVES 2

PEARS IN CASSIS CREAM

Pear desserts always suggest a special treat. This one is sophisticated— and quick, easy, and foolproof as well. The pears should be beginning to ripen, but they don't need to be fully ripe. You might want to try this recipe with other liqueurs—orange, blackberry, or hazelnut would be delicious—or replace the liqueur with fruit juice.

▶ *PREPARATION TIME: 10 minutes*
COOKING TIME: 20 minutes

---

1 cup heavy cream
1 tablespoon sugar
3 firm ripe pears, peeled, halved, and cored
3 tablespoons crème de cassis liqueur
2 tablespoons toasted chopped hazelnuts

---

1. Place the cream and sugar in a microwave-safe 1-quart glass measure. Microwave uncovered on high power for about 10 minutes, until reduced by half, watching and stirring every couple of minutes so that it doesn't boil over.

2. Place the pears in a micro-wave-safe 8-inch glass cake dish, cutside down, with the widest parts at the outside of the dish. Stir the crème de cassis into the cream and pour the mixture over the pears. Microwave the pears uncovered on high power for 3 minutes.

3. Turn the pears over and spoon the sauce over them. Microwave for 1 to 3 minutes longer, or until the pears are tender when pierced with a fork.

4. Remove the pears to a plate with a slotted spoon and keep warm. Return the dish with the cassis cream to the oven and microwave on high power for 2 to 4 minutes, until it's the consistency of a thick sauce. Serve the warm pears with the sauce spooned over them, and topped with the toasted hazelnuts.

SERVES 6

BROWN-SUGAR-GLAZED BANANA SLICES

Fast, simple, and luscious, this dessert is a banana lover's ultimate dream come true.

▸ *PREPARATION TIME: 5 minutes*
COOKING TIME: 2 minutes

2 bananas, peeled
1 tablespoon fresh lemon juice
2 tablespoons unsalted butter, cut into small pieces
2 tablespoons dark brown sugar
Softened vanilla ice cream or frozen vanilla yogurt
2 tablespoons broken pecans or walnuts (optional)

1. Cut the bananas into ¼-inch-thick diagonal slices; transfer to a small bowl; sprinkle with the lemon juice.

2. Place the butter in a microwave-safe 9-inch glass pie plate and sprinkle with the brown sugar. Microwave uncovered on high power for 1 minute; stir to blend. Add the bananas and stir to coat. Microwave for 1 minute and 15 seconds; stir once.

3. Spoon into dessert dishes and serve hot with ice cream or frozen yogurt. Sprinkle with pecans or walnuts, if desired.

SERVES 2

BAKED HONEY, BUTTER, AND CINNAMON PEARS

Bosc pears have more texture than Anjou, Bartlett, or Comice pears, which is why we recommend using them in this dessert.

▸ *PREPARATION TIME: 5 minutes*
COOKING TIME: 10 minutes
STANDING TIME: 5 minutes

---

4 Bosc pears, rinsed, halved, cores and stems removed
2 tablespoons unsalted butter, cut into 8 small pieces
2 tablespoons honey
Ground cinnamon
Plain yogurt or sour cream (optional)

---

1. Arrange the pears, cut-side up, in a microwave-safe 10-inch glass pie plate. Place a piece of butter in the cored section of each pear. Cover with microwave-safe plastic wrap and vent one side. Microwave on high power for 5 minutes, turning the dish a half-turn once halfway through the cooking.

2. Drizzle with the honey and sprinkle lightly with the cinnamon. Cover with microwave-safe plastic wrap and vent one side; microwave for 5 minutes. Let stand 5 minutes before serving. Serve warm with the juices, and topped with a spoonful of yogurt or sour cream if desired.

SERVES 4

FRUIT CRISPS

Fruit crisps are especially well suited for "baking" in the microwave. In fact, they are one of the few baked items we instinctively felt would work—and we were right. The fruit bottom emerges hot, bubbly, and juicy, and the top—thanks to the dryness and rough texture of the oatmeal—gets more luscious and crisp as it heats up. And to top it all off, microwave crisps bake in at least half the time it would take conventionally. We recommend popping one in your microwave just before you sit down to dinner. When it is time for dessert, the crisp should be still warm enough to melt that half-scoop of ice cream you just might be tempted to add.

CRANBERRY-APPLE CRISP

▸ **PREPARATION TIME:** 10 minutes
COOKING TIME: 10 minutes

Filling:
1 16-ounce can whole cranberry sauce
1 cup diced (¼ inch) peeled
  apple

Topping:
½ cup **each** packed light brown
  sugar, all-purpose flour,
  and quick-cooking (not instant) oatmeal

1 teaspoon ground cinnamon
¼ cup cold unsalted butter (½
  stick), cut into small pieces
Softened vanilla ice cream or
  softly whipped heavy
  cream, for serving

1. Lightly butter a microwave-safe 9-inch glass pie plate. Add the cranberry sauce and apples; stir just to blend.

2. In a large bowl, combine the brown sugar, flour, oatmeal, and cinnamon. Work in butter with a fork or pastry blender until the mixture forms coarse crumbs; sprinkle evenly over the fruit.

3. Microwave uncovered on high power for 5 minutes. Turn the dish a half-turn and microwave 4 to 5 minutes longer, or until the fruit is bubbly. Cool slightly before serving, topped with softened vanilla ice cream or whipped cream.

SERVES 4

LEMONY PEAR AND CURRANT CRISP

A richer, more buttery version of the following recipe can be made by increasing the amount of butter to ½ cup. Let your mood—or your conscience—be your guide.

▶ *PREPARATION TIME: 15 minutes*
COOKING TIME: 15 minutes

Filling:
2½ pounds (4 to 6) firm ripe pears, quartered, cored, and peeled
2 tablespoons dried currants
1 tablespoon fresh lemon juice
1 tablespoon granulated sugar
1 teaspoon grated lemon zest
⅛ teaspoon ground nutmeg

Topping:
½ cup each packed light brown sugar, all-purpose flour, and quick-cooking (not instant) oatmeal
¼ cup cold unsalted butter (½ stick), cut into small pieces
Softened vanilla ice cream, for serving

1. Lightly butter a microwave-safe 10-inch glass pie plate. Arrange the pears in a single layer; sprinkle with the currants, lemon juice, granulated sugar, lemon zest, and nutmeg.

2. In a large bowl, combine the brown sugar, flour, and oatmeal; stir to blend. Work in the butter with a fork or pastry blender until the mixture forms coarse crumbs; sprinkle evenly over the fruit.

3. Microwave uncovered on high power for 8 minutes. Turn the dish a half-turn and microwave until the pears are tender and the topping is crisp, about 6 to 7 minutes longer. Cool slightly before serving, topped with softened vanilla ice cream.

SERVES 6

STRAWBERRY-RHUBARB CRISP

The cool tang of plain yogurt is good with the assertive fruit flavors of strawberry and rhubarb in this crisp. A little flour is added to the sweetened fruit to compensate for its juiciness.

▶ **PREPARATION TIME:** 10 minutes
COOKING TIME: 17 minutes

Filling:
¼ cup granulated sugar
1 tablespoon all-purpose flour
2 cups sliced (½-inch) trimmed rhubarb
1 pint strawberries, hulled and halved
1 tablespoon finely chopped candied ginger (optional)

Topping:
½ cup **each** packed light brown sugar, all-purpose flour, and quick-cooking (not instant) oatmeal
¼ cup cold unsalted butter (½ stick), cut into small pieces
Plain yogurt or softly whipped cream, for serving

1. Lightly butter a microwave-safe 10-inch glass pie plate. In a separate bowl, combine the sugar and flour until blended. Add the rhubarb, strawberries, and candied ginger, if using; toss to blend. Spread in an even layer in the prepared pie plate.

2. In a large bowl, combine the brown sugar, flour, and oatmeal. Work in the butter with a fork or pastry blender until the mixture forms coarse crumbs; sprinkle evenly over the fruit.

3. Microwave uncovered on high power for 8 minutes. Turn the dish a half-turn and microwave 8 to 9 minutes longer, or until the fruit is thickened and bubbly and the topping is crisp. Cool slightly before serving. Top each serving with a dollop of yogurt.

SERVES 6

APPLE-ALMOND CRISP

Select firm, crisp apples—Winesap, Cortland, or Jonathan are best—for this homey dessert. The crumb crust is a good place to use up those few tablespoons of leftover nuts; here we use ground toasted almonds, but almost any nut will do.

▸ **PREPARATION TIME:** 10 minutes
COOKING TIME: 16 minutes

Filling:

1 1/2 pounds apples, peeled, cored, and cut in 1/4-inch wedges
2 tablespoons light brown sugar
1/4 teaspoon ground cinnamon

Topping:

1/4 cup toasted blanched almonds
1/2 cup **each** packed light brown sugar, all-purpose flour, and quick-cooking (not instant) oatmeal
1/2 teaspoon ground cinnamon
5 tablespoons cold unsalted butter, cut into small pieces
Softened vanilla ice cream, whipped cream, or vanilla yogurt, for serving

1. Lightly butter a microwave-safe 10-inch glass pie plate. Combine the apples, brown sugar, and cinnamon and toss to blend. Spread in an even layer in the prepared pie plate.

2. Finely grind the almonds in a food processor or with a Mouli grinder.

3. In a large bowl, combine the almonds, brown sugar, flour, oatmeal, and cinnamon. Work in the butter with a fork or pastry blender until the mixture forms coarse crumbs; sprinkle evenly over the fruit.

4. Microwave uncovered on high power for 8 minutes. Turn the dish a half-turn and microwave 7 to 8 minutes longer, or until the fruit is tender and the topping is crisp. Cool slightly before serving, topped with softened vanilla ice cream.

SERVES 6

APPLE SAUCES

Cooking apples down in the microwave to make a quick batch of applesauce is something we both do now as nonchalantly as boiling water in the kettle for tea. The real advantage to cooking applesauce in the microwave is that you don't need to worry about scorching the apples on the bottom of the pot. Furthermore, the apples cook down in half the time it takes to cook them conventionally.

We like leaving the skins on the apples and then separating the skins from the sauce by pushing them through a food mill. But, if you prefer—or you don't happen to have a food mill (you should get one, they are great!)—the apples could be peeled before cooking and then mashed when soft with a spoon.

CHUNKY APPLESAUCE
WITH PEARS*

▶ **PREPARATION TIME:** 10 minutes
COOKING TIME: 10 minutes
STANDING TIME: 10 minutes

1 pound tart, flavorful apples (Winesap, Granny Smith, Jonathan, Northern Spy, or Gravenstein), peeled, quartered, cored, and cut into ½-inch pieces

1 pound firm ripe pears, peeled, quartered, cored, and cut into ½-inch pieces
Granulated sugar (optional)
Ground cinnamon

Place the apples and pears in a microwave-safe 3-quart glass casserole with a lid. Microwave covered on high power for 5 minutes. Uncover; stir and mash slightly with a fork. Microwave covered 5 minutes longer. Let stand, covered, until slightly cooled, about 10 minutes. Taste, and add sugar if desired. Sprinkle with cinnamon and serve warm or chilled.

SERVES 4

WARM BAKED APPLESAUCE

This sinfully rich version of a simple traditional recipe is sure to be a stunning gastronomic success fit to serve at even the fanciest dinner party.

▶ *PREPARATION TIME: 5 minutes*
COOKING TIME: 15 minutes
STANDING TIME: 5 minutes

6–8 large flavorful apples (preferably Empire, Jonathan, Winesap, Cortland, or Rome, or a mixture of these), washed thoroughly, quartered, and cored
5 tablespoons brandy
4 tablespoons unsalted butter, at room temperature, cut into small pieces
¼ cup packed light brown sugar
¼ teaspoon ground cinnamon, plus more for serving
Softened vanilla ice cream

---

1. Combine the apples, brandy, butter, sugar, and ¼ teaspoon cinnamon in a microwave-safe 3-quart glass casserole with a lid. Microwave covered on high power for 15 minutes. Let stand, covered, 5 minutes.

2. Set a food mill over a heatproof bowl and puree the hot apples. Discard the apple skins. Spoon into dessert dishes while still warm and top with a spoonful of softened ice cream. Sprinkle with cinnamon and serve warm.

SERVES 4

ROSY APPLESAUCE*

The quality and freshness of the apples you select will determine the final flavor of the applesauce. Try mixing and matching some of your favorite eating apples and you will be amazed at the range of flavors. Because the apples are cooked in their skins it is imperative to wash and rinse them thoroughly in at least two changes of warm water.

▶ **PREPARATION TIME:** 10 minutes
COOKING TIME: 14 minutes

2 pounds fresh apples (use at least two varieties: e.g., McIntosh, Winesap, Empire, Jonathan, Cortland), well washed (see headnote), quartered, and cored (about 8–9 cups wedges)
1 cinnamon stick

1. Place the apples in a microwave-safe 3-quart glass casserole with a lid; microwave covered on high power for 12 to 14 minutes, or until the apples are evenly softened, stirring once after 10 minutes of cooking. Cool slightly.

2. Set a food mill over a large bowl and press the cooked apples through the mill. Discard the apple skins. Stir the cinnamon stick into the warm applesauce and cool. Refrigerate, covered, until ready to serve. For those who prefer extra sweetness, serve with a shaker of cinnamon sugar to sprinkle on each serving.

SERVES 4

PLUM APPLESAUCE*

Here is a perfect dessert for a hearty early-fall meal—the color is stunning. The butter in this recipe is optional.

▶ **PREPARATION TIME:** 10 minutes
COOKING TIME: 10 minutes

4 medium cooking apples, peeled, cored, and coarsely chopped (about 1 pound)

4 medium Santa Rosa purple
 plums, washed, pitted, and
 coarsely chopped
⅓ cup sugar, or to taste
1 tablespoon minced crystallized ginger
1 tablespoon unsalted butter

1. Stir together the apples, plums, sugar, and ginger in a microwave-safe 2-quart glass casserole with a lid. Microwave covered on high power for 10 minutes, stirring three times.

2. Puree in a food mill over a heatproof bowl; discard the skins. Stir in the butter until melted. Serve warm or chilled.

SERVES 4

HOMEMADE ICE CREAM

I ce cream based on a "from scratch" custard sauce has a rich, creamy, dreamy texture—not to be matched in store-bought ice creams at any price. But custard sauces are time-consuming and tricky, even for experienced cooks. Now, thanks to the microwave, all that has changed. Lori first discovered the stress-free joy of microwave custard sauces and although Marie was skeptical, after the very first attempt she was convinced—and there is nothing like the conviction of a convert.

The custard bases for the ice creams in this section are smooth and creamy, practically fail-proof, and can be made in at least half the time it would take to make them conventionally.

BITTERSWEET CHOCOLATE ICE CREAM

T his ice cream is incredibly smooth and has lots of chocolate flavor, which can be set off with our Peanut Butter Fudge Sauce (page 300).

▸ **PREPARATION TIME:** 15 minutes
COOKING TIME: 7 minutes
CHILLING TIME: 10 minutes
FREEZING TIME: 30 minutes

1 cup heavy cream
1 cup half-and-half
2 teaspoons instant espresso coffee powder

6 ounces bittersweet (not unsweetened) or semisweet chocolate, finely chopped
1 ounce unsweetened chocolate, finely chopped
4 large egg yolks
½ cup superfine sugar
Pinch salt

1. Microwave the cream, half-and-half, and espresso powder uncovered in a microwave-safe 2-quart glass measure on high power, whisking three times, just until boiling, about 4 to 5 minutes; set aside.

2. Microwave both chocolates together in a microwave-safe medium bowl on high power, just until melted 1 to 2 minutes, stirring four times.

3. Beat the yolks and sugar with an electric mixer on high speed until very light and fluffy, about 5 minutes. Fold in the melted chocolate with a rubber spatula, then fold in the cream mixture. Set the bowl in a larger bowl of ice water and whisk the mixture until cold, about 10 minutes.

4. Freeze in an ice cream maker according to the manufacturer's instructions. Store in the freezer until serving.

SERVES 4

CARAMEL ICE CREAM

Caramelizing sugar is an exact science, whether you are doing it on top of the stove or in the microwave. The process is faster in the microwave, plus, because of the moist heat, it won't crystallize. Although this technique has been carefully tested, it is important that you not walk away and ignore the microwave while the sugar is cooking. This ice cream is so delicious, it is well worth the few minutes (and it really is a very short time) that it takes to make it. Try it with our Mocha Sauce (page 283).

▶ *PREPARATION TIME: 5 minutes*
COOKING TIME: 18 minutes
CHILLING TIME: 10 minutes
FREEZING TIME: 30 minutes

½ cup sugar
¼ cup water
1 cup heavy cream
1 cup half-and-half
3 egg yolks

1. Combine the sugar and water in a microwave-safe 3-quart glass casserole. Microwave uncovered on high power for 4 minutes, stirring once and scraping down sides of the casserole with a spatula. Microwave undisturbed for 5 minutes, or until you begin to smell the aroma of caramelizing sugar. The caramel should be golden, but not amber. Remember, it will continue caramelizing as it stands. Microwave 1 to 1½ minutes

longer; check the caramel at 30-second intervals; protect your hands with pot holders and turn the casserole a quarter turn gently so the syrup will agitate slightly, preventing scorched spots. Remove from the microwave and let stand, uncovered, 5 minutes.

2. Meanwhile, combine the heavy cream and half-and-half in a microwave-safe 1-quart glass measure. Microwave uncovered on high power for 4 minutes, or until almost boiling. Meanwhile, whisk the egg yolks until lighten in color. Gradually whisk the hot cream mixture into the egg yolks until blended.

3. Add the hot custard mixture to the slightly less hot caramel syrup and carefully and firmly stir the mixtures together until the caramel syrup is completely blended with the hot cream. Pour back into the 1-quart measure. Microwave the caramel and cream mixture 1 minute. Whisk to blend. Microwave 60 seconds more, stirring every 20 seconds, until the custard is thickened. (It will register 180°F. on an instant-read thermometer.)

4. Scrape into a bowl and place in a larger bowl filled with ice water; chill, stirring occasionally, 10 minutes. Freeze in an ice cream maker according to manufacturer's instructions. Store in the freezer until serving.

SERVES 4

CAPPUCCINO ICE CREAM

For a delicious treat, serve this with a generous topping of Hot Fudge Sauce (page 282).

▸ **PREPARATION TIME:** 5 minutes
COOKING TIME: 6 minutes
CHILLING TIME: 10 minutes
FREEZING TIME: 30 minutes

1 cup half-and-half

1 cup heavy cream
2 tablespoons instant espresso coffee powder
3 large egg yolks
1/2 cup sugar
1 teaspoon vanilla extract

1. Whisk the half-and-half, heavy cream, and espresso powder in a microwave-safe 1-quart glass measure. Microwave uncovered on high power for 4 minutes, stirring once, until almost boiling.

2. Meanwhile, whisk or beat the egg yolks and sugar until light in color. Gradually whisk the hot cream mixture into the egg yolks until blended. Pour back into the 1-quart measure. Microwave uncovered for 1 minute. Whisk to blend. Microwave 60 seconds more, stirring every 20 seconds, until the custard is thickened. (It will register 180°F. on an instant-read thermometer.) Stir in the vanilla.

3. Scrape into a bowl and place in a large bowl filled with ice water; chill, stirring occasionally, 10 minutes. Freeze in an ice cream maker according to manufacturer's instructions. Store in the freezer until serving.

SERVES 4

FOR CHOCOLATE LOVERS ONLY

Then microwave takes the mess and the guess out of melting chocolate. In fact, it is one of the first things we did in our spanking new microwave ovens way back when. There's no double boiler to clean, no need for constant stirring, and the possibility of scorching is remote.

But, appearances can be deceiving because *chocolate melted in the microwave does not look melted.* Here are a few tips for smooth, runny chocolate every time:

▶ Finely chop or grate the chocolate into small pieces (use a food processor); smaller pieces melt more quickly and evenly than large pieces.

▶ Do not cover the bowl because condensation can cause the chocolate to harden or stiffen, reversing the melting process. For the same reason, always use a thoroughly dry bowl and utensils.

▶ Melt on 100% power, but *stir every 10 seconds* to avoid overcooking or scorching. Chocolate will only look melted after it is stirred.

HOT FUDGE SAUCE

This hot fudge sauce is very chocolatey, very thick, and very dark. It will get chewy when served over cold ice cream. Serve it hot or warm; at room temperature or cold it will be too thick.

▶ **PREPARATION TIME:** 5
 minutes
COOKING TIME: 4 minutes

───────────

¾ cup heavy cream
4 tablespoons unsalted butter,
 cut into small pieces

¼ cup granulated sugar
¼ cup packed dark brown
 sugar
Pinch salt
½ cup Dutch-process cocoa
 powder
1 teaspoon vanilla extract

1 ounce bittersweet (not un-
sweetened) or semisweet
chocolate, finely chopped

1. Place the cream and butter in a microwave-safe 1-quart glass measure and microwave uncovered on high power just until boiling, 2 to 3 minutes. Add the sugars and whisk until dissolved.

2. Whisk in the remaining ingredients until completely blended. Microwave uncovered on medium power (50%) for 1 minute. Strain the sauce and serve hot. Sauce can be reheated on medium power (50%) for 1 to 2 minutes until heated through.

MAKES 1½ CUPS

MOCHA SAUCE

It is easy to get hooked on this scrumptious coffee-flavored chocolate sauce. It's a knockout served with our Cappuccino Ice Cream (page 280). Keep the ingredients on hand so you can whip it up at a moment's notice. Serve warm or at room temperature.

▶ **PREPARATION TIME: 2**
   minutes
COOKING TIME: 4 minutes

1 cup heavy cream
1 cup semisweet chocolate
   chips
2 teaspoons espresso coffee
   powder

Combine the heavy cream, chocolate chips, and espresso powder in a microwave-safe 1-quart glass measure. Microwave uncovered for 4 minutes, stirring thoroughly three times, until the chocolate is melted and the sauce is thick and smooth.

MAKES ABOUT 1½ CUPS

CHOCOLATE-LEMON TART

Chocolate and lemon are a combination that's really tough to beat. These tarts would make a great ending to a romantic dinner for two.

▸ **PREPARATION TIME:** 15
  minutes
COOKING TIME: 16 minutes
COOLING TIME: 30 minutes
CHILLING TIME: 3 hours

8 tablespoons unsalted butter
10 chocolate wafers,* finely
  crushed
6 tablespoons sugar
¼ cup fresh lemon juice
Grated zest of 1 lemon
3 large egg yolks
⅓ cup heavy cream
Chocolate curls (see page 286),
  for garnish (optional)
Lemon slices, for garnish
  (optional)

1. Preheat the conventional oven to 350°, then prepare the crust: Melt the 2 tablespoons butter in a microwave-safe medium bowl on high power for 30 to 60 seconds. Add the crushed wafers and mix until the crumbs are moistened. Press the crumb mixture over the bottoms and sides of two 4½-inch metal tart pans with removable bottoms. Bake in the conventional oven for 10 minutes. Cool completely on a wire rack.

2. Meanwhile, prepare the filling: Melt the remaining 6 tablespoons butter in a microwave-safe 1-quart glass measure, about 1 minute. Stir in the sugar, lemon juice, and zest. Microwave for 2 minutes, stirring once. Whisk the egg yolks with about one quarter of the hot lemon mixture in another bowl, then return the lemon-yolk mixture to the glass measure and whisk gently to blend. Microwave for 2 minutes, whisking once. Let cool completely.

3. Whip the cream until stiff peaks form and gently fold into lemon curd mixture; spoon into the cooled tart shells. Refrigerate until firm, about 3 hours. Serve garnished with chocolate curls and/or lemon slices, if desired.

SERVES 2

HEAVENLY HAZELNUT FUDGE

The holiday season just isn't quite complete without fudge. This one couldn't be easier, so it's a great gift for all your friends—a wonderful way to show them that you really care. But don't wait for the holidays to make it—enjoy this all year round.

▶ **PREPARATION TIME:** 10 minutes
COOKING TIME: 3 minutes
CHILLING TIME: 2 hours

---

3 6-ounce packages semisweet chocolate chips
1 14-ounce can sweetened condensed milk
½ cup coarsely chopped toasted hazelnuts
1 tablespoon chocolate or hazelnut liqueur (optional)
1 teaspoon vanilla extract

---

1. Butter an 8-inch-square glass or metal baking pan.

2. Microwave the chocolate chips uncovered in a microwave-safe 2-quart glass measure on high power just until melted, about 2 to 3 minutes, stirring four times, being careful not to scorch the chocolate.

3. Stir in the condensed milk, hazelnuts, liqueur (if using), and vanilla extract and blend completely. Pour into the prepared pan and refrigerate for about 2 hours, or until firm. Cut into 1-inch squares and keep cool or store chilled in an airtight container.

MAKES 64 ONE-INCH PIECES

CHOCOLATE CUSTARD

This luxurious chocolate custard is wonderful garnished with raspberries and mint sprigs or with chocolate curls.

▶ **PREPARATION TIME:** 5 minutes
COOKING TIME: 20 minutes
STANDING TIME: 15 minutes
CHILLING TIME: 4 hours

⅔ cup **each** heavy cream and half-and-half
1 strip lemon zest, 2 inches × ½ inch
3 ounces bittersweet (not unsweetened) or semisweet chocolate, finely chopped

2 large eggs
1 large egg yolk
¼ cup sugar
Raspberries and mint sprigs or chocolate curls, for garnish

---

1. Microwave the cream, half-and-half, and lemon zest uncovered in a microwave-safe 1-quart glass measure on high power for 2 minutes.

2. Microwave the chocolate in a microwave-safe small bowl just until melted, 1 to 2 minutes, stirring every 30 seconds.

3. Whisk together the eggs, yolk, and sugar in a mixing bowl. Whisk in the hot cream mixture and then the chocolate; whisk until smooth. Strain the mixture and divide evenly between four 6-ounce microwave-safe ramekins.

4. Place the ramekins 1 inch apart on an automatic turntable in the microwave; start the turntable. Microwave uncovered on low power (20%) until the top is barely set, 13 to 15 minutes. Transfer to a wire rack, cover with a kitchen towel, and let stand 15 minutes. Cool to room temperature and then chill. Refrigerate for 4 hours or overnight. Or, if you're really in a hurry, place the ramekins in a large pan of ice water; let stand 30 minutes before chilling in the refrigerator. Serve very cold.

SERVES 4

NOTE: *To make chocolate curls,* place a bar of bittersweet or semisweet chocolate on a microwave-safe plate. Microwave at medium-low (30%) for 30 to 60 seconds, until just barely warm. To form the curls, hold the chocolate bar upright on its edge and pull a swivel-blade vegetable peeler toward you across the edge of the chocolate in a continuous even motion.

FROZEN CHOCOLATE AND COFFEE PIE

This fast and festive dessert really shows off your microwave. It's great for a party, but quick enough for a weekday dinner as well. You can make it ahead, freeze it, and drizzle with chocolate sauce before serving.

▶ **PREPARATION TIME:** *10 minutes*
COOKING TIME: *3 minutes*
COOLING TIME: *15 minutes*
FREEZING TIME: *30 minutes*

5 tablespoons unsalted butter
1⅓ cups crushed chocolate wafers*

2 pints coffee ice cream, softened
1 ounce bittersweet (not unsweetened) or semisweet chocolate
2 tablespoons heavy cream

1. Melt the butter in a microwave-safe 9-inch glass pie plate on high

* Preferably Nabisco Famous Wafers.

power until melted, about 1 minute. Stir in the chocolate wafer crumbs until evenly coated with butter. Using your hands, press the crumbs evenly over the bottom and sides of the plate to form a pie shell. Microwave uncovered on high power for 2 minutes, turning the dish halfway around after 1 minute. Transfer to a wire rack and let cool to room temperature, about 15 minutes.

2. Scoop the ice cream into the pie shell and spread evenly, mounding slightly in the center. Freeze until firm, about 30 minutes.

3. Just before serving, place the chocolate and cream in a microwave-safe 1-cup glass measure. Microwave uncovered until melted, about 1 minute, stirring once. Drizzle the chocolate over the pie and serve at once.

SERVES 8

OLD-FASHIONED CHOCOLATE PUDDING

Years ago—before the microwave—this was an easy pick-me-up for a rainy, lonely Saturday afternoon. It's even easier now!

▶ *PREPARATION TIME: 5 minutes*
COOKING TIME: 6 minutes

⅓ cup sugar
2 tablespoons cornstarch
2 cups milk
4 ounces semisweet or bittersweet chocolate, coarsely chopped
1 teaspoon vanilla extract
Pinch of salt
Whipped cream (optional)

1. Stir the sugar and cornstarch in a microwave-safe 1-quart glass measure until blended. Gradually stir in the milk. Add the pieces of chocolate. Microwave uncovered for 6 minutes, stirring thoroughly with a whisk every 2 minutes, until the pudding is smooth.

2. Whisk in the vanilla and salt. Divide evenly among six small custard cups or ramekins. Let stand until cooled, if you have the willpower. Serve with a spoonful of whipped cream, if desired.

SERVES 6

FRUIT AND CHOCOLATE

ORANGE SEGMENTS WITH CHOCOLATE SAUCE*

This dessert may include chocolate and heavy cream, but it is still relatively low in calories.

▶ **PREPARATION TIME:** 5 minutes
COOKING TIME: 1 minute

4 navel oranges
⅓ cup miniature semisweet chocolate chips
5 teaspoons heavy cream
Fresh mint leaves, for garnish (optional)

1. Using a small, sharp knife, cut the peel and white pith from the oranges, then cut the segments from between the membranes. Refrigerate until ready to serve.

2. Mix the chocolate chips and 2 teaspoons of the heavy cream in a microwave-safe 1-cup glass measure. Cover with microwave-safe plastic wrap and vent one side. Microwave on high power for 30 seconds. Stir well. Add the remaining cream; microwave, covered and vented, for 30 seconds. Stir well.

3. Spoon the oranges onto chilled dessert plates, drizzle the chocolate over them, and garnish with mint if desired.

SERVES 4

CHOCOLATE-DIPPED STRAWBERRIES

There's nothing more romantic than strawberries dipped in chocolate, and with this recipe nothing is easier.

▸ **PREPARATION TIME:** 15
minutes
COOKING TIME: 30 seconds
CHILLING TIME: 30 minutes

---

3 ounces bittersweet (not un-
sweetened) or semisweet
chocolate, very finely
chopped
1 1/2 teaspoons safflower oil
1 pint strawberries, preferably
with long stems

---

1. Mix the chocolate and oil thoroughly in a microwave-safe 9-inch glass pie plate. Microwave uncovered on high power for 15 to 20 seconds, then stir until smooth. If the chocolate is not completely melted, microwave 10 seconds longer. Transfer to a narrow tea cup.

2. Wipe off the strawberries, but do not wash or hull. Holding the hull or stem, dip each berry into the chocolate so that three-quarters of it is covered. Shake the excess chocolate back into the cup and place the berries on a baking sheet lined with waxed paper. Refrigerate 30 minutes before serving.

SERVES 2

FROZEN CHOCOLATE-DIPPED BANANAS

Just like they used to sell on the boardwalk at the beach. These are a great treat for kids and adults, and they don't take much work—but you'll get lots of thanks.

▸ **PREPARATION TIME:** 15
minutes
COOKING TIME: 4 minutes
FREEZING TIME: 1 1/2 hours

---

2 medium bananas
5 ounces bittersweet (not un-
sweetened) or semisweet
chocolate, coarsely chopped
1 tablespoon unsalted butter
1/2 cup chopped pecans

---

1. Cover a large plate with waxed paper. Peel the bananas and skewer them lengthwise with sturdy wooden skewers. Put the bananas on the plate, cover with more waxed paper, and freeze for at least 1 hour.

2. Microwave the chocolate and butter in a microwave-safe 9-inch glass pie plate on high power, stirring every 30 seconds, just until melted, 1 to 2 minutes. Microwave the pecans uncovered on a microwave-safe din-

ner plate, stirring once, until heated through, 1 to 2 minutes.

3. Coat the frozen bananas with the warm chocolate and then with the pecans. Return to the freezer on the waxed-paper-covered plate, cover with waxed paper and freeze until the chocolate hardens, at least 30 minutes. Serve frozen.

SERVES 2

HASTY PUDDINGS

FRUITY INDIAN PUDDING

You can save a lot of time by preparing this classic New England dessert in your microwave, and you won't give up any flavor. It's best served warm topped with vanilla ice cream.

▶ **PREPARATION TIME:** 20 minutes
COOKING TIME: 28 minutes
STANDING TIME: 10 minutes

2 tablespoons unsalted butter
1 cup milk
1 cup half-and-half
½ cup molasses
¼ cup sugar
¼ cup cornmeal
5 dried apricots, diced
2 tablespoons dried currants
1 teaspoon ginger preserves (optional)
¼ teaspoon ground cinnamon
3 large eggs
½ teaspoon vanilla extract
Vanilla ice cream (optional)

1. Melt the butter uncovered in a microwave-safe 2-cup glass measure on high power for 30 to 60 seconds.

2. Mix the milk, half-and-half, molasses, sugar, cornmeal, apricots, currants, ginger preserves (if using), and cinnamon in a microwave-safe 3-quart glass casserole with a lid. Microwave covered for 5 minutes; then stir. Microwave until thickened, 7 to 10 minutes, stirring three times.

3. Whisk the eggs into the melted butter, then whisk the egg mixture into the cornmeal mixture. Stir in the vanilla.

4. Pour the pudding into six 6-ounce microwave-safe porcelain ramekins. Arrange 1 inch apart in a circle in the microwave. Microwave on medium power (50%) until a knife inserted ½ inch from the center comes out clean, about 10 to 12 minutes; turn the dishes a half-turn after 5 minutes. Let stand 10 minutes. Serve warm, topped with vanilla ice cream if desired.

SERVES 6

CHERRY-LEMON RICE PUDDING

This is a really creamy, custardy rice pudding, and the cherries add a lovely dimension.

▸ **PREPARATION TIME:** 10 minutes
COOKING TIME: 24 minutes
STANDING TIME: 5 minutes

2 cups milk
¾ cup long-grain rice
¼ cup coarsely chopped dried cherries
¼ cup brown sugar
1 tablespoon all-purpose flour
¾ cup half-and-half
1 large egg yolk
Pinch grated lemon zest, or to taste
1 teaspoon vanilla extract

1. Combine the milk and rice in a microwave-safe 3-quart glass casserole with a lid. Microwave covered on high power to boiling, about 7 minutes. Microwave on medium power (50%) without stirring, until the rice is tender, 14 to 15 minutes. Sprinkle with the cherries and let stand, covered, 5 minutes.

2. Meanwhile, combine the sugar and flour in a 1-quart microwave-safe measure. Whisk in the half-and-half, egg yolk, and lemon zest. Microwave on high power, whisking four times, until thickened, about 1 to 2 minutes. Stir in the vanilla.

3. Fold the custard into the rice. Serve warm.

SERVES 4

ORANGE BREAD PUDDING WITH CHOCOLATE SAUCE

This dessert is both homey and flashy, and the orange and chocolate are a great flavor combination.

▸ **PREPARATION TIME:** 20 minutes
COOKING TIME: 20 minutes
STANDING TIME: 15 minutes

¾ cup milk
¾ cup half-and-half
¾ cup sugar
2 large eggs

1 teaspoon vanilla extract
1 teaspoon grated orange zest
6 ounces unsliced challah or
    white bread, cut into 1-inch
    cubes
1/2 cup semisweet chocolate
    chips
1/4 cup heavy cream
2 teaspoons orange liqueur like
    Grand Marnier or Cointreau
    (optional)

---

1. Butter a microwave-safe 8-inch-square glass baking dish.

2. Pour the milk and half-and-half into a microwave-safe 2-quart glass measure. Microwave uncovered on high power until hot but not boiling, about 2 minutes. Whisk the sugar, eggs, vanilla, and orange zest in a small bowl until blended, then whisk into the milk mixture. Microwave on medium power (50%), stirring once, until thickened, about 2 minutes.

3. Spread the bread cubes in the prepared dish and cover with the custard. Let stand 5 minutes.

4. Microwave the pudding uncovered on medium power (50%) until a knife inserted 1 inch from the center comes out clean, 10 to 14 minutes. Cover with waxed paper and let stand 10 minutes.

5. Meanwhile, combine the remaining ingredients in a microwave-safe 2-cup glass measure. Microwave on high power for 30 seconds, then whisk well. Continue to microwave to melt the chocolate completely, 30 to 60 seconds longer. Serve the pudding warm, topped with the warm chocolate sauce.

SERVES 4

DESSERT SAUCES

The microwave allows you to make fabulous dessert sauces almost effortlessly. Since small amounts consistently microwave most quickly and evenly, sauces yielding less than two cups work the best.

Dessert sauces can turn a simple slice of pound cake or dish of ice cream into something festive. The sauces we present run the gamut from a simple sauce of cooked fresh blueberries laced with grated lemon zest to a rich, sinful concoction of heavy cream, butter, and brown sugar famous among ice cream sundae cultists as caramel sauce. Look in the chocolate section of this chapter for a classic hot fudge sauce and a scrumptious mocha sauce.

All these sauces can be prepared at a moment's notice.

RED PLUM SAUCE*

Toward the end of each summer the market is suddenly bursting with many varieties of red plums. This red plum sauce is pretty, versatile, and delicious. Use it on ice cream, fruits, shortbread, yogurt, or sorbet.

▶ **PREPARATION TIME:** 5 minutes
COOKING TIME: 13 minutes
STANDING TIME: 5 minutes
CHILLING TIME: 1 hour

½ cup sugar, or to taste (depending on sweetness of plums)
2 tablespoons water (optional)
2–3 teaspoons fresh lime juice

1½ pounds ripe fresh red plums, washed thoroughly, quartered, and pitted

1. Toss the plums and sugar in a microwave-safe 3-quart glass casserole with a lid. If the plums seem juicy, do not add the water; if the mixture is dry, add the water. Microwave covered on high power, stirring once, for 10 minutes, or until the plums have softened and collapsed. Microwave 2 to 3 minutes longer, if necessary. Stir thoroughly; let stand, covered, 5 minutes.

2. Puree the plums in a food mill or press through a sieve set over a large bowl. Refrigerate, uncovered, until cold, about 1 hour. The sauce will thicken as it chills. Just before serving stir in lime juice to heighten the flavors. Serve cold.

MAKES ABOUT 2 CUPS (Serves 4 to 6)

BLUEBERRY SYRUP*

Blueberry syrup is a great luxury to have on hand, and very simple to prepare. You can get it going while you're preparing dinner and it'll take very little time. If you have some stored in your refrigerator you can use it for a million things—on French toast, waffles, or pancakes; with rich custard ice cream; as a topping for a tart lemon mousse or pound cake; on an orange custard; drizzled over chunks of cantaloupe or honeydew melon; or combined with carbonated water and served over crushed ice to quench an unrelenting thirst. This also makes a great gift.

▶ *PREPARATION TIME: 5 minutes*
COOKING TIME: 18 minutes
COOLING TIME: 10 minutes

---

1 pint fresh blueberries
*1/2 cup **each** water and sugar*
3 tablespoons lemon juice
1/8 teaspoon ground cinnamon

---

1. Place the blueberries in a food processor and process until coarsely chopped. Stir together the blueberries and the remaining ingredients in a microwave-safe 2-quart glass measure. Cover with microwave-safe plastic wrap and vent one side. Microwave on high power for 8 minutes, stirring four times.

2. Strain through a very fine strainer, pressing hard to extract all the liquid. Discard the solids. Put the liquid back in the clean 2-quart glass measure and microwave uncovered for 10 minutes, stirring four times. Let cool to room temperature and store tightly covered in the refrigerator.

MAKES 1¾ CUPS

BLUEBERRY-LEMON SAUCE*

This sauce is great on vanilla ice cream, lemon sherbet, or lemon pound cake or drizzled over a compote of sliced fresh summer fruits.

▶ **PREPARATION TIME: 5 minutes**
COOKING TIME: 5 minutes

¼ cup sugar
2 teaspoons cornstarch
1 pint fresh blueberries, rinsed and sorted, or 2 cups frozen unsweetened blueberries
1 tablespoon fresh lemon juice
½ teaspoon grated lemon zest

Stir the sugar and cornstarch in a microwave-safe 1-quart glass measuring cup until blended. Add the blueberries and stir to coat. Microwave uncovered on high power for 5 minutes; stir thoroughly. Add the lemon juice and lemon zest and let stand until ready to serve. Good served warm or chilled.

MAKES ABOUT 2 CUPS (Serves 4 to 6)

BROWN SUGAR AND BANANA SAUCE

Everyone loves ice cream, and it will taste even better with this delicious and speedy topping. It's inspired by the famous Bananas Foster from New Orleans, but it contains less fat, it's quicker, and the cleanup is really easy. It's great served over vanilla ice cream—but try it on vanilla-chocolate chunk, dark chocolate, rum raisin, or our favorite, pecan praline.

▶ **PREPARATION TIME: 10 minutes**
COOKING TIME: 10 minutes

---

2 tablespoons plus 1 teaspoon unsalted butter
¼ cup plus 1 teaspoon dark brown sugar
Pinch ground cinnamon

¼ cup chopped pecans
2 large bananas, peeled, sliced diagonally ½-inch thick
2 tablespoons tangerine or orange juice
Pinch grated tangerine or orange zest
2 pints ice cream

1. Microwave 1 teaspoon of the butter uncovered in a microwave-safe 9-inch glass pie plate on high power until melted, abut 30 to 60 seconds. Stir in the 1 teaspoon brown sugar and the cinnamon. Microwave on high power for about 1 minute, until the sugar is dissolved. Stir in the pecans. Microwave uncovered for 2 to 3 minutes, stirring every minute, until the pecans are beginning to toast. They will continue to cook after removing them from the oven. Place in a small bowl and reserve.

2. Microwave the remaining 2 tablespoons butter uncovered in the same pie plate until melted, about 30 to 60 seconds. Stir in the remaining ¼ cup brown sugar. Microwave uncovered for 1 minute, or until the sugar is dissolved.

3. Stir the bananas, tangerine juice, and zest into the brown sugar mixture and blend completely. Microwave uncovered on high power for 3 minutes, stirring three times. Serve the warm bananas over ice cream and sprinkled with the toasted pecans.

SERVES 4

GINGER CUSTARD SAUCE*

This is a lowfat version of custard sauce, containing lowfat milk and less egg yolk. It's delicious, and you'll never miss the extra fat.

▶ *PREPARATION TIME: 5 minutes*
COOKING TIME: 2 minutes
STANDING TIME: 10 minutes

⅓ cup lowfat milk
2 tablespoons minced crystallized ginger
Pinch grated lemon zest
1 tablespoon sugar
1½ teaspoons all-purpose flour
1 large egg yolk

1. Place the milk, ginger, and lemon zest in a microwave-safe 2-cup glass measure. Microwave uncovered on high power for 1 minute. Let stand 10 minutes.

2. Mix the sugar and flour and add to the warm milk. Add the egg yolk and whisk until well blended. Microwave uncovered for 45 seconds, stirring three times. If desired, strain the sauce into a bowl. Serve immediately, or chill and serve cold.

MAKES ABOUT ½ CUP
(Serves 2)

CUSTARD SAUCE

The satisfying, creamy consistency of a custard sauce can help many desserts be even better, and custards are a microwave specialty. There's none of that lengthy stirring over a hot stove; delicate custard sauce microwaves smooth and creamy with a minimum of stirring and time. You can serve this sauce immediately, or store it tightly covered in the refrigerator for about a week—letting it warm slightly before serving.

Custard sauce works really well with poached or fresh fruits—such as peaches, nectarines, plums, pears, figs, or berries (or try a mixture of berries—blueberries, strawberries, blackberries, and raspberries).

Soufflés, and simple cakes can also be improved by serving with a custard sauce. It's not only terrific with summer desserts—serve it in winter with persimmon pudding, apple crisp, or gingerbread. For an elegant presentation, try putting the sauce on a plate (an oversized plate, for more drama) and tilting the plate to spread the sauce evenly (there should be just enough sauce on the plate to coat it in an even layer). Then, to show off the flavors, colors, and textures to their best advantage, place the dessert on top of the sauce. Decorate with fresh mint, candied violets, or toasted almond slices.

▶ **PREPARATION TIME: 5 minutes**
COOKING TIME: 6 minutes

1 cup half-and-half
1 cup milk
3 large egg yolks
¼ cup sugar
½ teaspoon vanilla extract

1. Microwave the half-and-half and milk uncovered in a microwave-safe 2-quart glass measure on high power for 4 minutes, until very hot but not boiling.

2. Meanwhile, whisk together the yolks and sugar in a medium bowl until fluffy and pale, about 2 minutes. Gradually pour the hot milk into the egg mixture, whisking constantly. Pour back into the glass measure and microwave uncovered for 2 minutes, whisking once. If not quite thick enough to coat the back of a spoon, continue to microwave, checking and whisking at 20-second intervals. Whisk in the vanilla. Serve warm or at room temperature.

MAKES 2½ CUPS (Serves 6 to 8)

BUTTERSCOTCH SAUCE

> **PREPARATION TIME:** *5 minutes*
> **COOKING TIME:** *7 minutes*

8 tablespoons unsalted butter (1 stick)
1 cup light brown sugar
⅓ cup light or dark corn syrup
Pinch salt
1 cup heavy cream
1 teaspoon vanilla extract
1 teaspoon fresh lemon juice

Melt the butter in a microwave-safe 1-quart glass measure, about 2 minutes. Stir in the brown sugar, corn syrup, and salt. Microwave uncovered on high power for 3 to 5 minutes, stirring twice, until the mixture reaches boiling and 234°F. on a candy thermometer. Whisk in the cream, vanilla, and lemon juice until smooth. Serve warm or at room temperature.

MAKES ABOUT 3 CUPS
(Serves 8)

CARAMEL SAUCE

E veryone loves caramel sauce, and the microwave is the best way to make it.

> **PREPARATION TIME:** *5 minutes*
> **COOKING TIME:** *9 minutes*

¼ cup unsalted butter (½ stick)
¾ cup dark brown sugar
¼ cup light corn syrup
1 cup heavy cream

1. Melt the butter uncovered in a microwave-safe 1-quart glass measure on high power, about 1 minute.

Stir in the sugar and corn syrup. Microwave uncovered on high power until the mixture registers 240°F. on a candy thermometer, about 3 to 4 minutes.

2. Remove from the oven and stir in the cream. Microwave uncovered on high power until the mixture reaches 200°F. on a candy thermometer, about 3 to 4 minutes. Stir well, and strain if desired. Serve warm or at room temperature.

MAKES ABOUT 2 CUPS
(Serves 6)

PEANUT BUTTER-FUDGE SAUCE

▸ **PREPARATION TIME:** 5
minutes
COOKING TIME: 10 minutes

1 14-ounce can sweetened condensed milk
4 ounces bittersweet (not unsweetened) or semisweet
chocolate, finely chopped
2 tablespoons smooth peanut
butter
¼ cup heavy cream
½ teaspoon vanilla extract

Microwave the condensed milk uncovered in a microwave-safe 2-quart glass measure on medium power (50%) for 10 minutes, whisking four times. Whisk in the chocolate and peanut butter and continue whisking until melted and completely smooth. Whisk in the heavy cream and vanilla. Serve warm. Gently reheat on medium power (50%) if necessary.

MAKES ABOUT 2 CUPS (Serves 8)

CANDIES

MEXICAN COFFEE TRUFFLES

Even kids and noncooks can make these truffles, and they are as flavorful as they are easy to prepare.

PREPARATION TIME: 10 minutes
COOKING TIME: 3 minutes
CHILLING TIME: 2 hours

1 cup heavy cream
2 strips lemon zest, 2 inches × ½ inch
8 ounces bittersweet (not unsweetened) or semisweet chocolate, very finely chopped
1 tablespoon plus 1 teaspoon instant espresso coffee powder
1 tablespoon coffee liqueur
¼ cup unsalted butter (½ stick), at room temperature
¼ cup Dutch-process cocoa powder

1. Place the cream and lemon zest in a microwave-safe 1-quart glass measure and microwave uncovered on high power until slightly thickened, 2½ to 3 minutes. Discard the zest. Add the chocolate and stir vigorously until melted. Add 1 tablespoon of the espresso powder and the coffee liqueur and stir until well blended. Let cool to room temperature, then stir in the butter. Refrigerate or freeze covered until firm enough to shape, about 1 to 2 hours.

2. Mix the remaining 1 tablespoon espresso powder with the cocoa in a small bowl.

3. Using your hands, shape the truffle mixture into 1-inch balls and roll each ball in the cocoa mixture. Store in refrigerator up to 1 week, but warm at room temperature about 10 minutes before serving.

MAKES 3 DOZEN

CHOCOLATE-DIPPED GINGER AND CASHEWS

This would make a great gift for one of your favorite friends, and it couldn't be easier. And here's a tip: Buying crystallized ginger in small bags in Oriental markets rather than the expensive little spice jar size in specialty stores can be much less expensive.

▶ **PREPARATION TIME: 5 minutes**
COOKING TIME: 2 minutes
STANDING TIME: 30 minutes

8 ounces bittersweet (not unsweetened) or semisweet chocolate, finely chopped
¼ cup minced crystallized ginger
¼ cup coarsely chopped toasted cashews

1. Melt the chocolate uncovered in a microwave-safe 1-quart glass measure on high power for 1 to 2 minutes, stirring three times. Stir in the ginger and the cashews.

2. Drop 20 candies by rounded teaspoonsful onto a baking sheet covered with wax paper. Let stand until hardened (about 30 minutes), placing in the refrigerator if necessary. Store in a cool place for up to 3 weeks.

MAKES 20 CANDIES

CHOCOLATE HAZELNUT CLUSTERS

You can try this substituting your favorite nut, or your favorite combination of nuts.

▶ **PREPARATION TIME: 10 minutes**
COOKING TIME: 2 minutes
STANDING TIME: 30 minutes

1 pound bittersweet (not unsweetened) or semisweet chocolate, finely chopped

1¼ cups coarsely chopped toasted hazelnuts

1. Microwave the chocolate uncovered in a microwave-safe 8-inch glass cake dish on high power for 1 minute; stir. Microwave, stirring every 30 seconds, just until melted, about 1 minute. Add the hazelnuts and stir to mix well.

2. Line a large baking sheet with waxed paper. Using soup spoons, drop the chocolate and hazelnuts evenly in 24 mounds on the waxed paper. Let stand until hardened, about 30 minutes, refrigerating if necessary. Store in an airtight container in refrigerator up to 3 weeks.

MAKES 2 DOZEN

CANDIED ORANGE PEEL*

This recipe can also be made with grapefruit—use two large grapefruits, either yellow or pink will work well. Candied orange peel takes more time than some candies, but since much of it is unattended time, you can be doing something else at the same time.

▶ **PREPARATION TIME:** 10 minutes
COOKING TIME: 35 minutes
SOAKING TIME: 30 minutes
DRYING TIME: 24 hours

---

4 large navel oranges
4½ cups water
3 cups sugar

---

1. Using a swivel-blade vegetable peeler, cut the peel from the oranges. Cut it into strips about 2 inches long and ¼ to ⅓ inch thick.

2. Place the peel in a microwave-safe 2-quart glass measure and add 2 cups of the water. Cover with microwave-safe plastic wrap and vent one side. Microwave on high power for 8 minutes. Drain off the liquid and add 2 cups fresh water. Microwave, covered and vented, another 8 minutes. Stir the mixture, cover, and let stand until the peel is soft, about 30 minutes. Drain the peel and discard the liquid.

3. Stir 2 cups of the sugar and ½ cup water together in the same clean 2-quart glass measure. Microwave uncovered for 4 minutes. Stir well and microwave until the sugar is dissolved, about 2 minutes.

4. Add the peel to the syrup. Microwave, covered and vented, for 15 minutes, stirring three times. Drain; roll the hot peel in the remaining 1 cup sugar until completely coated. Let the candied peel dry on a wire rack for 24 hours. Store in an airtight container up to 3 weeks.

MAKES 3 CUPS

HAZELNUT BRITTLE

This is terrific candy, and is also wonderful if made with peanuts or pecans.

½ cup **each** granulated sugar, packed dark brown sugar, and light corn syrup
1 tablespoon water
1 cup hazelnuts, coarsely chopped
¼ cup marzipan (almond paste), coarsely chopped
1 tablespoon unsalted butter
1½ teaspoons vanilla extract
⅛ teaspoon ground cinnamon
Pinch salt
½ teaspoon baking soda

1. Butter a baking sheet.
2. Mix both the sugars, the corn syrup, and the water in a microwave-safe 2-quart glass measure. Microwave uncovered on high power for 4 minutes. Stir in the hazelnuts and marzipan. Microwave 3 minutes, stirring three times. Stir in the butter, vanilla, cinnamon, and salt. Microwave until a candy thermometer inserted in the mixture registers 300°F., about 3 minutes. Add the baking soda and stir until light and foamy.
3. Immediately pour the mixture onto the prepared baking sheet and smooth lightly with a metal spatula. Let cool completely, about 30 minutes, then break into pieces. Store in an airtight container.
MAKES 1 POUND

CHOCOLATE-ALMOND CARAMELS

Surprise and impress your family and friends with these delicious and sophisticated caramels.

¾ cup sugar
6 tablespoons light corn syrup
2 tablespoons unsalted butter, cut into small pieces

1 tablespoon cold water
2 teaspoons chocolate liqueur
2 ounces unsweetened choco-
    late, coarsely chopped
1 cup heavy cream
5 ounces blanched almonds,
    toasted and coarsely
    chopped
1 teaspoon vanilla extract
Pinch salt

---

1. Butter an 11 × 15-inch baking sheet.

2. Place the sugar, corn syrup,
butter, water, and chocolate liqueur
in a microwave-safe 2-quart glass
measure. Microwave uncovered on
high power until the sugar is dissolved, 3 to 4 minutes. Add the chocolate and cook until a candy

thermometer inserted in the mixture
registers 240° F., 2 to 4 minutes.
Slowly whisk in the cream. Microwave until the thermometer registers
248° F., about 3 minutes. Stir in the
remaining ingredients.

3. Pour the chocolate mixture
onto the prepared baking sheet to
cover about three quarters of the surface. Let cool to room temperature,
about 30 minutes.

4. Cut the sheet of candy into six
even strips. Roll each strip into a ½-
inch-thick rope. Cut each rope into
six 1¾-inch-long pieces. Tightly
wrap each candy in a 4-inch × 6-
inch piece of waxed paper or plastic
wrap and twist the ends tightly. Store
in a cool place.

MAKES 36 CARAMELS

PIES

PEAR-APPLE PIE

This is a really comforting, delicious pie, perfect in the fall during the apple harvest.

> **PREPARATION TIME:** 20 minutes
> **COOKING TIME:** 15 minutes
> **COOLING TIME:** 15 minutes

2 Granny Smith apples
4 firm ripe pears
4 tablespoons brown sugar
2 tablespoons fresh lemon juice
7 tablespoons unsalted butter, at room temperature
1 cup crushed oatmeal cookies
Crème fraîche or sour cream, for serving

1. Peel and core the apples and two of the pears, then cut into ¾-inch chunks. Combine the apple and pear chunks, 2 tablespoons of the brown sugar, and 1 tablespoon of the lemon juice in a microwave-safe 1-quart glass measure. Cover with microwave-safe plastic wrap and vent one side. Microwave on high power for 8 minutes; stir in 1 tablespoon of the butter after 4 minutes. Transfer to a food processor or blender and process with four on/off pulses so that fruit is still chunky. Let the filling cool to room temperature.

2. Meanwhile, microwave 5 tablespoons of the butter uncovered in a microwave-safe 9-inch glass pie plate until melted, about 1 minute. Stir in the cookie crumbs until evenly coated with butter. Using your hands, press the crumbs evenly against the bottom and sides of the plate to form a pie shell. Microwave the shell uncovered about 2 minutes, turning the dish halfway around after 1 minute. Let cool to room temperature on a wire rack, about 15 minutes.

3. Meanwhile, peel, core, and thinly slice the remaining pears. Mix the remaining 2 tablespoons sugar, 1 tablespoon butter, and 1 tablespoon lemon juice in another microwave-safe 9-inch glass pie plate. Microwave uncovered for 1 minute, stir, and add the pear slices. Microwave until pears are softened, about 3 minutes, stirring halfway through the cooking.

4. Pour off the juices from the pears into the cooled filling. Just before serving, spoon the filling into the pie shell and arrange the pear slices on top. Serve warm or at room temperature with crème fraîche or sour cream.

SERVES 8

LEMON-STRAWBERRY PIE

S erve this tangy delicious pie in the spring or summer, when strawberries are at their most flavorful and beautiful.

▶ **PREPARATION TIME:** 20 minutes
COOKING TIME: 12 minutes
COOLING TIME: 30 minutes
CHILLING TIME: 2 hours

3/4 cup (1 1/2 sticks) plus 5 tablespoons unsalted butter
1 cup crushed graham crackers
3/4 cup sugar
5 tablespoons fresh lemon juice
3 tablespoons fresh lime juice
Grated zest of 1 lemon and 1 lime
6 large egg yolks, lightly beaten
1/2 cup heavy cream
1 pint strawberries, hulled and sliced

1. Microwave the 5 tablespoons butter in a microwave-safe 9-inch glass pie plate on high power until melted, about 1 minute. Stir in the cracker crumbs until evenly coated with butter. Using your hands, press the crumbs evenly against the bottom and sides of the plate to form a pie shell. Microwave the shell uncovered for 2 minutes, turning the dish halfway around after 1 minute. Let cool to room temperature on a wire rack, about 15 minutes.

2. Meanwhile, combine the remaining 3/4 cup butter, the sugar, juices, and zests in a 1-quart microwave-safe glass measure. Cover with microwave-safe plastic wrap and vent one side. Microwave for 4 minutes, stirring four times.

3. Whisk one third of the citrus mixture into the egg yolks in a small bowl, then return it to the remaining citrus mixture and whisk until completely blended. Microwave uncovered for 4 minutes, stirring once. Whisk vigorously until cooled and smooth, about 2 minutes. Let cool to room temperature, then refrigerate until chilled, about 2 hours.

4. Just before serving, whip the cream to stiff peaks. Fold the cream into the citrus mixture and spread in the pie shell. Arrange the sliced strawberries on top and serve at once.

SERVES 8

INDEX

INDEX OF LIGHT
AND LOWER CALORIE RECIPES

"Especially Good for Your Recipes"
(These recipes are indicated by a * in the text.)